THE

CIVILIZATIONS OF THE EAST

❖ ❖

The Near and Middle East

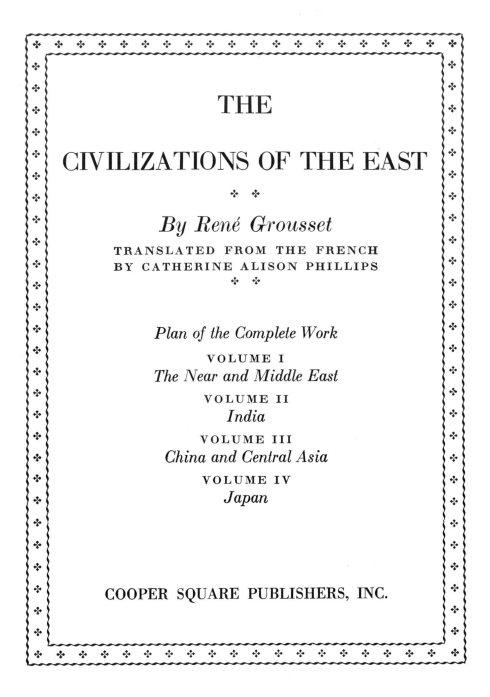

THE

CIVILIZATIONS OF THE EAST

❖ ❖

By René Grousset

TRANSLATED FROM THE FRENCH
BY CATHERINE ALISON PHILLIPS

❖ ❖

Plan of the Complete Work

VOLUME I
The Near and Middle East

VOLUME II
India

VOLUME III
China and Central Asia

VOLUME IV
Japan

COOPER SQUARE PUBLISHERS, INC.

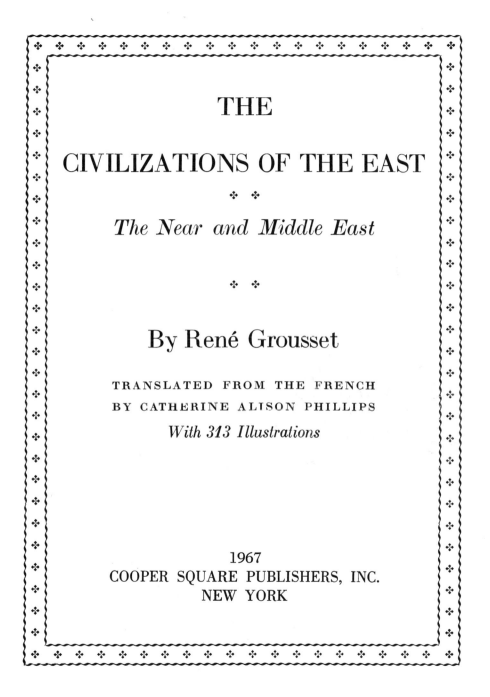

THE

CIVILIZATIONS OF THE EAST

✢ ✢

The Near and Middle East

✢ ✢

By René Grousset

TRANSLATED FROM THE FRENCH
BY CATHERINE ALISON PHILLIPS
With 313 Illustrations

1967
COOPER SQUARE PUBLISHERS, INC.
NEW YORK

Originally Published as
LES CIVILISATIONS DE L'ORIENT
Copyright by Les Éditions G. Crès et Cie 1929
Copyright 1931 by Alfred A. Knopf, Inc.
Reprinted by Permission of Alfred A. Knopf, Inc.

Published 1967 by
Cooper Square Publishers, Inc.
59 Fourth Avenue, New York, N. Y. 10003
Library of Congress Catalog Card Number: 66-30807

TRANSLATOR'S NOTE

The Civilizations of the East

Volume I: The East

The translator desires to express her grateful thanks to PROFESSOR MINORSKY *for kindly reading the chapters on Persian art and giving her the benefit of his advice on questions of transliteration.*

TABLE OF CONTENTS

The Civilizations of the East

Volume I: The East

CHAPTER IV

PERSIAN PRE-ISLAMIC CIVILIZATION

❖ ❖

CHAPTER V

ARAB CIVILIZATION

❖ ❖

CHAPTER VI

PERSIAN ISLAMIC CIVILIZATION

INTRODUCTION

The Civilizations of the East

Volume I: The East

I HAVE BEEN ASKED TO WRITE A GENERAL INTRODUCTION TO THE study of the arts in Asia for the cultivated public, and the present work is an attempt to meet this request. I may say that I make no pretence of giving a detailed account of the archæological and artistic data within this short compass. It is my more modest hope that the book may provide a guiding thread among the various styles and periods and give an adequate and correct idea of the various schools and works. With this object in view, it has been my aim to present the history of art in its due relation to general history, not, of course, by repeating the significant interpretation of the facts which I have given at greater length elsewhere, but by re-creating their historical setting. In order to call this up in all its living reality, I have provided as many illustrations as possible, both photographic and literary, by which I mean quotations from literary works, and more especially poetry. In so doing I may perhaps incur the criticism of having produced a work both impersonal and subjective; but the best answer to this criticism is that, in my opinion, this is the best method of making my readers understand and love the subject of this study.

The present volume is devoted to the Near and Middle East, in which is included Iran. The second will be devoted to India, Farther

India, and the Malay Archipelago, the third to China and central Asia, the fourth to Japan and Tibet.

At the end of the last volume will be found a certain amount of bibliographical material and an index of the proper names, technical terms, and words from Oriental languages contained in the four volumes.

These volumes could never have appeared but for the kindness of all those collectors, travellers, and curators of museums who have been so good as to give me permission to reproduce works or photographs in their possession. The present volume, in particular, owes everything to MESSIEURS HENRI VÉVER, ANDRÉ GODARD, DOUCET, HENRI VIOLLET, EUSTACHE DE LOREY, GERVAIS COURTELLEMONT, CHARLES VIGNIER, PROFESSOR SARRE, and CAPTAIN RENÉ BERTRAND, besides MESSIEURS CHARLES BOREUX, DUSSAUD, DRIOTTON, CONTENAU, and many other Orientalists, all of whom I cannot enumerate here, but to whom I have expressed my sincere gratitude in the course of my work.

THE

CIVILIZATIONS OF THE EAST

❖ ❖

The Near and Middle East

❖ ❖

CHAPTER I

The Earliest Civilizations of the East:
The Neolithic

NEOLITHIC REMAINS IN THE EAST

T HE CIVILIZATIONS OF ASIA UNDOUBTEDLY GO BACK, FOR THE most part, to a prehistoric origin, which, if not common to all, is, at least, obviously homogeneous. Indeed, although the study of prehistoric remains in the East has only been pursued during the last thirty years or so, it already affords some insight into the deep affinities which originally formed a more or less intimate link between the great historic civilizations, however sharply these may have been differentiated subsequently.

Setting aside the Atlantic, Danubian, Ukrainian, and Ægean civilizations, which do not fall within the scope of this work, the first prehistoric civilization with which we meet is that of Egypt. Along the Libyan tributaries of the Nile, which are now dried up, have been found palæolithic settlements, with thousands of ax-heads of chipped stone of the " Lower Palæolithic " types known to French archæologists as " Chellean " and " Acheulian," from the palæolithic finds at Chelles, Seine-et-Marne, and Saint-Acheul, near Amiens. But then comes a gap: so far, not a trace had been found of neolithic civilization properly so called; but we now find flourishing on the banks of the Nile at Nagada, Abydos, and Al-Amrah a rich " aeneolithic "

3

civilization — that is, the end of the stone age, when copper was beginning to make its appearance, " the approximate date of which is at least 5000 B.C." At this far-distant period the inhabitants of the valley, the majority of whom no doubt belonged to a race or races with Mediterranean affinities, had domesticated the dog, the ass, the ox, the sheep, and the gazelle and were cultivating barley, millet, and wheat. Their arms, implements — sickles and ploughshares — and domestic utensils were of flint. Their knives, in particular, slightly curved blades of yellowish flint, with a polish as of metal, are unusually perfect; but their vases, above all, fill us with astonishment. These vessels, whether cylindrical or globular, graceful or massive, these drinking-vessels carved out of sandstone, granite, marble, diorite, obsidian, alabaster, or crystal, are among the most beautiful which have come down to us from prehistoric days. The jewellery is partly of the neolithic type — bracelets and necklaces of bone, ivory,

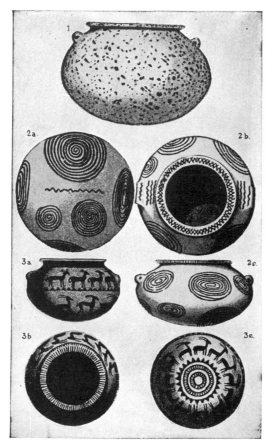

FIGURE 1

Pre-dynastic Egyptian vases, after de Morgan. — *By permission of Messrs. Paul Geuthner* or flint — and, already, partly of copper, especially the pins. There are abundant examples of the ceramic art, including (to follow the probable chronological order) first vases of smooth red clay, decorated round the upper edge with a band of black glaze; next rough red vases; and lastly red or buff pottery decorated in various ways. There is also an infinite variety of shapes — bowls, cylindrical pots, amphoras, spherical vases, pots with three feet, etc. All these pieces were shaped by hand, without any wheel, and the painting was applied without firing. The patterns are either geometrical — speckled, chequered with a rectangular pattern or patterns of concentric lozenges, serrated, or decorated with alternating crescent- or bobbin-shaped designs, parallel wavy lines, spirals, and snail-shaped designs — or else borrowed from plant and animal forms — processions of conventionalized aquatic birds, trees, etc.; sometimes, too, the painted decoration consists of regular pictures: funerary boats,

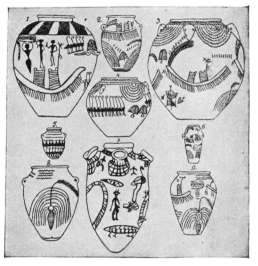

FIGURE 2

Pre-dynastic Egyptian painted ware, after de Morgan.
— *Photo, Leroux*

libation urns, or ritual dances, all equally conventionalized (Fig. 1 and 2).

It may be noted here that Egyptologists distinguish between two phases of this aeneolithic civilization in Egypt: a first phase, between 7500 and 5000, which had its centre at Nagada, in Upper Egypt, and seems to have been African in character; and a second phase, between

FIGURE 3
Pre-dynastic Egyptian schist palette of King Narmer.
— *Cairo Museum*

5000 and 3500, which had its centre in the north and seems to have
been Asiatic in character.

On the other hand, in the period following upon the latter — a
period which may properly be designated as " proto-historic " — the
schist palettes, representing war and hunting scenes, which have come
down from the pre-Pharaonic tribes, show signs of decidedly realis-

FIGURE 4
The lion king. Pre-dynastic Egyptian schist palette.

tic tendencies. It is remarkable that the animals — lions, bulls, antelope — and even the human figures which appear on these slabs display sometimes an obvious affinity with similar products of archaic
Chaldean art in the general outline and the treatment of the muscles.
The lions, in particular, as Mr. Hall points out, remind one of the
lions of Chaldeo-Assyrian art rather than of those of Egypt under the
Pharaohs. This point may well be stressed, for it undoubtedly points

to commercial and artistic relations between the earliest Egyptian and the earliest proto-Sumerian civilization (Fig. 3 and 4).

FIGURE 5
Bowl from Susa, first style.
— *Louvre. Archives photographiques*

There are no palæolithic remains in Chaldea or Elam, no doubt because at the beginning of the quaternary age these regions were still under water. During the aeneolithic age (end of the neolithic and beginning of copper), a magnificent civilization sprang up round Susa, the future capital of Elam. In the lowest deposits at Susa, known as " Susa I," and of Tepe-Mussian, some ninety-five miles to the west (known as the epoch of Susa I b), de Morgan found traces of a population engaged in agriculture and cattle-breeding, which was still making flint weapons and vessels of steatite or alabaster, but was at the same time familiar with weapons and mirrors made of a copper containing ninety per cent of the pure metal. The pottery produced by this people was very fine. The vessels, in the shape of beakers, bowls, or cooking-pots, were undoubtedly thrown on the wheel, unlike the Egyptian pottery

FIGURE 6
Bowl from Susa, first style.
— *Louvre. Archives photographiques*

of the same period; the painted ornamentation was fired, and varied in colour from pink to brown or black, according to the degree of firing. Here again the decorative motives were in part purely geometrical — consisting of an infinite number of combinations of wavy lines, serrated lines, chequered patterns, zigzags of every description, bands of lozenges, triangles joining at the apex and spread out like the wings of a butterfly, and even Maltese crosses and swastikas (Fig. 5 to 7) — and in part borrowed from animal or vegetable forms: thus we find at Susa I or Mussian conventionalized palm-trees, processions of ibex or wild goats with enormous horns, and aquatic or wading birds, all completely conventionalized, in a style which shows a remarkable sense of decorative effect (Fig. 8 to 10). On various fragments from Mussian, however, we find a few designs showing realistic observation of nature, among others a charming head of a hind (Fig. 13 to 15).

FIGURE 7

Susian painted ware, second style, from Tepe-Mussian.
— *Louvre. De Morgan mission. Archives photographiques*

How did the artists of Susa I arrive at this conventionalized art, with its breadth, power, and faculty for synthesis? Apparently by starting from a realistic observation of nature. The proto-historic inhabitants of Susa, at the opening of the aeneolithic age, probably began by drawing the vegetable or animal forms that they had before their eyes. Gradually, and by dint of repetition, they came to assimilate these forms to a decorative pattern of a geometrical character. The theory on this subject developed by Monsieur Pottier in Volume XIII of the *Délégation de Perse* seems to us to be final, in spite of Monsieur Frankfort's objections. But, as Dr. Contenau points out, if this naturalistic style is anterior to the conventionalized ornament which triumphed as early as the period of Susa I, then we are forced to assume an enormously long period of incubation for the art of that place. This art of Susa I, which seems primitive to us because we are ignorant of its origins, was really the result of a process of evolution which had already gone on for thousands of years. Indeed, an incredibly ancient habit of picture-drawing is already presupposed by this conventionalized representation of the human body in its typical form of a figure with a slender waist, of impossibly delicate girth, and broad shoul-

FIGURE 8
Susian painted ware, first style.
— *Louvre. De Morgan mission. Archives photographiques*

ders and bust which have been compared to a coat-hanger (Fig. 11);
or the type of wild goat with horns of enormously exaggerated size,
almost forming a complete circle (Fig. 8 and 12); or, again, the
aquatic birds with inordinately long but very elegant necks or legs,

FIGURE 8b, 9, 10
Susian painted ware, first style.
— *Louvre. De Morgan mission. Archives photographiques*

and the rows of flying beasts, ranged as though on a spit (also reproduced in Fig. 8 and 12). This consideration alone would lead
us to assume that before Susa I there existed a Susa of incredibly
remote antiquity.

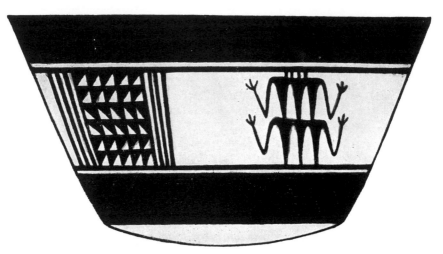

FIGURE 11

Susian ware with human figures, from Tepe-Mussian.
— *Louvre. De Morgan mission. Archives photographiques*

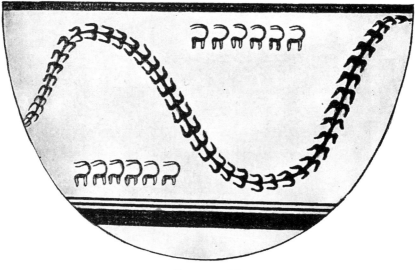

FIGURE 12

Susian ware with birds and ibex, from Tepe-Mussian.
— *Louvre. De Morgan mission. Archives photographiques*

The chronology of this advanced civilization of Susa I has recently undergone revision. Not long ago it was still assigned to between 3500 and 3000 B.C.; but now it is assigned by general consent
to a much earlier date,
towards 5000 and the fifth
millennium. It seems to
have come to an end about
3500. Moreover, a gap in
civilization represented by
a thickness of about five
yards of earth seems to divide it from the civilizations represented by the
proto-historic and historic
deposits; but, according to
recent works, there does not
seem to be an absolute gap;
at any rate, we must admit
the existence of a style I b,
forming a transition be-
tween Susa I and Susa II,
and represented chiefly at
Tepe-Mussian. It was not
till later, towards 4000 or
3500, that a new civilization
was to appear, with "Susa
II," which was character-
ized by a return to pottery

FIGURE 13

Fragment of painted Susian ware, from
Tepe-Mussian.

— *Louvre. De Morgan mission. By permission of
Messrs. Leroux*

and the appearance of writing (curved script). Later still, about
2800 or 2200, was to come the stage of "Susa III," marked by the
triumph of linear script.

We may here indicate the profound artistic revolution which

occurred during the period separating Susa I and I b from Susa II. As we have seen, the style of the pottery of Susa I was characterized by an astonishingly elegant conventionalization. The figures on the ware of Susa II are much less artistic, but far more naturalistic. Though this return to the naturalistic style coincides with an undeniable falling-off in artistic power, it shows that the art of Susa was once more turning to the fountain-head of observation. "Instead of wading birds with exaggeratedly long legs, we find the swan and partridge appearing, with their short legs, the eagle with outspread wings, the wild goat with horns now of reasonable dimensions, and represented in natural attitudes — for instance, turning the head to look behind it." Thus we come to the earliest cylinders of Susa, dating from the year 3000 B.C., with their fights between lions or bulls, their charg-

FIGURE 14

Fragment of Susian painted ware, from Tepe-Mussian.

— *Louvre. De Morgan mission. By permission of Messrs. Leroux*

ing bulls, with head down and lowered horns, their pairs of leaping beasts of the goat tribe, one on each side of the tree of life, their wild beasts corralled in enclosures, works of astonishing spontaneity and realism — so great, indeed, that, though they already contain the germ of the whole of the animal art of Assyria, yet Assyrian technique seems cold and academic by comparison with them, the Minoan art of Crete alone, with its bull-fights and springing lions, having produced anything equal to them in freedom of treatment.

Following on the art of Susa, and in close connexion with it, we may mention the recent discoveries of Professor Herzfeld in Persian Kurdistān and Fārs. In 1927 and 1928 the German archæologist brought to light at Damāghān and Persepolis a remarkable civilization which he considers to be purely neolithic and anterior to the discovery of copper. If this view meets with confirmation, then this civilization would be anterior to that of Susa I, which, as we have seen, is already aeneolithic. Professor Herzfeld is even of opinion that it was neolithic Persia which gave birth to the civilization of Susa. But whatever view may be taken of this question of priority, the affinity between the two cultures is obvious. The " neolithic " painted pottery of Damāghān and Persepolis immediately reminds us of the ware of Susa I and I b, both by its geometrical motives and by its human or animal figures (ibex, moufflon, or figures of " suppliants "). But whereas there seems to be, if not a gap, at least a period of cultural stagnation between Susa I and II, the pre-Aryan pottery of Kurdistān and Fārs would seem to bear witness to a remarkable continuity of development.

FIGURE 15

Fragment of Susian painted ware, from Tepe-Mussian.
— *Louvre. De Morgan mission. By permission of Messrs. Leroux*

Signs of this continuity will be found even at the height of the bronze age. In fact, in the region of Nehāvend Professor Herzfeld has found a series of painted vases of the bronze age, some of them showing animal motives of a curiously realistic nature, and some bearing, side by side with processions of wading birds, which recall Susa I, the heraldic eagle, a favourite motive of Susa II. At the same time the great animal art which was to be characteristic of Mesopotamia appears both on these painted vases and on the seals or amulets likewise found at Nehāvend; for instance in a drawing of a prowling hyena, amazingly realistic in action, or in a group of a beast of the feline tribe devouring a beast of the deer tribe, a motive which became classic in Sumerian art, as afterwards in that of the steppes.[1]

At Anau, near Askhabad in Russian Turkestan, in the vicinity of the Persian frontier, the Pumpelly mission discovered three successive prehistoric sites. On the first of these sites (Anau I), nowadays dated about 3000 B.C. (the period at the end of Susa II and the beginning of Susa III or a little later), the inhabitants, who cultivated wheat and barley and had domesticated the sheep, the ox, and the pig, belonged to the end of the aeneolithic age, characterized by polished stone and copper; on the second (Anau II), we see the domestication of the camel, goat, and dog; on the third, which came to an end about 2000, we are at the height of the copper age. The various sites at Anau have yielded, side by side with vessels of alabaster and marble, a whole series of painted pots, in the earliest period with a pink, light-red, or light-yellow ground, sometimes monochrome, sometimes decorated with geometrical ornaments in brown; these ornaments are generally composed of straight lines, and offer instances, among other motives, of bands of trellis-work formed of lozenges with their lateral angles touching one another, as in Elam; we may also draw attention to a few conventionalized branch-like forms offering an analogy with those of Susa, and, at Anau III, to some figurines representing the " nude goddess " whom we also find in Elam and Chaldea during the archaic period.

In 1916 Sir Aurel Stein discovered some ancient aeneolithic sites, more or less analogous to those of Anau, in southern Seistān, to the south-east of Iran. Side by side with stone utensils of a type which is

[1] Thanks to a donation from Messrs. Migeon and Nazare-Agha, some of these vases from Nehāvend have recently been added to the collections of the Louvre. See G. Contenau: *Bulletin des Musées de France*, February 1930.

still neolithic, though accompanied by copper objects, he discovered
a number of earthenware pots varying in colour, according to the degree of firing, from buff, reddish, or greenish, to red, grey, or shot
with various colours. The workmanship of these pieces seems to
point to the use of the wheel, as well as various technical processes
characteristic of Anau. As at Anau, no handles are to be found,
though the handle is beginning to take shape on the aeneolithic pots
of Mesopotamia and Egypt. The principal decorative motives are
geometrical in character: parallel wavy or zigzag lines, triangles
joined at the apex " butterfly-fashion," chains of lozenges, S-shaped
curves (which we shall find again in China), semicircles fitting into
each other in such a way as to form leaves, arranged in stars on a
cross-hatched ground. The leaf is also treated as an independent motive. Besides these we find a few silhouettes of animals which are remarkably realistic in character, notably some heads of ibex and
goats. Not far away, at Nal, in Baluchistan, the Archæological Survey of India has discovered some pottery of a similar nature, which
Mr. Mackay assigns to the date of Susa I. The ground is light red;
the decoration, in dark red or black, consists of parallel horizontal
bands between which run wavy lines, crosses, triangles, lozenges, and
concentric circles, the general effect, as we shall see, somewhat
resembling the neolithic pottery of China.

THE NEOLITHIC AGE IN THE FAR EAST

FROM BALUCHISTAN WE PASS TO THE AENEOLITHIC AND CHALCO-
lithic settlements of north-western India, Harappa and Mohenjo-
Daro, both situated in the Indus basin, the first in the Punjāb, the second in Sind. We are here dealing with regular cities, the importance
of which is apparent from their massive brick substructures and
vaulted drains. At Mohenjo-Daro Sir John Marshall found three
cities, one above another, the lowest of which he dated provisionally

at about 3300 B.C., the other two at about 3000 and 2700 B.C., but which are perhaps rather more recent, as is shown by the chronology established for Chaldea. The unknown people which inhabited these

FIGURE 16

Seal from Mohenjo-Daro.

Drawn by Jean Buhot after The Archæological Survey of India *and Coomaraswamy:*
History of Indian . . . Art.
— *By permission of Messrs. Goldston*

towns made cotton stuffs and had domesticated the ox, the sheep, and the pig. The objects found by the Archæological Survey of India at various depths on these two sites between 1920 and 1925 include the usual polished stone and copper implements, flint weapons side by

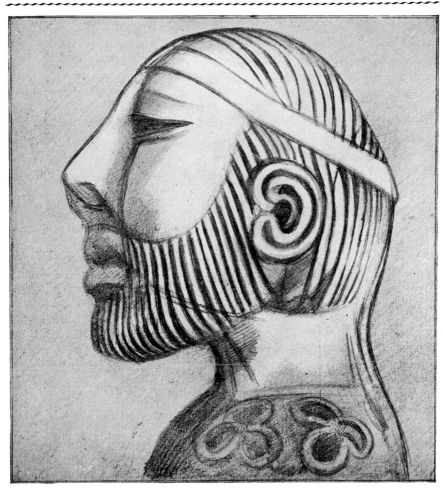

FIGURE 16b
Statue from Mohenjo-Daro.
Drawn by Jean Buhot after The Archæological Survey of India *and Coomaraswamy:*
History of Indian . . . Art.
— *By permission of Messrs. Goldston*

side with copper instruments and utensils and gold and silver jewellery. We also note a glazed blue and white faience and some unpainted pottery, side by side with pottery painted in black on a red

ground, recalling that of Baluchistan and Seistān. But the most remarkable find consists of a thousand or so limestone tablets, used as
seals, with animal designs — generally oxen, zebu, tigers, and elephants — and an unknown pictographic writing which is still very
near to the hieroglyph (Fig. 16). The resemblance was at once remarked between these seals and those of Sumerian Chaldea, the bulls,
in particular, also suggesting those of the Mesopotamian cylinders.
At Mohenjo-Daro was also discovered a limestone bust of a person
the reed-like treatment of whose beard suggested at first sight a comparison with certain Mesopotamian types (Fig. 16 b). Many writers,
indeed, have been inclined to see in the remains at Harappa and
Mohenjo-Daro a directly Mesopotamian and Sumerian civilization.
It certainly appears as though this civilization had deep affinities
with that of Chaldea and Elam in the proto-historic period, though it
none the less preserved a distinct individuality. Thus the animal and
vegetable forms represented on the seals of Mohenjo-Daro and
Harappa are largely confined to indigenous types: the zebu, the elephant, the rhinoceros, the tiger, the serpent (nāga), and the wild fig-
tree. Moreover, the pictographic writing of the Indus valley is quite
distinct from the earliest Sumerian or Susian cuneiform. Lastly, the
only seals that occur in the valley of the Indus are rectangular tablets,
and never round cylinders, as in Chaldea. Yet commercial relations
must certainly have existed between Mesopotamia and the Indus;
and as a matter of fact the Anglo-American mission of Messrs. Hall
and Woolley has recently discovered at Kish, in Chaldea, a seal
from the Indus dating from about 2500–2350,[1] and even bearing a
pictographic inscription of the Harappa type. These two archæologists have also found at Ur, in Chaldea, a steatite seal of about the
same date, with an intaglio of a bull quite in the manner of Harappa,
but this time with a cuneiform inscription. However, the most ele-

---

[1] This date, which is that of the third dynasty of Ur, is suggested by our friend
Monsieur Watelin, who collaborated with Mr. Woolley in the excavations at Kish.

mentary prudence would suggest that commercial, or even cultural, relations do not necessarily indicate identity of race and language. We shall have the same remark to make apropos of the analogies which have been pointed out between prehistoric remains in China and those of Anau, Susa, and the Ukraine; while the question of aeneolithic civilization in India and of that of Harappa and Mohenjo-Daro will be examined at greater length in Chapter i of the second volume of this work.

For long nobody had suspected the existence of palæolithic remains in China, but they were discovered about 1920 by Messrs. Licent and Teilhard de Chardin. Under the loess beds in the Ordos district, where the Yellow River makes a bend, the two missionaries found deposits of chipped flints of Mousterian and Aurignacian workmanship. After a gap of several millenniums considerable neolithic settlements make their appearance, separated from these palæolithic deposits by the whole of the period during which the loess was being formed. These were discovered between 1920 and 1924 by the Swedish scholar J. G. Andersson and his companions at Ho-nan and Kansuh and in Manchuria. The two chief sites are Ts'i-kia-p'ing, in Kansuh, and Yang-chow, in Ho-nan, the former of which Andersson and Arne propose to date somewhere about 3500 B.C., and the latter between 3000 and 2700 B.C., these dates being based on the old chronology of Susa. We are unable to follow those whom more recent theories as to the dates of Susa would lead to assign these most ancient Chinese sites to an earlier date in the past. However this may be, here too both weapons and implements are still neolithic, with bone sickles, flint knife-blades, marble or shell rings, etc. The Ts'i-kia-p'ing stage, which yielded an unpainted pottery, together with a smaller quantity painted in monochrome, belongs, properly speaking, to the end of the neolithic age. When we come to the Yang-chow stage, which serves to determine the antiquity of the various sites, not only in Ho-nan, but also in Kansuh, we are undoubtedly witnessing

the transition from the neolithic to the aeneolithic. An abundance
of pottery, both painted and unpainted, was excavated there, the unpainted vessels being either of a grey clay-like tone, or grey inside
with a red surface produced by firing, or light red, or even beige.
These pots are made of carefully worked clay, often with handles,
and seem to have been thrown on the wheel. Certain shapes among
these unpainted pieces seem to foreshadow those of the Chinese
bronzes of later days; this is notably so of the three-footed vases,
which remind us of the bronzes of the " Ting " period. We may remember, however, that vases with three feet also appear among the
objects found in the earliest city on the site of Troy, as well as on
Egyptian sites of the aeneolithic period. In like fashion the loop-
shaped handles which appear on certain of these vessels are akin to
those of the vases of pre-dynastic Egypt, just as other handles from
Ts'i-kia-p'ing, of the type through which ropes were passed for sling-
ing the jars, recall those of Chaldean vessels from Kish. Moreover, on
certain neolithic Chinese vessels the designs seem to have been produced by means of a rope, as in southern Russia, or even by rolling
the pot on a mat.

In the painted vessels of the Chinese neolithic age the colour of
the ground is often reddish, varying from brick-red to red-brown according to the degree of firing, though often, too, it is yellowish white,
dull white, or grey, on which the patterns stand out in red or black,
sometimes tending towards orange or dark grey. On the grey vessels
the ornamentation is usually in red, on the red ones in black or dark
red. The decorative motives are almost exclusively geometrical, and
include: a leaf-shaped ornament, dotted, striped, or divided by a line
down the middle; the motive, which we have already met with in
eastern Asia, of two triangles jointed at the apex like the wings of a
butterfly, in this case expanding in such a way as to form a protuber-
ance at the point where they touch; a chequer pattern of triangles or
lozenges; bands of a " snake-skin " ornament (Fig. 17 and 18);

stripes (Fig. 19); or bundles of bands converging to form a spiral (Fig. 20) — the last of these ornaments being as harmoniously decorative as the Ægean motives borrowed from submarine flora — or a sort of lenticular motive surrounded by a fringe, possibly representing a mouth or an eye; serpentine patterns somewhat resembling those of Greek work, but shallower than those of Dipylon ware; longitudinal bands covered with a dotted pattern, and with a serrated edge,

which are known as "the death motive" or "the way of death," because they are found only in tombs. This subject will be treated in greater detail in Chapter i of the third volume of this work, dealing with the aeneolithic civilization of China. Andersson also found a few patterns based on animal forms (zoomorphic), though these appear to be exceptional; semicircles suggesting a flight of birds, and even, on one

FIGURE 17
Chinese aeneolithic vase from Kansuh.
— *Louvre. Photo, Wannieck*

pot from Kansuh, a band of conventionalized birds (possibly aquatic), somewhat analogous to those of Susa or pre-dynastic Egypt. Here we undoubtedly have a specimen which establishes an undeniable point of contact between Chinese neolithic and that of the Near East. We may add that in strength of form, toughness of material, and beauty of colour (we may draw attention to some admirable reds), as well as in the splendid rhythm of the decorative motives, whether stripes, wavy bands, or spirals, the painted vases of Ho-nan and Kansuh may be reckoned among the most perfect works of prehistoric art. We may also add that the preliminary examination made by Dr. Black of the skulls found with these objects would seem to indicate that the race with which we are dealing here is already the Chinese race of the present day. The neolithic and aeneolithic remains in Japan will be examined in Chapter i of the fourth volume of this work.

FIGURE 18

Chinese aeneolithic vase of painted ware from Yang-Chow, Kansuh.
— *From Andersson:* Preliminary Report . . .

From this rapid general survey we may conclude that during the aeneolithic age — that is, towards the end of the age of polished stone, when copper was beginning to be introduced — Egypt, Mesopotamia (especially Elam), eastern Iran, north-west India, western Turkestan, and northern China formed so many centres of civilization. The populations of these various regions tilled the soil and raised cattle. They were undoubtedly accustomed to trade, for aeneolithic China, in particular, made use of jade, which may have come from Kashgaria, and of cowries, or shells used as currency, which had to be brought from the Gulf of Chih-li to Kansuh. In the painted pottery we find curious affinities here and there between Egypt and aeneolithic Susa, between Susa and Anau, between Anau and the Chinese aeneolithic, between Susa, Anau, and Seistān, and between Seistān, Baluchistan, and the finds at Harappa and Mohenjo-Daro in India. On the strength of this we may at once set aside as most improbable the belief that the great prehistoric civilizations were completely isolated from one another, while we may reject the hypothesis of migrations as useless. Let us be content to draw the conclusion that at the dawn of history there existed a common civilization extending from Egypt to the Yellow River and the Indus, which we may call the " painted pottery civilization," equipped with more or less the same implements, whose art had ideals, processes, and subjects of a decidedly similar nature,[1] though this general harmony as regards fundamental motives in no way impaired the industrial and

FIGURE 19
Painted ware from Yang-chow, Kansuh.
— *From Andersson:* Preliminary Report . . .

[1] See W. Percival Yetts: " Painted Neolithic Pottery in China," *Burlington Magazine*, December 1925 (with comparative illustrations of the various aeneolithic ware of Susa, Anau, Tripolje, and China).

artistic independence of the several centres. We may add that this civilization of unknown identity produced some masterpieces.

We shall see how these different centres of a common civilization of the aeneolithic age gave rise, by a process of divergent develop-

FIGURE 20
Painted ware from Yang-chow, Kansuh.
— *From Andersson:* Preliminary Report . . .

ment and progressive differentiation, to the four great historical civilizations of the Eastern world: the Egyptian, the Mesopotamian (which was itself to give rise to the pre-Islamic and Islamic civilization of Persia), the Indian, and the Chinese.

CHAPTER II

Egyptian Civilization

MEMPHITE CIVILIZATION

THE BRILLIANT CIVILIZATION OF AENEOLITHIC EGYPT HERALDED that of Egypt under the Pharaohs, so that we see the latter growing directly out of the former.

On the eve of the unification of Egypt under the Pharaohs, the Egyptian race had already been homogeneous for a long time, though no doubt made up of varied elements of a Mediterranean character, with Berber, Semitic, and African affinities. For centuries it had been split up into a large number of principalities, distinguished from one another by their tribal totem-animal and tribal god: the sparrow-hawk of Horus, the jackal of Anubis, the phœnix of Osiris, the lion of Ra, the ram of Ammon, etc. In course of time these principalities were reduced to two, those of Upper Egypt and of the Delta; and Egyptian civilization has left signs of an intense creative activity about this time. To their painted ware and neolithic vases of hard stone (which were to continue down to the time of the last three dynasties, and even longer) the Egyptians added copper weapons and implements and copper and gold jewellery; on their palettes of schist they carved historical reliefs — scenes of war and the chase and religious scenes — of a realism and delicacy which are already almost classical in character. Above all, they invented writing — a writing at first quite primitive and pictographic, which we shall see develop

27

FIGURE 22
Diorite head of Khephren, IVth dynasty.
Front view.
— *Cairo Museum. Photo, Molleni-Radiquet*

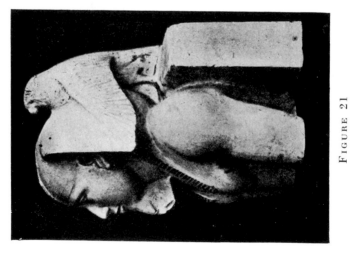

FIGURE 21
Diorite head of Khephren, IVth dynasty.
— *Cairo Museum. Photo, Molleni-Radiquet*

into the convention of hieroglyphs on the one hand, and into a pho-
netic system on the other.

In the second half of the fourth century, or at the opening of the
third (about 3315 B.C., or, according to the approximate dating

most recently arrived at
by Eduard Meyer, about
3197), the two Egypts were
united under the monarchy
of the Pharaohs. From the
first the character of this
monarchy was essentially religious. The Pharaoh was regarded as a god incarnate.
On ceremonial occasions,
wearing the uræus of gold
upon his brow, and holding
in his hands the crook and
the flail, the insignia of divinity, he would appear before the adoring multitude
in his set ritual attitude, im-
passive, superhuman, and,
though still alive, partaking
of eternity.

Thus his religion made
every Egyptian the slave and

FIGURE 23

Group of Mykerinos and two female figures.
— *Cairo Museum. Photo, Molteni-Radiguet*

pious worshipper of his king, and the monarchy of the Pharaohs was
based upon the most sacred beliefs of the race.

On this unshakable foundation, and in spite of the social trans-
formations, or even profound revolutions, of which Monsieur Moret
has recently reconstituted the memory, the twenty-five Egyptian
dynasties followed one another in majestic succession for centuries

FIGURE 24

The Sheikh-al-balad. Wooden statue of the
Vth dynasty.
—*Cairo Museum. Photo, Giraudon*

and millenniums. Their history falls into four main periods: the Memphite Empire, lasting from 2895 to 2360 B.C., or rather, perhaps, from 2778 to 2242; the first Theban Empire, from 2160 to 1660; the second Theban Empire, from 1580 to 1100; and the Saïte period, which lasted down to 525 B.C.

The Memphite Empire reached its apogee under the IVth dynasty (from about 2840 to 2680), which included kings Cheops, Khephren, and Mykerinos, who built the Great Pyramids and extended the influence of Egypt as far as Byblos in Phœnicia, as is proved by Monsieur Montet's quite recent discoveries.

Memphite art has left us some imperishable works. It was the age of the Great Pyramids, of the great Sphinx of Gizeh, and the portrait statues of the Cairo Museum. This art, like the monarchy of the Pharaohs itself, was very intimately bound up with the religious beliefs of the Egyptians, and particularly with their ideas of the future life. The pyramids, which were regular mountains built by the hand

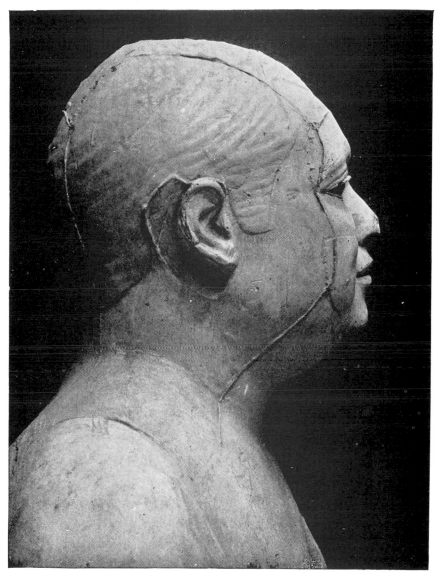

FIGURE 25
Head of Sheikh-al-balad.
— *Cairo Museum. Photo, Giraudon*

FIGURE 26
Scribe seated on the ground, Vth dynasty.
— *Louvre. Photo, Giraudon*

of man, and reached a height of almost as much as five hundred feet, were intended to be the tombs of the Pharaohs, and most of the statues or bas-reliefs which have come down to us are simply funerary statues or designs. The reason for this is that the whole Egyptian people, from the Pharaohs down to the lowest fellaheen, spent their lives in preparation for their future destiny. The Egyptians believed in the survival of the soul, or, rather, of the "double" which inhabited the body and continued to carry on its earthly existence in the tomb after death. In order to render possible this existence beyond the grave, certain conditions were necessary: the preservation of the mummy and the presence in the tomb of statues and paintings representing the departed, his associates, and his various occupations upon earth, which he was supposed to continue in the under-

FIGURE 27
Scribe seated on the ground, Vth dynasty.
— *Cairo Museum. Photo, Molteni-Radiguet*

world. The more perfect the resemblance of these pictorial representations, the more chance the dead man had of a secure and comfortable survival. Thus the religious ideas with which Egyptian society was entirely permeated contributed towards the development of art, and in particular of the plastic arts.

Egyptian art, which could already look back on an existence of

almost thirty centuries, reached its highest point under the IVth
dynasty. The statues of this period are real portraits, highly natural
in their poses, sometimes broadly idealized in treatment, sometimes
reproducing the peculiari-
ties of the person and
his surroundings to the
point of satire. Among
these idealized figures we
may cite the great diorite
portrait statue of Khe-
phren, with the hawk standing with outspread wings
behind the head of the
King. This work is a
product of a very great art
and is impressive in its
nobility. " Rarely," says
Maspero, " has the majesty
of royalty been rendered
with so much breadth "
(Fig. 21, 22). In the same
style are the schist group
of Mykerinos and his wife,
now in the Metropolitan
Museum, New York, and
the Mykerinos group of
three figures in Cairo (Fig.
23). Quite different in

FIGURE 28
Bust of painted limestone, IVth dynasty.
— *Louvre. Photo, Giraudon*

style is the wooden statue of Ka-Aper, known as the " Sheikh-al-
balad," or surveyor of works at the pyramids under the Vth dynasty; this is a highly realistic portrait of a fat, self-satisfied, and
consequential bourgeois of a powerful and somewhat vulgar cast

of countenance and an already rather ponderous gait, but, for the
rest, full of energy and dignity; it might be taken for a portrait
of a Roman tax-farmer of the best period (Fig. 24, 25). To the
same age belong the seated scribe in the Louvre, so strikingly lifelike

FIGURE 29
Egyptian head.
— Louvre. Photo, Giraudon

with his cold, hard look and keen glance (Fig. 26), and the seated
scribe in the Cairo Museum, with the almost malevolent expression
of a disillusioned official (Fig. 27); not to speak of many other busts
with an expression of such intense life that at times it becomes dis-
tressing, as though the old sculptor magician had really succeeded in

FIGURE 30
Wooden group, Memphite period.
— *Louvre. Archives photographiques*

imprisoning the soul of the departed in his effigy, so that it has continued all down the ages to carry on the same existence, whether aristocratic or bourgeois, as in the time of King Cheops (Fig. 28 to 30). In fact, all this statuary bears witness to a realism of inspiration, a richness and flexibility of expression, that Egyptian art was never to recover to the same extent in succeeding ages, for it rapidly forged its own bonds.

Indeed, the chief interest of these Memphite portrait statues consists in this very quality, this almost exclusive preoccupation with the reproduction of personality — in what we may call their strongly bourgeois character. Neither Greek sculpture, which is always more or less idealized and Olympian, nor

FIGURE 31
Head of a royal personage, Middle Empire.
— *Louvre. Archives photographiques*

the portrait statues of Imperial Rome herself were to succeed to the same extent in giving us this disturbing impression of a " real presence," this sense of a human brotherhood directly touching ourselves.

THEBAN CIVILIZATION

THE FIRST THEBAN EMPIRE REACHED ITS CULMINATING POINT UNDER
the XIIth dynasty (between about 2000 and 1788), under a succession of kings almost all of whom were named Amenemhet and Senusret. This period, like the last, was marked by a brilliant blossoming

FIGURE 32
Fresco from Beni-Hassan. XIIth dynasty.
— Archæological Survey of Egypt

and renaissance of art. The limestone statues of Senusret I found at
Licht, and now in the Cairo Museum, may be reckoned among the
purest masterpieces of Egyptian art; their heads, with full, smiling
faces of supreme elegance and dignity, are akin to the most noble
conceptions of the Greek genius in the harmonious ideal which inspires

them and the atmosphere of happiness in which they seem to be
bathed. Indeed, the whole art of the XIIth and XIIIth dynasties has
an infinite fascination. The portrait statues of the Memphite period
were doubtless more powerful and realistic, and sculpture under the

FIGURE 33
Fresco from Beni-Hassan, XIIth dynasty.
— *Archæological Survey of Egypt*

Rameses was to be more refined in its elegance and more aristocratic
in its delicacy; but the busts of the first Theban Empire, which mark
the transition between the two styles, offer such a happy blend of
strength and grace that we may regard them as, on the whole, the

most representative works of Egyptian classicism (Fig. 31). As for the painting of the first Theban Empire, it has left us some admirable frescoes, among which we may mention the wonderful cat in the chapel of the tomb of Khnumhetep II at Beni-Hassan, lying in wait among the reeds for its prey (Fig. 32): "Here we find every char-

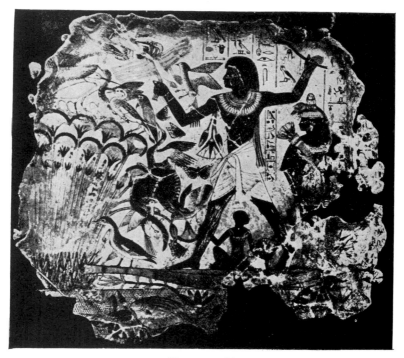

FIGURE 34
Painting of a fowling-expedition.
— *British Museum. Photo, Mansell*

acteristic of the creature," says Maspero: "the outstretched neck, the quivering spine, the spasmodic movement of the tail, the body drawn slightly back before the spring, and the intense fixity of the eyes, which arrest and fascinate the prey." We may also mention the bird-paintings in the same chapel, worthy rivals of all the most exquisite

productions of Chinese art in this line (Fig. 33) ; the charming scene
of peasants taming gazelles from the hypogeum of Khnumhetep,

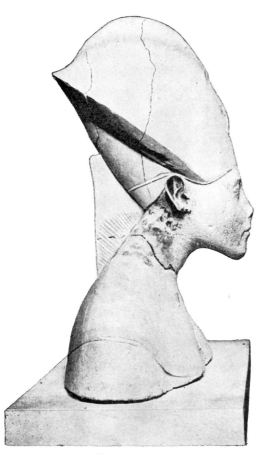

FIGURE 35
Bust of Amenophis IV, XVIIIth dynasty.
— *Louvre. Photo, Giraudon*

again at Beni-Hassan; and, lastly, those military scenes representing
war-dances and pugilistic combats which have been popularized
among us by the stock text-books. In spite of the conventions which

were adopted by Egyptian art once and for all — such as the invari-
able representation of the feet in profile, and of the eyes as seen
from the front — in these last-mentioned scenes we may admire a
freedom of line and a sense of movement which have, so to speak, an

FIGURE 36
King Tutankhamen, XVIIIth dynasty.
— *Cairo Museum. From Legrain:* Catalogue du Musée du Caire

almost cinematographic quality that we shall not find again in the
same degree, except perhaps in Japanese art.

We may note that in the days of the XIIth dynasty Egypt maintained political and artistic relations with Syria (as is shown by Monsieur Montet's excavations at Byblos and by those of Monsieur du
Mesnil du Buisson at Quatna-Mishrifeh in the region of Homs) and
with the Crete of the second Middle Minoan period (as is shown

FIGURE 37
Alabaster statue of Rameses II.
— *Turin Museum. Photo, Alinari*

FIGURE 38
Head of a queen, XVIIIth dynasty.
— *Louvre. Photo, Giraudon*

by the finding of Minoan vases of the Kamares type in Theban tombs).

Towards 1660 B.C., Egypt was invaded and partially conquered by some Asiatic nomads known to history under the name of the Hyksos. After a century of struggles they were expelled, and the Theban Empire was restored by the XVIIIth dynasty, the most glorious in the annals of Egypt (1580–1321). The great Pharaohs of this dynasty, Thothmes III (d. 1447) and Amenophis III (1415–1380), conquered Syria and entered into friendly relations with the kingdoms of Babylonia and Assyria, Mitanni (a kingdom of western Mesopotamia), and Crete of the Late Minoan period. In consequence of the disorders caused by the attempt at religious revolution made by the Pharaoh Amenophis IV (1380–1362), and in spite of the prudent policy of reaction followed by his successor, Tutankhamen (who died in

FIGURE 39
Head of a queen, Saïte period.
— Lou re. Photo, Giraudon

1350), the XVIIIth dynasty had to make way for a more orthodox house, the XIXth (1321–1200). In the mean time, northern Syria had been conquered by the Hittites, a people of Asia Minor, partly Asiatic and partly Indo-European, of which we shall have more to say later. After a long war the Pharaoh Rameses II (1300–1234) partitioned Syria with the Hittites and allied himself with them by marriage; but under the rule of his successors Egypt had twice to meet the attacks of the seafaring races of the Ægean, the Ægeans and Achæans, in 1229 and 1192. Victorious, but exhausted by these troubles, she withdrew into her valley, where, except for a short Assyrian invasion in the seventh century (670, 663), she was

Figure 40

Queen Nefertiti, XVIIIth dynasty.
— *Berlin Museum. Photo, Grantz*

to preserve her independence down to the Persian conquest of 525, various towns in the Delta serving as her capital — of which Saïs was her choice from 651 onward.

Thus in many respects the period of Rameses II is the last great period of the empire of the Pharaohs. It is also one of the best-known, particularly for its architecture. One can hardly find a single town in Egypt which does not possess some monument built or repaired by Rameses. He completed the great temples of Karnak and Luxor, and built the Ramesseum at Gurnah, which celebrates his fame.

All these temples are constructed on the same uniform and grandiose plan. They are led up to by colonnades or avenues of sphinxes and rams, followed by obelisks covered with reliefs, and open on to a forecourt, the portal of which was flanked by massive pylons. Next comes the hypostyle hall, with a flat roof supported by a forest of columns,

FIGURE 41

Blue glass head of a royal personage, XVIIIth dynasty.
— *Louvre. Archives photographiques*

sometimes sixty-five feet high (the hypostyle hall at Karnak contained as many as 134 of these). The walls of these columned halls

FIGURE 42
Blue glass head of the XVIIIth dynasty. Profile view.
— *Louvre. Archives photographiques*

were covered with paintings and sculptures representing the great exploits of the Pharaoh. On solemn festivals the great processions which formed part of Egyptian worship took place in the hypostyle

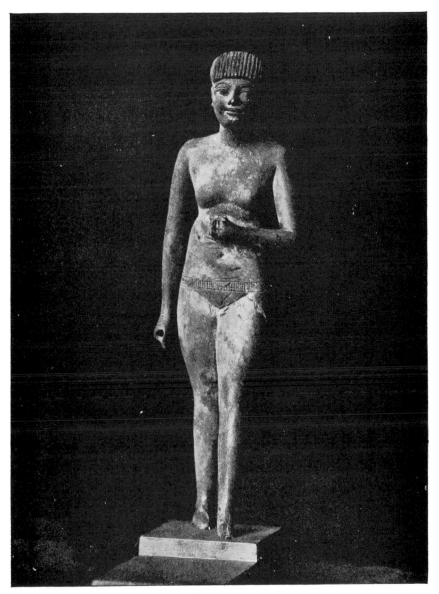

FIGURE 43
Wooden statuette.
— *Louvre. Archives photographiques*

hall. From it one entered the sanctuary, in which stood the shrine of the god, and to which none but the Pharaoh and the high priest had access.

" The impression emanating from these Theban temples is one of incomparable grandeur. The colossal proportions of the colonnades, the crushing massiveness of the general effect, the obsession of the giant statues with which they are peopled, the eternal silence of this assembly of granite figures, thrill the modern visitor with a sense of the superhuman." This impression must have been even more profound in the time of the Pharaohs, when a dread mystery hovered about these columns, and everything worked together to intensify the sanctity of the spot. A gradation in the lighting was skilfully contrived, ranging from the forecourt, which was open to the brilliance of the Eastern skies, to the hypostyle hall, which was bathed in a mysterious half-light, and the sanctuary, where the mighty shadow of the god moved in a vague dimness. Here, remote from the glance of any profane eye, the enigmatic gods of Egypt, those gods with the head of a ram, a jackal, or a hawk, communed face to face on equal terms with the Paraoh, the god made manifest, their representative upon earth.

But the Egypt of the ancient theogonies, the sanctuaries and tombs is not the whole of Egypt. Side by side with it existed an Egypt full of delicacy, prettiness, and charm, revealed to us in the statues or statuettes of women with their jewels, toilet appliances, and furniture. While the former thrills us with a sense of the eternal, the latter fascinates us by its incredibly modern quality, by its keen feeling for dress — in short, by its femininity. We have to go as far as the Greece of Tanagra, or Japan in the eighteenth century, to find such subtle talent expressed in trifles. In many of the royal statues of the second Theban Empire, such as those of Amenophis IV, Tutankhamen, and Rameses II (Fig. 35 to 37), we already notice more aristocratic elegance than majesty. This elegance is most freely expressed

FIGURE 45
Woman at her toilet.
— Louvre. Photo, Giraudon

FIGURE 44
Kneeling woman.
— Louvre. Archives photographiques

in most of the heads of queens and great ladies of this or the Saïte periods (Fig. 38 to 42). But its chief triumph is in the nude female figure, a triumph which is not without merit when one thinks of all the conventions — such as the law of the frontal pose, and the arms held close to the sides — which hampered Egyptian sculpture to the end. In spite of this initial disadvantage, the nudes of the Theban and Saïte periods give proof of a freshness and vigour the memory of which even the Alexandrine school itself cannot efface (Fig. 43 to

FIGURE 46
Gathering lilies. Bas-relief of the neo-Memphite period.
— *Louvre. Archives photographiques*

46). There are, moreover, a quantity of trifles and toilet appliances, such as spoons for cosmetics or perfumes, which show how thoroughly the artists of Thebes and Saïs had grasped the decorative value of the female body (Fig. 47 to 49). They and the Greeks were the only sculptors of antiquity capable of a free reproduction of the nude. While the Assyrians, for example, stifled the body under heavy draperies, the Egyptians did not hesitate, even in representing the wife or daughters of the Pharaoh, to indicate a rounded breast, a soft abdominal line, or the curve of a hip beneath the diaphanous stuff

FIGURE 47
Egyptian cosmetic spoon.
— *Louvre. Archives photographiques*

FIGURE 48
Egyptian toilet spoon.
— *Louvre. Archives photographiques*

(Fig. 50 to 52). Still more transparent were the stuffs which clothed the singers and dancers so frequently represented in the paintings found in the tombs (Fig. 53), of which it has been said: " The calculated indiscretions of this sort of veil were an invitation to the sculptor or painter to show off the slenderness and elegance of the body by closely following the contours of the body."

FIGURE 49
Swimming female figure with duck. Wooden cosmetic spoon of the later
Theban Empire.
— *Louvre. Archives photographiques*

The fact is that woman occupied a far more important position in Egyptian society than in other Oriental countries. She was really " mistress " of the house and, according to the testimony of Herodotus, enjoyed a prestige and a freedom of conduct already foreshadowing the *Syracusan Women* of Theocritus. The Egyptian storytellers give us glimpses of the same light flutter of pleasure-loving life in the cities of the Pharaohs as might be seen later in the Alexandria of the Lagides. They call up before our eyes the forms of women " gentle in love, hair blacker than night, teeth more brilliant than splinters of flint, a slender figure, and a firm and well-placed

FIGURE 50
Bronze female statue. Bubastite period.
— *Louvre. Photo, Giraudon*

bust." In the course of a tale of magic, such as that of " Khufui and the Magicians," dating perhaps from the first Theban Empire, they sketch for us a love-romance of the year 2000 B.C.: " One day when His Majesty was visiting with his suite the house of the scribe who was his chief reader, the eye of the chief reader's wife fell upon one of the vassals in the train of the King; no sooner had she caught sight of him than she no longer knew what place in the world held her. . . ." And there are love-songs of the days of the Pharaohs, translated by Monsieur Moret, which remind us, not only of the Song of Songs, but also of the Greek Anthology.

At the end of this rapid sketch the question which suggests itself to us is: what was the contribution of Egypt to the civilization of the East? At first sight it would seem as though the particularism of the Nile valley was too pronounced, and the historical individuality of the world of the Pharaohs too exclusive, for the essential qualities of Egyptian culture to spread to the rest of the Eastern world. And, as a matter of fact, we see no direct transmission of the heritage of Egyptian culture to other peoples, comparable to the process by which the material civilization of Assyria and Elam passed to Achæmenid Persia.

But this impression can only persist if we neglect the intermediate links of the chain. For throughout the whole of the second millennium and down to the Persian period a mixed zone of common influence existed, for instance, between Egypt and Assyria, a transitional zone represented by Syria and Phœnicia. As we have seen, from a very early period, as early as the ancient Memphite Empire, the maritime populations of Tyre, Sidon, Byblos, and other Phœnician cities had accepted the influence of the empire of the Pharaohs. At the same time these Semites, like all the other inhabitants of Syria, felt the attraction of the elements of their own race in Babylonia. Thus historic Phœnician art, in the sarcophagi or specimens of goldsmiths' work which have come down to us, presents the character of an empirical

FIGURE 51
Figure in painted wood. First Theban Empire.
— *Louvre. Photo, Giraudon*

FIGURE 52
The lady Naiya. Wooden statuette.
— *Louvre. Archives photographiques*

combination of Egyptian with Chaldeo-Assyrian technique. As examples of this highly composite Syrian art we will merely mention the delicate reliefs on plates of ivory, with animal figures, discovered by Messieurs Thureau-Dangin and Barrois in 1928 at Arslān-Tāsh, to the north of Aleppo, on the east bank of the Euphrates, which are now in the Louvre. These plates adorned the ivory bed of Hazael, king of Damascus (844–812), and were handed over by his son Ben-Hadad

FIGURE 53
Musicians and dancing-girls. Egyptian painting.
— *British Museum. Photo, Mansell*

(812–773) as tribute to Adad-Nirari III, king of Assyria from 812 to 783, when the latter was besieging Damascus (see R. Dussaud: *Bulletin des Musées de France*, July 1929). Such works as these clearly show how Egyptian influence was spreading in the direction of Mesopotamia and came in contact with Chaldeo-Assyrian influences. We shall have occasion to point out the same influence in Hittite art, and even in that of Sargonid Assyria — for instance, in the Sphinx of Assarhaddon. Finally, it was from Egypt that the Achæmenid Persians borrowed the idea of their columned halls, which made their way from Thebes to Persepolis, until the colonnades of Persepolis were in turn imitated by the Indians of the Maurya period in the palaces of Pātaliputra (Patna).

CHAPTER III

Chaldeo-Assyrian Civilization

SUMERO–AKKADIAN CIVILIZATION

FROM THE VERY DAWN OF HISTORY THE LAND OF CHALDEA AND Elam, which, like Egypt, had been an active centre of aeneolithic civilization, was in like fashion the seat of powerful organized states.

From the very beginning of its history — that is, according to the tablets most recently deciphered by Monsieur Legrain, towards the middle of the fourth millennium — we find Chaldea already divided into two regions, as it had no doubt been for a long time past. These were the lands of Sumer and Akkad, which seem, indeed, to have corresponded to two distinct races and languages: the Sumerian race and tongue, and the Semitic.

The Sumerian tongue was a very peculiar language, of a non-Semitic character, spoken in the southern towns of Chaldea, such as Ur, Lagash, etc. According to the bas-reliefs, the Sumerian race seems to have been characterized by " a globular head, rather of the brachycephalic type, and a prominent nose like an eagle's beak, with a shaven face and head." It is supposed that the cuneiform script — or, rather, hieroglyphic writing, which gave rise to cuneiform script as it became conventionalized — was invented in Chaldea for the Sumerian language.

The Akkadian tongue spoken in the Chaldean cities of the north

59

FIGURE 53b

Ur-Nina and his family, about 2900 B.C.
— *Louvre. Photo, Giraudon*

— at Kish, Agade, and Babylon — was a Semitic language. According to the most ancient bas-reliefs, the population of Akkad had " a somewhat concave profile, with a straight nose, fuller at the tip "; besides which they did not shave their heads and wore beards.

At the time when history begins, the lands of Sumer and of Akkad were still quite distinct politically, but the Chaldean civilization was already a mixed, or " Sumero-Akkadian," one, in which it is rather difficult to distinguish the part played by either element. This is particularly so both where the gods are concerned — for the two races had, no doubt, for long past shared a common pantheon — and as regards the cuneiform script, which was adopted by Semites and Sumerians alike.

Chaldea, on the other hand, always retained its own distinctive characteristics, though it none the less followed the same course of evolution as its neighbour Elam, of which we have spoken above (pages 8–14). Thus the earliest aeneolithic settlements of Chaldea (possibly to be assigned to the fifth millennium) [1] have as their counterpart the remains of Susa I b, while the most ancient Sumerian civilization corresponds to the epoch of Susa II, about 3500–3100. There are, moreover, some very archaic sculptures from the *tell* of Susa, carved out of blocks of bitumen, with figures of a type fairly analogous to the Sumerian mentioned above, with " globular heads and hooked noses like the beak of an eagle." In spite of this, the first language spoken in Elam which has been deciphered, known as *Anzanite*, appears to have been as distinct from Sumerian as from Semitic.

At the head of every Chaldean city, whether Semitic or Sumerian, was a prince, or *patesi*, who was at the same time high priest of the local god. Among these gods we may mention Anu, god of the heavens, Enlil, the elements let loose, Adad, the beneficent elements, Ea, the god of the waters, Sin, the moon-god, Shamash, the sun, Marduk,

[1] See Moret: *Histoire ancienne*, I, i, p. 124.

the planet Jupiter, Ishtar, the goddess of fertility and war, etc. Many of these cults had an astronomical character — in fact, astronomy,

FIGURE 53c

Golden dagger with lapis handle
and its sheath, Ur.
— *From Childe:* The Most Ancient East

FIGURE 53d

Gold toilet-set and case, Ur.
— *From Childe:* The Most Ancient East

or rather astrology, played a preponderant part in Chaldean society. It was in order to study the movements of the stars that the Chaldeans built their first temple observatories, massive brick constructions,

FIGURE 53e

Bas-relief showing chariot, Ur.

— *From Childe:* The Most Ancient East

FIGURE 53f

Silver boat from royal tomb, Ur.

— *From Childe:* The Most Ancient East

which as a rule took the form of a seven-storeyed pyramid rising in stepped tiers.

The wealth of the country is explained by the fertility of the soil of Chaldea, or, rather, by the way in which the Sumero-Akkadians took advantage of it. The cuneiform tablets are witness that from the very dawn of history Chaldea, like Egypt, was subjected to an intensive exploitation. One of the principal functions of the kings was the construction and upkeep of irrigation canals, thanks to which Chaldea bloomed like a garden and left in the memory of the peoples the tradition of an *earthly paradise.*

This agricultural prosperity gave rise to industrial enterprise. No people has shown greater invention in the arts of luxury than the Chaldeans. With a mastery which has never been surpassed, their craftsmen produced stuffs of brilliant hues, sumptuous carpets, precious furniture, and goldsmiths' work which was sought after throughout the whole Orient. To dispose of these products the merchants of Chaldea followed the Euphrates road and the desert tracks as far as the mountains of Armenia and Cappadocia and the coasts of Syria. Together with their wares they carried to the neighbouring races their cuneiform script, which was scratched on clay tablets with an iron instrument shaped like a nail. They were the only race in the Asia of that period which possessed a complete culture. Hence throughout the whole of the third millennium, and even down to the fourth century B.C., this culture played somewhat the same role in the East as did Hellenic culture during the Greco-Roman period. As the Amarna and Boghaz-Keui tablets bear witness, in the fourteenth century B.C. it was to Chaldean scribes that the kings of Mitanni, the Hittite sovereigns, the little Canaanitish princes, and the Pharaohs of the XVIIIth dynasty had recourse in order to conduct their correspondence with one another.

The most ancient traces of the historic civilization of Chaldea were discovered in 1927–8 at Ur (Tell-el-Muga'yir) and at Tell-el-Ubaid,

FIGURE 53g
Stone vase carved with procession of animals, Erech.
— *From Childe:* The Most Ancient East

FIGURE 53h
Circular bas-relief showing a hunt in the marshes. British Museum.
— *From Childe:* The Most Ancient East

near Ur, by Messrs. Hall and Woolley's Anglo-American mission. Part of them go back to the first dynasty at Ur (from about 3100 to 2800 B.C.), and part to a period previous to this first dynasty, which may be provisionally dated at about 3500 to 3200 B.C. The finds, which represent Sumerian culture, consist of steatite or alabaster vases analogous to those of pre-dynastic Egypt, gold jewellery (head-dress of Queen Shub-ad), statues such as the amazing bull's head in gold with a beard of lapis lazuli, mosaics of coloured stones, one of which represents a royal banquet with animals offered as tribute, and some limestone reliefs, one of which represents a chariot drawn by asses or creatures part ass, part gryphon, with human figures of a decidedly Sumerian type.

Our first impression when faced with these works dating from the year 3100, or earlier, is one of astonishment at the high civilization and subtle art of which they are the revelation. We need only glance at the objects brought to light by Mr. Woolley, which are so many masterpieces. For instance, there is a plate of shell, representing a sort of game of chess, in which we already find, in a more realistic form, those pairs of animals face to face which formed a conventional motive in later ages: rearing lions tearing to pieces beasts of the deer tribe, which are also standing on their hind legs, and pairs of animals of the bovine or deer tribe standing in a heraldic posture on opposite sides of the tree of life. In these figures thirty centuries of Mesopotamian civilization already live before us. Again, on a plate of engraved shell forming the front of a royal harp, we find the subject (which was already known!) of the hero Gilgamesh grasping the two bulls; or animals endowed with human attributes in a fashion unknown in Egypt till a later age — lions, jackals, and bears on their hind legs, carrying food or playing the harp, with that animal humour which we shall find in Japan four thousand years later, in Toba Sojo; or, better still, on the so-called " Standard " we already find a regular epic scene, with those great ordered groups which we shall find again twenty centuries later on the Assyrian reliefs: we see the war-chariots in action, with their drivers and lancers, trampling the conquered enemy beneath their horses' hoofs; or the king, surrounded by his attendants, and with his chariot behind him, receiving the captives; or, again, the same king and his courtiers after the victory, pouring libations to the gods in token of gratitude. Next come processions of harpists and dancers, and, to conclude the picture, the booty passing before the king — cattle, bales of wares, etc. When, long afterwards, in the seventh century B.C., we come to the triumphs of the kings of Assyria, we should not forget these ancient prototypes of the epic scenes of Sumerian history. Above all, when we come to the realistic animal sculpture of the Sargonid age, we must remember the fragments excavated on this same site at Ur by Mr. Woolley: the silver head of a cow from the tomb of Queen Shub-ad, the gold and lapis lazuli head of a bull found near it, from the front of the harp mentioned above. In their brutal elegance and powerful realism — so powerful as to breathe a spirit of absolute despotism — these heads show us that the whole principle of Chaldeo-Assyrian, Achæmenid, and Sāsānid animal sculpture was already in existence. We may even wonder whether this powerful Sumero-Akkadian realism did not lose some of its spontaneity by the time it arrived at the historic period, by developing into a system and a classical convention, and whether what is known as " Moslem aridity " was not already beginning as early as the time of Khammurabi.

Again, in the implement for holding reins from the tomb of Shub-ad, the style of the ass which surmounts it already foreshadows the whole art of the Caucasus and of the steppes, with their bronze ornaments for harness and standards, adorned with figures of deer (Fig. 53 i).

We cannot but be filled with a profound emotion as we witness, not the process of development, but the sudden revelation of the whole æsthetic canon of the Near and Middle East, which was already fully

FIGURE 53i

Rein ring and mascot from Queen Shub-ad's
chariot.

— *From Childe:* The Most Ancient East

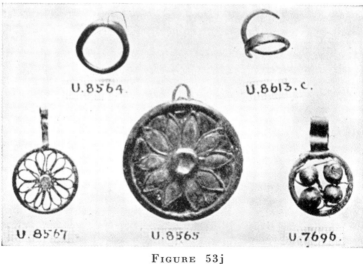

U.8564.   U.8613.C.

U.8567.   U.8565.   U.7696.

FIGURE 53j

Ear-rings and pendants from graves at Ur.
— *From Childe:* The Most Ancient East

constituted at such a remote period. For let us but consider the dates. The tomb of Queen Shub-ad, as we have seen, dates from about 3100 B.C., the period of the first dynasty of Ur. But deeper still, the fourth grave at Ur, known as the grave of the Standard, takes us back, according to Mr. Woolley, to 3500 B.C.

In connexion with the same remote age in Chaldea, we may also mention the antiquities of Kish, dating from the Sumerian period of that city, and discovered in 1928–9 by the archæological expedition of the University of Oxford and the Field Museum of Chicago, consisting of Messrs. Langdon, Mackay, Charles Watelin, and T. K. Penniman. The terracotta figurines yielded by these excavations — including a chariot with driver and horses, polychrome Sumerian heads, bands with reliefs of animals of the deer tribe with great horns — date from about the year 3000. But we may observe that in the lower strata on the same site at Kish, after a great flood — suggesting *the* Flood — which is marked by a gap in civilization, we find far more ancient deposits, containing objects which already bear witness to an advanced civilization: for example, a copper dagger-handle with an elegant interlaced pattern, which Monsieur Watelin assigns to about 3200, and some cylinders which he assigns to 3500. Lower still, aeneolithic deposits have been reached which Monsieur Watelin dates at about 4000.[1]

The antiquities of Tello, the ancient Sumerian city of Lagash, belong to the same civilization, though they have been known to us for longer. One of the most venerable of the finds at Tello, dating from about 3000 B.C., is the little bas-relief in the Louvre known as the " figure with the plumes." The person represented here displays all the characteristics of the Sumerian type mentioned above: the hooked nose like an eagle's beak, the clean-shaven face; the upper part of the body is bare, in accordance with the customary etiquette

___

[1] See Ch. Watelin: "*Rapport sur les fouilles de Kish*," *Journal Asiatique* (Paris), July–September 1929 (which appeared in 1930), pp. 111–12.

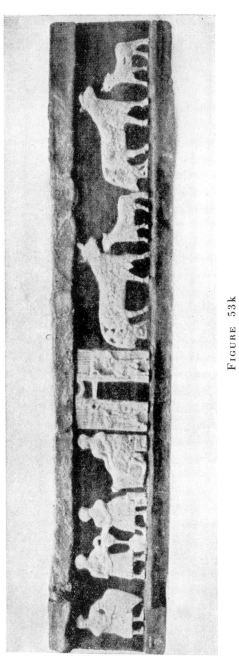

FIGURE 53k

Milking-scene, from walls of A-anni-padda's temple at el-Ubaid.
— *From Childe: The Most Ancient East*

of religious ceremonies, and it wears a long skirt. In the same style, and likewise dating from about 3000 B.C., is the limestone slab in the Louvre representing Ur-Nina, the *patesi* of Lagash, surrounded by his family, the prince and the other figures being of the same Sumerian type, which is all the more characteristic here because all of them are bare-headed and have their heads clean-shaven as well as their faces (Fig. 53 b). Still more remarkable is the famous " Vulture stele " set up by Eannatum, the next king but one of Lagash after Ur-Nina, to commemorate his victory over the rival cities. The front of the stele represents Eannatum leading his troops to victory. Both King and soldiers are represented as belonging to the usual Sumerian type, but wearing helmets: the soldiers, in a dense phalanx, are armed with long lances and protected by long, square shields; the King is brandishing a lance in one hand and

FIGURE 54
Vulture Stele from Tello.
— *Louvre. Archives photographiques*

a sort of scimitar in the other; in the distance vultures are devouring the corpses of the enemy. On the reverse side we see the god of Lagash bearing a mace in one hand, his emblem, an eagle with outstretched wings and lions gripped in its claws, in the other, while the vanquished enemies are contained within a net (Fig. 54).

In this stele Sumerian sculpture already gives proof of those qualities of composition, strength, and vigour which were to remain the heritage of Assyro-Chaldean art throughout its fifteen centuries of history. Lastly, Entemena, king of Lagash, and grandson of

Eannatum, has left us a magnificent silver vase, now in the Louvre, on the body of which are represented four lion-headed eagles holding in bonds a series of lions, deer, and wild goats alternately, while each lion is at the same time biting the muzzle of the deer or wild goat in the next group. Thus, as Monsieur Pottier points out, even at this archaic period the Chaldeans had already definitively laid down the traditional principles of heraldic art and figures face to face, as they were handed down through the ages by the Hittites, the Assyrians, the Persians of the Achæmenid and Sāsānid ages, and through the latter to the Altaic races. This decorative motive is closely connected with the preference displayed by the ancient Chaldeans for combats between monsters and men or animals. The cylindrical seals, such numbers of which have come down to us through the excavations at Tello, are full of such scenes, inspired chiefly by the ancient epic of Gilgamesh and the monster Enkidu, and symmetrical in design. Contemporaneously with this heraldic pose, indeed, we find on these cylinders a certain number of types of monster, such as the two-headed eagle and the " *kherubim*," or human-headed bulls, which were to be so profusely developed by the Assyrians later, but were already fixed as early as the period of Lagash and Agade; or such as the winged dragon, often represented as standing, with a scaly body, having the fore-paws of a lion, the hind feet of a bird of prey, and the head and tail of a serpent, like the one on the body of the libation urn from Gudea in the Louvre. In this, again, all the arts of nearer Asia and central or northern Asia, from the Sāsānid to the Siberian textiles — the transitional stage between which is marked by the arts of the Caucasus and southern Russia — owe a tribute to the ancient masters of Sumer.[1] The same groups of animals — not fully conventionalized as yet — are found on the cylinders of Susa, dating from about 3000 B.C. We may point out, in particular, fights between lions and bulls, charging bulls or leaping beasts of the deer tribe, with a vivid

[1] See Vol. III, Fig. 88–101.

realism and freedom of movement which are, oddly enough, very similar to those of Cretan art, and which Assyrian art was never to recover again to the same degree. (See G. Contenau: *Manuel d'archéologie orientale*, Vol. I (1927), pp. 381–401, Fig. 287–302.

During the following period, that of the Empire of Agade, this art, which was already full of promise, made amazing progress. Agade was at that time the chief city of the Semitic land of Akkad. Its kings, Sargon the Old, or Sarru-kinu, and Naram-Sin (between 2875 and 2712, or else between 2700 and 2600), subdued the whole of Mesopotamia. This first Semitic Empire has left us one admirable work of art, the triumphal stele of Naram-Sin, now in the Louvre, on which that King is represented as leading his army to the attack on a mountainous region, the inhabitants of which are being surprised and massacred. The vigorous qualities displayed by the Vulture stele are still to be found here, but the artist further displays a freedom of technique and a knowledge of anatomy which are a real innovation. The King, wearing on his head the lofty helmet with bull's horns, is a heroic figure, standing in a spirited attitude, with a bow in his left hand, and his lowered lance in his right hand. The modelling and supple rendering of the nude are no less remarkable in the figures of the soldiers, whose action as they ascend the mountain is most happily indicated beneath the light stuff of their skirted garment. But it is perhaps the figures of the vanquished which are most remarkable in this respect. The figure whom the King is trampling underfoot, the corpse that is being hurled down from the mountain, and, lastly, facing the King, the conquered enemy who is turning in his flight to beg for mercy, and his companion who is falling back on his knee in his attempt to turn aside the javelin as it strikes him, are all worthy of the Æginetan pediments. Moreover, the happy grouping of the figures, and the care with which the landscape is indicated without over-emphasis or heaviness, are significant of the remarkable skill in composition (Fig. 55).

FIGURE 55
Stele of Naram-Sin.
— *Louvre. Archives photographiques*

After the fall to Agade the Sumerians recovered the hegemony under the Ur dynasty, whose empire embraced the whole of Mesopotamia between 2475 and 2358, as that of Agade had formerly done. But the Sumerian art of this period is chiefly known to us from the works of a little prince who played only a secondary part politically, Gudea, the local *patesi* of Lagash, who flourished about 2492 B.C.

Before the period of Gudea, Chaldean sculpture, with the exception of the figurines and pottery, had still as a rule been confined to incised work upon stone and bas-relief. It now shook off the last traces of this timidity, and, like the sailor who ventures at last to lose sight of shore in order to launch out upon the high seas, it now grappled with works in the round; and, at a single blow, it produced masterpieces. The animal-sculptors have left us such works as Gudea's mace, now in the Louvre, with its two lions' heads back to back, which already possess all the realism of

FIGURE 56
Statue of Gudea.
— *Louvre. Archives photographiques*

the Sargonid lions. The metal-workers cast statuettes such as the copper " prophylactic divinity " of Ur-Bau (Gudea's predecessor at Lagash), a little bearded divinity resting his knee on the ground while he drives a nail into it, who, by the delicacy of his profile and the grace of his movement, is worthy, not only of Assyrian, but of Greek art. Finally, when we come to statues on a large scale, we have the diorite portraits of Gudea brought from Tello to the Louvre (Fig. 56, 57). The most beautiful of these statues is undoubtedly the one —

FIGURE 57
Statue of Gudea.
— *Louvre. Photo, Giraudon*

unfortunately h e a d l e s s — which represents the old monarch seated with folded hands, holding on his knees the plan of one of the buildings founded by him. In all these works Gudea is draped in a piece of stuff which leaves his right arm and shoulder bare. As on the stele of Naram-Sin, the modelling of the muscles in the nude portions — the right arm and shoulder — is rendered with admirable realism, and all the more boldly because the artist is working in the round; even in the draped portions the stuff in no way obscures the limbs — unlike the later developments of Assyrian art; we have only to look at the play of the masses of muscle on the back: " we feel that the body is alive beneath the thin stuff." In the same way, contrary to the fashion of Assyrian art, the somewhat squat appearance of the racial type is here corrected by the breadth of the treatment; and the style, though robust, remains restrained and sober. The whole produces an uncommon effect of balanced strength and constructive force. As for the heads, which are shaven in the Sumerian fashion, and generally surmounted by a sort of turban with a roll of stuff round the head, their powerful build recalls certain heads of the archaic period of Greek art (Fig. 58). Indeed, as Dr. Contenau has pointed out, we are here dealing with works " which ought soon to have led up to an art as pure as that of the Greeks almost two thousand years later " (see Fig. 59). But this art, weighty and sure of itself though it might be, and already so emancipated that anything might be expected of it, was to be to some extent checked in its development, no doubt as a result of the series of invasions which were to take the guidance of Chaldea's destinies out of her own hands.

FIGURE 58
Sumerian head wearing turban.
— *Louvre. Archives photographiques*

BABYLONIAN CIVILIZATION

THE LAST SUMERIAN EMPIRE, that of Ur, was overthrown about 2358 by two foreign peoples: the Elamites on the east, and the Amorites on the west. The Elamites set up a dynasty of their own race in the south of Chaldea, while the north fell into the power of the Amorites, a Semitic people coming from Syria. The Amorites established their centre at Babylon, a city which, thanks to them, was to become the capital of Chaldea. One of their kings, Khammurabi (2123–2081?), overthrew the Elamite dynasty in the south and founded the Babylonian Empire, whose power extended over the whole of Mesopotamia.

Whether they were purely Semitic or merely assimilated to the Semitic type, it is certain that the Amorites were very rapidly absorbed into the Akkadian stock, and brought about the triumph of the Semitic element in Chaldea. In this respect Khammurabi was a true successor to the ancient kings of Agade. He had remarkable powers of administration and gave orders for the compilation of a

FIGURE 59
Chaldean relief, about 2500 B.C.
— *Louvre. Photo, Giraudon*

celebrated code of laws which is still one of the best sources of our knowledge of Chaldean society.

The art of the period of Khammurabi has left us several works of capital importance, notable among which is the diorite stele found at Susa, now in the Louvre, on which is engraved the code of the Chaldean monarch. On it Khammurabi is represented as standing in an attitude of supplication, wearing a sort of turban, and dressed in a long robe which leaves his right arm bare; the sun-god Shamash is seated on a throne facing him, dictating to him his laws (Fig. 60).

This relief has been justly admired for the purity of its lines, the " sober grandeur " of its composition, and the majesty of pose of god and King alike. But in comparing it with that of Naram-Sin, Dr. Contenau justly points out that, though it reveals " a certain advance in refinement of technique, a greater sureness of touch, and perhaps even a more just care for proportion," the progress goes no further than these formal virtues. The time is approaching when the body was to cease to have any life beneath the draperies, and when, under the hands of the Assyrians, the latter came to be treated for their own sake alone. Dr. Contenau concludes that, though the Amorite princes may have become the zealous disciples of their Sumero-Akkadian subjects and to a certain extent perfected the technique of the age of Agade and Lagash, yet, far from seeking anything further, they seem, on the whole, to have taken care to adhere to the traditional canons of art.

FIGURE 60
Stele of Khammurabi.
— *Louvre. Photo, Giraudon*

In the sphere of literature the age of Khammurabi set itself in like fashion to codify, catalogue, and preserve the treasures of Chaldean thought, which were already considerable. And now the Semitic, Akkadian element decidedly gained the upper hand over the Sumerian. For this very reason care was taken to translate most of the old Sumerian epics into Semitic; at the same time the Semitic works themselves were edited for the royal library and the temple libraries, so that the Amorite period had somewhat the same importance for the preservation of Chaldean literature as Athens had in the age of Peisistratus and his successors for the preservation of the Homeric literature in its definitive form.

In fact, the Semitic recensions of the epic of Gilgamesh seem to date from this period — Gilgamesh being a sort of Sumerian Hercules, the son of a goddess, but pursued by the wrath of another goddess, Ishtar, whose love he had rejected. To the same period belong the Chaldean versions of the Creation and the Deluge, mighty epics which have the very note of the book of Genesis, just as we find something of the lyric grief of the Hebrew Psalms in the Chaldean litanies and in the famous "Poem of the Suffering Righteous Man," which has such analogies with the book of Job. In this violence and harshness of tone, in this picture of the misery of man before his god, who is conceived as jealous and terrible, in these pathetic and sometimes despairing cries, and in the power with which the whole moral problem is here presented, as well as in the gloomy and powerful imagery drawn from the ancient theogonies, the Chaldean genius has, indeed, a certain affinity with that of the Bible. Thus Chaldean thought, the humanism of the East in its most ancient period, did really exercise a decisive influence upon the intellectual evolution of the neighbouring races. In the same way, as we shall see, Chaldean motives were for many centuries to inspire the decorative art of later peoples: the Hittites, the Assyrians, and the Persians of the Achæmenid and Sāsānid periods.

HITTITE CIVILIZATION

THE DYNASTY OF KHAMMURABI AND THE GREAT BABYLONIAN EMPIRE were destroyed about 1925 B.C. by a raid of the Hittites, invaders who descended upon it from Asia Minor. In the confusion which ensued, the Kassites, who inhabited the mountains bounding Chaldea on the east, seized Babylon, which remained in their possession for more than five centuries, from 1760 to 1185. While still preserving the results of her civilization, Babylon experienced a perceptible check in her artistic evolution under this foreign domination, and fell into a state of political decline which enabled first the Egyptian Pharaohs of the XVIIIth dynasty, then the Hittites, and lastly the Assyrians to seize the hegemony of the East.

When the Hittites first appear in history, in the twentieth century before our era, they are found living on the plateau of Anatolia and had as their centre Cappadocia, where stood their capital, Hattushash, the modern Boghaz-Keui. They seem to have been a composite people. It is quite probable that the nucleus of the Hittite confederation was Asianic — that is, genuinely Anatolian. It is also quite possible that an Indo-European aristocracy had arrived by way of the Bosporus and superimposed itself upon this indigenous mass. As for their culture, side by side with the native elements we can distinguish others which were borrowed from Chaldea. Part of the Hittite texts, and notably the inscriptions on the rocks, are written in a special hieroglyphic script which has not yet been entirely deciphered and represents this people's national writing. At the same time the Hittites used the cuneiform script which had originated in Chaldea. German archæological missions have discovered at Boghaz-Keui a whole store of royal archives written on cuneiform tablets, but composed, some in Babylonian Semitic, the diplomatic language of the period, others in the various dialects of the Hittite confederation, which are as yet but imperfectly identified. As for their religion, it included the cult of a great god, a divinity of thunder and the mountain heights, named Teshub, whose attributes were the ax and the bull; and of a great goddess who was the prototype of the Greek Cybele.

The Hittites were firmly established in Asia Minor, where they occupied Cappadocia, Pontus, and part of Armenia and Cilicia and from whence they dominated Phrygia and Lydia; and in the twentieth century B.C. they began to make their power felt in northern Syria and Mesopotamia. In 1925 B.C., as we have seen, they swept down and sacked Babylon in the course of a sudden raid. And towards 1370 they subdued the powerful kingdom of Mitanni, situated in the north-west of Mesopotamia, in the great bend of the Euphrates.

At that time the sway of the Hittite kings extended from the Black Sea and Lydia to the frontiers of Assyria. In the south they detached northern Syria from its dependence upon Egypt and, towards 1350, established their own suzerainty there. In spite of the victory gained over them by the Pharaoh Rameses II in 1295 at Kadesh (now Tell-Nebi-Mend, near Homs), Egypt ended by partitioning Syria with them, the north remaining in the hands of the Hittites, the south in those of the Egyptians. This peace was followed in 1279 by a close alliance. The great Hittite Empire, thus firmly established in Asia Minor, western Mesopotamia, and northern Syria, lasted for almost two centuries. But, like Egypt, it sustained a shock from the invasions of the maritime races of the Ægeans and Achæans between 1229 and 1192, after which it was simultaneously attacked on the north-west by the Thraco-Phrygians, who obtained possession of the Hittite domains in Asia Minor, and on the south-east by the Assyrians, who proceeded to encroach incessantly upon the remaining Hittite possessions in northern Syria and western Mesopotamia from the twelfth century onwards. As early as 1110 the Assyrians subdued for the first time this greatly shrunken Hittite kingdom of Carchemish. Towards 1060 the Hittites shook off their domination, but were crushed again in 850 and 715, on the latter of which occasions they were absorbed once for all into the Assyrian Empire.

As we see, in the fourteenth and thirteenth centuries B.C. the Hittites played a leading part in the political history of western Asia. During the whole of this period they and the Egyptians were the true successors of the old Chaldean emperors in the hegemony of the East, and played a scarcely less important part in the history of civilization. While Babylon slumbered, so to speak, under the Kassite kings, they formed, in many respects, the connecting link between the ancient Chaldean and the later Assyrian civilizations.

Hittite art, which has been revealed by the excavations at Boghaz-Keui and Yasili-Kaya in Cappadocia, Ibriz in Lycaonia, Malatia in Lesser Armenia, Carchemish on the Euphrates, and Zenjirli on the Syro-Cilician frontier, has now asserted its individual character, thanks to the work of German scholars, of Monsieur Hrozny of Prague, and of Messieurs Pottier and Contenau in France. Though inspired by the ancient art of Chaldea and, to a lesser degree, by certain Egyptian conventions, it shows signs of real originality and often proved its powers of invention.

Whereas everything built by the Chaldeans was entirely constructed of plain brick, the Hittites, though also using brick for the upper part of the buildings, employed stone for the foundations. Moreover, unlike the Chaldean architects, who seem to have been ignorant of any pillars but those of brickwork, they made a wide use of the column properly so called, the form which they affected being a wooden column standing upon a stone base — a system which was also adopted in Mycenæan Greece. Finally — and this is their essential contribution — they conceived the idea of decorating the plinths of their buildings and the bases of their columns with a number of bas-reliefs; these bas-reliefs on the plinths and sculptured bases of columns are as characteristic of Hittite art as reliefs on the frieze and sculptured capitals are of Greek art. For the rest, the Hittites seem to have had such a predilection for bas-reliefs that they covered whole walls of rock with them as well; a notable instance is the base of the temple of Yasili-Kaya, situated on a rock near Boghaz-Keui, where the marriage of the god Teshub and the Great Goddess is carved in the rock in the form of two processions of divine characters, standing on their symbolic animals and advancing to meet each other. As Dr. Contenau has pointed out, in this work, which must go back to the period of the great Hittite Empire, about the fourteenth century, we find all the essential characteristics of Hittite art, " a predilection for sculptures arranged in long rows, a desire for movement, a taste for broadly conceived compositions, eliminating detail and confining itself to great masses, the use of animals to adorn doorways, whether flat against the wall or so disposed that the front part of the creature seems to be emerging from the wall." Indeed, when we consider the processions of divinities at Yasili-Kaya, or the splendid relief of the sun-god on a limestone block at Boghaz-Keui, we have the impression that here we are concerned with a branch of the art of Mesopotamia, as powerful as Chaldean art and perhaps possessing a superior sense of movement, but, in this first period at least, neglecting those episodical details which were to characterize Assyrian art.

The second Hittite archæological group is that of Carchemish, which has been so strikingly analysed by Monsieur Pottier and seems to extend in a regular series from the fourteenth to the ninth century. Certain of the most ancient reliefs in this group represent a combination of divine genii and animals — lions, bulls, or deer — which, as Monsieur Pottier points out, display a greater affinity with ancient Sumero-Akkadian art than with that of Assyria. On the most recent reliefs, for example, scenes of royal and everyday life, such as hunting-scenes, predominate over religious subjects. In both types the animals, and, above all, the lions, deer, and bulls, are treated with remarkable power, which, as was also to happen in Assyrian art, often accentuates the relief of the principal articulations of the body, as well as with a breadth and sense of realism which, in spite of a certain naïveté of technique, are remarkably successful in rendering the distinctive characteristics of species, pose, and movement in these beasts (Fig. 61). The Assyrian art of the Sargonid period had only to develop these qualities in order to arrive at the masterpieces of the animal-sculptors of Khorsābād. Often, too, animal forms are combined with human heads, or vice versa, in such a way as to produce fantastic monsters, inspired by both Egypt and Chaldea, but preserving a local character. The Hittite sphinx, in particular, is distinguished by the treatment of an Egyptian subject with a technique borrowed from Chaldea; but it

FIGURE 61
Royal hunting-scene, Hittite.
— *Louvre. Archives photographiques*

sometimes assumes the quite typical form of a two-headed creature, a sort of chimera, having at the same time a human head in the normal position, and a lion's head issuing from the breast. On the other hand, we may note at Carchemish some processions of soldiers in which the costume of the warriors, with their plumed and crested helmets, seems to be intermediate between that of Assyrian and that of Mycenæan soldiers.

According to Monsieur Pottier, the finds at Zenjirli also seem to form a regular series extending from about the fourteenth to the eighth centuries. Some fine column-bases have been found there, formed of two sphinxes joined together, these monsters being here treated quite in the Mesopotamian manner; in the same style are a number of lions guarding doorways, with the body in relief and the head in the round — lions and sphinxes which, if we think of the date, may well seem to have inspired the lions and *kherubim* guarding the doors of the Sargonid palaces. In the bas-reliefs at Zenjirli, as in those of Carchemish, we may also note some hunting-scenes which, though rather naïve, are full of movement; some representations of the god Teshub armed with a thunderbolt; and some fine types of Hittite warrior, which can be recognized by their national costume: the high head-dress shaped like a tiara, or Phrygian cap, the roll of hair lying on the neck, the girdle with a long, fringed end falling down on the thigh, and the shoes with a long, pointed toe turned up at the end. Malatia, to the north of Zenjirli, has yielded a fine bas-relief, now in the Louvre, representing a prince in his chariot hunting the deer (Fig. 61). In view of the date attributed to this work (about 1000 B.C.), there is some justification for regarding such works as this as the prototype of the similar hunting-scenes which are so frequent on the Assyrian bas-reliefs.

ASSYRIAN CIVILIZATION

WHATEVER THE RACIAL CONSTITUENTS OF THE ASSYRIAN PEOPLE may have been — and it contained Sumerian, Semitic, Mitannian, and other elements — by the time it arrived at the classical period of its history, it presented an exclusively Semitic aspect. At this time it was a strong military race, tougher and more virile than its Babylonian cousins. As we see the Assyrians on their bas-reliefs, they were squat and muscular, with aquiline noses and coarse nostrils, thick lips, large and piercing eyes, and a vigorous cast of countenance. And as they reveal themselves to us in their inscriptions, they were

Spartan while on campaign, sensual and ostentatious when victorious, and cruel to the vanquished. At the time when they entered the main current of world-history, about the thirteenth century B.C., they already formed a sort of military state, of which war was to remain the national industry to the end.

The earliest gods of Assyria were the high priests of the two national divinities, Assur, the eponymous god of the country, and Ishtar, the planet Venus, the goddess of war and also of fertility. In spite of these sacerdotal origins the Assyrian monarchy never possessed a religious character like that of the monarchy of the Pharaohs. It was in the first place a military monarchy, to whose nature any sort of mysticism was foreign. For two centuries (the fourteenth and thirteenth) it waged war against the Kassite kings of Babylon with the object of wresting their supremacy from them, which it succeeded in doing for the first time under Tiglath-pileser I (about 1115–1100). After a century of obscurity, kings Assur-nazir-pal II (884–859) and Shalmaneser III (859–824) gradually brought the various states of Mesopotamia and Syria under their suzerainty. After a fresh period of eclipse, during which the neighbouring peoples shook off the yoke, King Tiglath-pileser III (746–727) conquered Damascus in 732 and Babylon in 728. His work was carried on by the dynasty of the Sargonids (722–612). The founder of this house, Sargon II (722–705), who built the palace of Khorsā-bād, destroyed the kingdom of Israel (722) and crushed Urardhu (Ararat), a state peopled by a Caucasian race settled in what is now Armenia (714). His son Sennacherib (705–681) definitively annexed Babylonia (in 689). Esar-haddon (681–669), son of Sennacherib, imposed his suzerainty upon Egypt (670). Finally, Assur-bani-pal (669–626), son of Esar-haddon, destroyed Elam (646), the last independent state in the Middle East. By this time Assyria had no rivals left in the East. The dominion of the Sargonids, based upon the terror of their arms, was now undisputed from Cappadocia to Iran, from Ararat and the Caspian to Egypt and the Persian Gulf; even Iran and Asia Minor, which did not form part of the Assyrian Empire, felt the influence of its civilization. Its capital, Nineveh, was the real capital of the world.

No people has been more severely judged than the Assyrians; and it is certainly difficult to find anything that inspires sympathy in their character. Ruthless in war and implacable in politics, they were a hard and despotic nation — so despotic and so hard that, compared with them, the other peoples of the ancient East seem to us almost compassionate, not even excepting the Phœnicians or the Jews. But they also possessed the qualities of their defects. Tenacious, vigorous, and muscular, they stood for the fine human animal with all its ardour and cunning; the warriors of Assur have the terrible beauty of a great wild beast. Moreover, it was the very brutality of the Assyrians that really led them to play a part in history. Unconsciously, their inhuman policy served the cause of civilization. Through blood and hatred, through terror erected into a system of government, these Romans of ancient Asia ended by uniting all the peoples of the East beneath the same yoke. They were the imperial race of the East and absorbed all the former civilized states of antiquity into one and the same empire. By devastation and massacre they caused peace to reign from the Nile to Mount Ararat. It is true that this empire collapsed at the very moment when the Sargonids had just put the finishing touch to its construction, and this deathlike peace gave place to a revolt of all the tormented peoples. But in this respect the work of the Assyrians outlived them, and the short and terrible peace of the Sargonids was the herald of the beneficent peace of the Archæmenids. The vast political unit which the Sargonids had really brought into existence did not disappear again. Under a variety of names and masters this Sargonid Empire, which was to be handed down in turn to the Chaldeans, the Achæmenids, the Macedonians, the Sāsānids, and the Arabs, this empire of the Middle East, was to remain one of the most constant of historical factors, and bore to the end the stamp of the materialistic civilization of Nineveh and Babylon.

The Chaldeo-Assyrian civilization already contained the germ of nearly the whole of the Arabo-Persian civilization; and the court of the Sargonids already expressed the whole spirit of the Orient in the brutality and pomp of its royal despotism, the luxury of its setting, and the blend of self-indulgence and savage energy which characterized all its members.

First the king. He was not a god, as in Egypt; he was the head of an army; for the whole Assyrian people was nothing but an army, which was nearly always on campaign. This " king of the legions, the great king, the mighty king, the king of the land of Assur," passed half his life on horseback or in his chariot, in hunting or in warfare, in the massacre of wild beasts or of peoples. When they were not at war, the kings of Assyria hunted the aurochs or the lion and fought them in single combat. War, which in their eyes was nothing but a more exciting form of the chase, provided them with the same brutal joys: they fought with lance or arrow like the most insignificant of their infantrymen, and then, when it came to the " kill," they flayed their prisoners alive, impaled or blinded them with their own royal hands.

The ferocious instincts which they displayed in action gave way in hours of repose to a life of indolence and unbridled indulgence. The whole Oriental temperament is revealed in these contrasts. The king who had fought single-handed with the lion or the aurochs, the Hittite and the Elamite, would next relapse for months or years on end into the delights of the harem, sated with pleasures and glory, besotted and effeminate as the Sardanapalus of legend. On ceremonial occasions he would appear beneath a blaze of canopies, parasols, and feather fans, dressed like an idol and decked out like a favourite of the harem. Let us picture the Sargonid to ourselves on these occasions of state, with his sensual lips, his powerful profile, and his eagle eye, dressed in the amazing costume of which the bas-reliefs have preserved the record. His face was carefully painted; his hair and beard, perfumed and curled with meticulous care, descended in tiers of ringlets on his shoulders and breast; on his head he wore a tiara of white woollen material striped with blue and shaped like a truncated cone, bound round the brow with a broad ribbon covered with a pattern of gold rosettes; his robe of deep blue with red rosettes was finished at the hem with a fringe adorned with four rows of precious stones; this robe, which left his arms bare, was confined at the waist by a broad embroidered girdle, in which was stuck a set of daggers; over his robe the king wore a chasuble-shaped garment open at the sides and simply loaded with embroidered flowers and sprays, with gold and silver trimmings and jewels of every kind. To this sumptuous costume was added a profusion of jewels: necklaces and ear-rings of gold, a short sword with a sheath covered with plates of gold and a gold lion in relief. This mass of precious stones, this blaze of gold on the plain white and blue of the woollen stuffs, must have produced a dazzling effect beneath the Eastern sun.

We may imagine, grouped round the Sargonid, the throng of dignitaries and courtiers, all decked out with the same care and massive luxury, from the Tartan, or grand vizier, down to the least of the young princes. And lastly, forming the background of the scene, we may imagine the Assyrian warriors, veterans of the old campaigns in Egypt, Ararat, and Elam, now victorious in some twenty battles, sated like their master with gold and blood, and like him celebrating their triumph by colossal orgies. Proud and menacing as the *kherubim*, the winged bulls of Khorsābād, they formed a heroic escort to the Sargonid. Here were the horsemen, the terrible horsemen of Assur, accustomed to guiding their horses by a mere pressure of the knee, and the sound of whose distant galloping troubled the night-watches of the prophets of Israel; here were the charioteers, three to each heavy chariot; here were the infantry, with their pikes or their bows, wearing a conical helmet, sometimes surmounted by a short crest, their leathern jerkins covered with overlapping metal scales to protect the chest and shoulders, and with a short waist-cloth falling to the knee, beneath which appeared their close-fitting breeches and high leather boots, laced up the front. Armed with a great wicker shield faced with metal, a bow, a short sword, and a six-foot lance, they advanced in serried ranks in the fine order shown on the bas-reliefs. Above their battalions, amid a forest of peaks and blades, rose the royal standard, the sacred disk of Assur, the divine archer, borne on two bulls' heads.

On days when a triumph was being celebrated, it must have been a stupendous sight to see this people in arms ascending the giant staircases of the palaces and temples in the train of the Sargonid. These palaces and temples were built upon platforms of unburnt brick, forming, as it were, an artificial eminence, so that they were visible over a vast extent of country. The monumental aspect of the Sargonid palaces, as we can reconstitute them from the reliefs at Khorsābād, was apparent at the very portal of the building — a colossal portal flanked by massive square towers and guarded by winged bulls with human faces, the grim *kherubim* which seemed like incarnations of the gloomy genius of Assur. Having crossed this dread threshold, one entered a great square courtyard, from which opened off the royal apartments. This was the Forbidden City, as sternly closed to all rumours from without as the seraglio of modern sultans. Here, in the cool shadow of the harem, the Sargonid could recall at leisure the memory of his hard campaigns beneath the terrible sun of Egypt or the Gulf, in the sands of the Syrian desert and the marshes of Elam. Every bas-relief in the palace, every tablet in the royal library, celebrated the monarch's pride, his wars, his hunting-expeditions, his pleasures, and his vengeance. The whole palace — a palace fortress whose luxury did not conceal its warlike character — was like a mighty hymn to the glory of Assur, its king and its gods.

The apotheosis of the Ninevite gods, which was so closely associated with the triumph of the Sargonid, was the apotheosis of the race itself. Their victory over the gods of Egypt, Judea, and Elam was the symbol of Assyrian world hegemony; the temple dominated the palace. The distinguishing mark of this temple, built on the model of the Chaldean temples, was the *ziggurat,* a square tower built in a series of diminishing tiers. There would be as many as seven of these tiers, each of which was consecrated to a star and painted a special colour — white, black, yellow, crimson, vermilion, silver, or gold. On top of the last storey, the golden one, stood the sanctuary of the god — either Assur, the eponymous divinity of the race, or Ishtar, the tutelary goddess of Arbela. It was here that, on their departure for their wars or hunting-expeditions, the Sargonid kings, surrounded by their soothsayers and astrologers, came to take counsel of the great gods their masters — the blazing stars of the Chaldean firmament.

This brutal people was highly cultured. Trained in the school of Chaldean letters, it collected this precious heritage and has handed it down to us. The last of its kings, Assur-bani-pal, collected an enormous library at Nineveh, thousands of tablets from which have been found and removed to the British Museum. This library covers the whole mass of scientific and literary knowledge which at that date had been accumulating for about two thousand four hundred years, during which Chaldeo-Assyrian society had been in existence; and it is partly through its agency that the Chaldean legends referred to above have been transmitted to us. But the most specifically Assyrian element in the texts of this period are the inscriptions of the kings. Here we have the heroic deeds of Assyria narrated from day to day by those who had performed them — and in what a tone! In this connexion nothing could be so expressive as the inscriptions of Assur-nazir-pal II, which throw a fierce glare of light upon the dread figures of the kings of Assyria and bring them to life before our eyes in all their colossal pride, with their savage joys and their thirst for blood: "One out of every two did I slay; I built a wall before the gates of the city; I flayed the chiefs alive and covered the wall with their skin. Some of them were walled up alive in the masonry, others were impaled along the wall; I had a large number of them flayed in my presence, and I covered the wall with their skin. I made wreaths of their heads and garlands of their corpses riddled with wounds." And he concludes his words with the announcement, like the roar of a wild beast: "As I stand on the ruins, my face beams with gladness. In the sating of my wrath I find satisfaction!"

ASSYRIAN ART

ASSYRIAN ART PROVIDES A FAITHFUL ILLUSTRATION OF THESE WORDS. The bas-reliefs of Nineveh and Khorsābād are simply a chronicle of royal acts narrated in frescoes of stone.

In this respect, as in so many others, Assyrian art is derived, not only from Chaldean art, but also from the Hittite, or, rather, from Chaldean art through the Hittite (Fig. 62). To convince ourselves of this, all we have to do is to compare the bas-reliefs of Yasili-Kaya, near Boghaz-Keui, described above, with such an Assyrian work as the procession of gods standing on the backs of animals from Mathai; the latter of these, which dates from Sennacherib (705–681) — that is, from a fairly late period — still faithfully follows the general subject, arrangement, and even style of the old Hittite model. More generally speaking, it was the Hittites who suggested to the Assyrians the idea of adorning the plinths of their buildings with processions of mythological or historical figures. Since the Assyrians did not, like the Hittites, employ blocks of stone for the base of their buildings, they had recourse to a mere facing of stone for their bas-reliefs, which produced the same effect. As the ruins of Carchemish prove, it was also the Hittites who taught the Assyrians to represent on these bas-reliefs not only mythological and religious subjects, but also, and in the first place, " secular " — that is, historical — subjects, such as the great exploits of the kings in war or the chase. Lastly, it was the Hittites, far more than the Chaldean masters of the Kassite age, who gave the Assyrian sculptors their love of life and sense of movement. Assyrian art can, however, be distinguished at

FIGURE 62
Lion, possibly Hittite. Azem Palace, Damascus.
— *Photo, E. de Lorey*

sight from that of the Hittites by its care for detail. The Hittites, as we have seen, were broad in composition and sober in ornament. The Assyrians, following in this respect the later Chaldeans, strove to render every curl of the hair or beard (Fig. 63), every detail of the chasing of a jewel, to the point of meticulousness. Their attention being absorbed by the ornamental detail of the fabrics, they stifled the body beneath the richness and heaviness of the stuff (Fig. 64 and 65). On the other hand, in the nude parts which are left exposed, such as the arms, this very love of detail causes them to exaggerate the treatment of the muscles to the point of violence. Such a wealth of detail of minor importance would soon become wearisome were it not that the unity of the whole is rigorously preserved by the clearness of the conception and the vigour of the execution. In spite of the heaviness of the racial type and the overloaded ornamentation which deprive Assyrian art of any aspiration towards elegance, it none the less achieves an effect of undeniable grandeur by its care for accuracy, its sense of proportion, and the natural majesty of the figures represented.

FIGURE 63
An Assyrian officer.
— *Louvre. Photo, Giraudon*

This nobility and majesty are strikingly present even in the earliest period, covering the reigns of Assur-nazir-pal II (884–859) and his successor, Shalmaneser III (859–824). The great standing statues of these princes are still, however, rather archaic and of too squat an appearance, the garment being in the form of a rigid column. The portraits in relief on the steles are more successful. In both, the work is distinguished by quite a pleasing simplicity, the ornamental details of the fabrics being still indicated with a certain sobriety; while in the winged bull and the colossal lion from Nimrud we notice a fire and mastery of technique which were to culminate in the masterpieces of the Sargonid animal-sculptors. As for the historical scenes containing a number of figures, they are characterized by the absence of any landscape (a few suggestive touches alone indicating the scene of action) and by the explanatory inscriptions in cuneiform with which the figures are almost entirely covered.

FIGURE 64
Sargon of Assyria and his viziers.
— *Louvre. Archives photographiques*

Under Sargon (722–705) a realistic setting appears, if not in the hunting-scenes, at least in the warlike ones, in which it begins to be possible to distinguish the various kinds of tree. The relief, which has hitherto been very low, becomes sharper, and the inscriptions are incised beside the figures and not on them. Under Sennacherib (705–681) the use of landscape backgrounds becomes general, the scene even being indicated with an exactitude which emphasizes the detail of trees and plants — palm-trees, pines, cypresses, vines, or reeds. The sculptor is interested in every episode of palace or camp life, thus combining " *genre* scenes " with his great historical compositions. Finally, under Assur-banipal (669–626) the bas-relief completes its development into a real picture crowded with figures. Beasts and men alike are full of amazing movement. The realistic episodes and *genre* scenes are treated with remarkable skill. Landscape in particular is lovingly reproduced. The

FIGURE 65
Barbarian archers.
— *Louvre. Delaporte donation. Archives photographiques*

figures are in general taller and less squat than before. As to the technique, it too reaches its highest perfection, every scene being chiselled with admirable finish.

As we watch this whole process of evolution, we can distinguish a certain number of general types which varied only in detail. Among the mythological beings we have first of all the winged bull with a man's head, used to flank a doorway — a statue when seen from in front, and a bas-relief when seen in profile (hence the visual artifice of its five paws). The body is that of a bull, but the curls and

FIGURE 66
Head of an Assyrian horse.
— Louvre. Photo, Giraudon

mane recall the lion, and the great wings are those of an eagle. This mythical creature, which is a mixture of man, bull, lion, and eagle, wears on its hairy, bearded face, crowned by the royal tiara, an expression of grave, noble serenity, which is already quite Olympian. It is " a combination of the great forces of nature " and has the majesty of a Zeus. The same characteristics are to be found in other creatures of the same order, in which the bust of a man is found in combination with the body of a lion.

In these mythological heads, as in those of the ordinary mortals, the Assyrian type is reproduced almost exclusively. It is an essentially virile type, not only in the kings and bearded warriors, but also in the beardless youths. In all of them we find the same forceful expression. But the individual types are not so marked as in Egypt, the personality being indicated only by the attributes and costume.

In spite of the qualities which we have pointed out, it must be ad-

mitted that the Assyrians did not render the human body so well as
the Egyptians, and the reason for this, as we have seen, was their
ignorance of the nude, due to the fact that the body was hidden from
them by the garment. On the other hand, the animal forms, which
they could study freely, are reproduced with a mastery which makes
these artists the greatest animal-sculptors of the ancient world. The
scenes illustrating the wars of Sennacherib and Assur-bani-pal are
certainly a vision of epic power, but it is among the royal hunting-
scenes of Koyunjik (Nineveh) and Khorsābād that we meet with the
real masterpieces.

The horse, man's companion in war and the chase, was naturally
the subject of impassioned study on the part of the Ninevite masters.
The sculptors of the bas-reliefs render its beautiful forms with the
loving care of connoisseurs, as well as every detail of its harness and
luxurious accoutrements (Fig. 66 to 68). Though it is a fairly near
relation of the Arab, the Assyrian horse, with its finely shaped head
and peculiarly expressive face, seems to belong to a rather less slender and more thick-set race. On these bas-reliefs we may admire
some magnificent specimens checked in their course, eager to start
off again, and quivering with impatience. In others, for instance at
Koyunjik, in a great scene representing Assur-bani-pal out hunting,
the galloping horses are beasts with superb muscles, while the King,
with drawn bow and arrow ready to let fly, is standing erect in his
chariot, full of the joyous animation of the chase (Fig. 69). Beside
this scene full of movement, we may admire the horses at rest in the
royal stables; they are eating out of mangers held by the palace
grooms, one of whom is rubbing down his horse, which is stretching
its limbs as the brush passes over them. The Assyrians have been
equally happy in their rendering of the other members of the horse
family. Everybody knows the reliefs of Assur-bani-pal hunting the
wild ass (onager), now in the British Museum: A herd of wild asses,
surprised by the King, is fleeing in disorder. Some, pierced by arrows,

FIGURE 67
Assyrian mounted archer.
- *Louvre. Photo, Giraudon*

FIGURE 68
Assyrian chariot.
— *Louvre. Photo, Giraudon*

FIGURE 69
Assur-bani-pal hunting.
— *British Museum. Photo, Mansell*

FIGURE 70
Hunting the wild ass.
— *British Museum. Photo, Mansell*

roll to the ground; others are bitten in the leg and pulled down by the
hounds; the more fleet of them make off at a gallop; a colt pauses to
kick up its heels, while a mare turns to call to her foal (Fig. 70 to 73).

FIGURE 71
Hunting the wild ass.
— *British Museum. Photo, Mansell*

These scenes are as graceful in line as they are rapid in movement.

The same grace is to be seen in two scenes representing an ibex or wild goat hunt: the goats are seen grazing while they are being stalked; one of them turns and snuffs the air, while the kids crop the

FIGURE 72
Hunting the wild ass.
— *British Museum. Photo, Mansell*

grass or trot behind their mothers; then the alarm is given, the arrows fly, and the flock breaks wildly into flight (Fig. 74).

Assur-bani-pal's hunting dogs must be given a place by themselves. They are superb mastiffs of a special breed, trained to stand up to a lion. Held in leash by the huntsmen, they strain at the rope and hurl themselves forward growling, in their eagerness for their prey and their impatience to be let loose (Fig. 75). A little further on, in one of the scenes described above, we see them at work, falling tooth and nail on a wounded wild ass.

But the supreme triumph of the Assyrians is in their representation

FIGURE 73
Wild ass pulled down by hounds.
— *British Museum. Photo, Mansell*

of the lion. They have really drawn him from the life, and compared with their lions, even those of the Greeks seem mere creatures of fancy. Not only did they hold frequent *battues* for hunting lions, but

FIGURE 74
Hunting the wild goat.
— *British Museum. Photo, Mansell*

they tamed them and brought them up in their palaces. Thus one of Assur-bani-pal's reliefs shows us a lion and lioness wandering at large in a royal park, among palm-trees and vines, the male beast standing in a noble attitude, the female lying inert on the ground, with her head on her outstretched paws (Fig. 76). Further on, a captive

FIGURE 75
Assur-bani-pal's hunting dogs.
— *British Museum. Photo, Mansell*

lion is being released from its cage for a fight in the arena and rushes forth with an expression of alarm and fury and a threatening snarl (Fig. 77). We may also cite the pathetic " wounded lioness " of the

British Museum: her hind quarters are paralysed by the arrow, but the beast braces herself to meet her death and, turning to face the enemy, lifts up her head in a last furious roar (Fig. 78). Another scene represents the single combat between King Assur-bani-pal and a lion, the episode being described in the inscription beside it: " I, Assur-bani-pal, king of the nations, king of Assyria, alone and on foot, in my majesty, did advance upon a mighty lion of the desert.

FIGURE 76
Lion and lioness in the royal park.
— *British Museum. Photo, Mansell*

I seized it by the ear, and, by the grace of Assur and of Ishtar, queen of battles, with my own hands I pierced its side with my lance" (see Fig. 79 to 81). Lastly, the Assyrian sculptors likewise excelled in representing the lion in the round, as the bronze statue from Khorsābād, now in the Louvre, bears witness; it shows us the beast crouched and roaring, with its powerful masses of muscle, its lean hind-quarters and redoubtable fangs, and "its muzzle wrinkled by its gaping jaws" (Fig. 82).

The treatment of the lion and the bull by the Assyrians was to a large extent to inspire the Persian sculptors of the Achæmenid age. The whole of Persian art, including that of the Sāsānids, was furthermore to inherit the heraldic motives of Assyria. Thus the griffons which are so largely represented in Assyrian decoration — for instance, on the mantle of Assur-bani-pal — were later to appear upon Sāsānid textiles; for instance the dragon-peacock on the garment of the equestrian figure of Khosrau II at Tāq-i Bustān. Among other figures which were to become very widespread was a sort of winged

FIGURE 77
Lions issuing from their cage.
— *British Museum. Photo, Mansell*

bull, with a slender elegance almost like that of a horse, which is found in pairs face to face, each standing on its hind legs in a perfectly symmetrical position, one on each side of a third figure or of the Plant of Immortality. Or, again, eagles, or monsters resembling eagles, standing on the heads of other animals. These decorative motives, dating back to the ancient Sumero-Akkadian cylinders, were developed by the Hittites, taken over by the Assyrians, and handed on by them to Persia and " Farther Iran." In this connexion we may note how Assyrian civilization filtered through into Ararat and among the other " Alarodian " peoples in the direction of the Caucasus, sowing

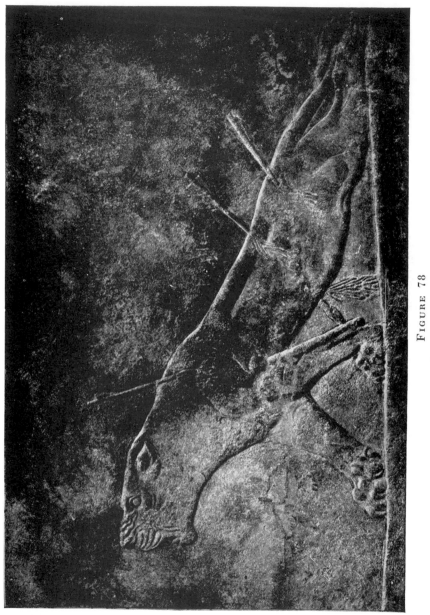

FIGURE 78
The wounded lioness.
— *British Museum. Photo, Mansell*

FIGURE 79
Assur-bani-pal's lion hunt.
— *British Museum. Photo, Mansell*

the seed which we shall see coming to life both in Iran and in
Transcaucasia, both in southern Russia and among the Altaic races
(see Volume III, Fig. 88 to 102).

FIGURE 80
Lion hunt.
— *British Museum. Photo, Mansell*

After this account of Assyrian sculpture we have now to say something about Assyrian painting. Up to the present time our information
on this subject was rather scanty; but in 1929 Monsieur Thureau-
Dangin, of the Louvre, discovered at Tell-Ahmar (formerly Til-

FIGURE 81
Assur-bani-pal's lion hunt.
— *British Museum. Photo, Mansell*

Barsib), in Jezireh, Syria, an Assyrian palace the interior of which
was decorated at a height of about six feet from the ground with
great frescoes, probably dating from the time of Tiglath-pileser III
(746–727). We find in them the same subjects as in the sculpture of

that time: scenes of battle and carnage and royal audiences, with the accustomed figures. The galloping horsemen are, in general, visions of epic splendour. The treatment of these frescoes has great affinities with that of the bas-reliefs. The different colours are always marked off from one another by a dark line. The colours consist of red (a

FIGURE 82
Bronze crouching lion from Khorsābād.
— *Louvre. Archives photographiques*

brownish red), white, and blue (a blue such as is seen in carpets). Yellow and green were not introduced into Assyrian painting till the time of Sargon.[1]

[1] Copies of these frescoes by Monsieur Cavro will shortly be exhibited in the Louvre. For further details see Thureau-Dangin: "*Les Spécimens de peintures assyriennes de Til-Barsib,*" in the review *Syria*, Vol. XI (1930), p. 113, with reproductions.

CHAPTER IV

Persian Pre-Islamic Civilization

ACHÆMENID CIVILIZATION

THE PERSIANS, THE MEDES, AND MOST OF THE OTHER PEOPLES of ancient Iran belonged to the Iranian race, a branch of the Indo-Iranian or " Aryan " family (the terms are synonymous), which itself forms part of the Indo-European group. We do not know at what period they established themselves in Iran; we need merely note that in the fourteenth century B.C. the north-west of Mesopotamia was inhabited by a people known as the Mitannians, whose kings bore Indo-Iranian names and worshipped gods which were also Indo-Iranian.

The primitive Iranian tongue was closely connected with Sanskrit. We find it in the form of two dialects: " Old Persian," the dialect of Fārs, or Persian proper; and Zend, which purports to represent a dialect of Media and is the language of the Mazdean Bible, or *Avesta*. There is a later form of Iranian, called Pahlavi (Pehlevi), which was the language of the Parthians and Sāsānids.

The first Iranians to make their appearance in history are the Medes, the inhabitants of what is now Iraq-i Ajami. In 612 their king Cyaxares took Nineveh and destroyed the Assyrian Empire, the possessions of which were then divided between the Medes, who took Assyria proper, and their allies, the Babylonians, who took Chaldea and Syria. Towards 550 or 549 the empire of the Medes was con-

112

quered by the other great Iranian people, the Persians. Cyrus, the Persian conqueror, annexed one after the other Media and its dependencies in 549, the kingdom of Lydia — that is, Asia Minor — in 546, eastern Iran as far as the Indus between about 545 and 539, and lastly the Chaldean or Babylonian Empire, with its Syrian dependencies, in 538. The empire thus constituted was governed till 330 by his dynasty, the great Achæmenid dynasty, and in 525 Cambyses, the son of Cyrus, further conquered Egypt. After a brief period of eclipse Darius I (521–486), who represented a collateral branch of the Achæmenids, ascended the throne and reorganized the empire. We know that this prince and his son Xerxes I after him (486–465) made an unsuccessful attempt to conquer Greece. The rest of the Achæmenids, of the close of the fifth century and the beginning of the fourth, generally Artaxerxes or Darius by name, contented themselves with diplomatic and financial intervention in the disputes between the Greek cities, until the last of them, Darius III, was vanquished by Alexander the Great, King of Macedonia, who conquered the Persian Empire between 334 and 327.

The Persians as they appear to us during this first phase of their history were unquestionably one of the noblest races of the antique world. Their sense of honour and humane and chivalrous character are a relief after the odious vices and savage cruelty of Assyro-Babylonian or Punic society. From the very moment when they enter history, we seem to feel that they are men of our own race. The Greeks were not mistaken when, throughout their struggle with the Persians, they always regarded them as worthy adversaries and were careful not to confound them with the common run of subject nations. "The young Persians," wrote Herodotus, "are taught three things: to ride, to shoot with the bow, and always to tell the truth."

The primitive religion of the Indo-Iranian tribes, before the Iranians split off from the Indians, included two principal groups of deities: the *Dēva,* or "celestial ones," the gods of the shining firmament; and the *Asura* or *Ahura*, the " lords " or " masters," who were of a more moral and less strictly naturalistic character. After the separation the Iranians and the Indians treated these two categories in a different fashion. The Indians turned the *Dēva* definitively into gods, degrading the *Asura* to the position of a sort of Titans, who

FIGURE 83

Fire-altar at Naqsh-i Rustam.
— *Photo, Sevruguin, Teheran*

were the enemies of the gods and soon developed into demons; while the Iranians, on the other hand, turned the *Dēva* into mere demons, known as the " *div*," and made the *Ahura* the only true gods. According to Darius I's rock-hewn inscriptions, the Iranians had already gone through another state of development by the time they reached the Achæmenid period, for one of the *Ahura*, Ahura-Mazdā, worshipped under the name of " the wise lord," was recognized, if not yet as the only god, at least as " the greatest of the gods "; what is more, under the Achæmenids, the cult of the royal house had Ahura-Mazdā as its sole object, ignoring all the other gods; and from this to monotheism is not a great step. The essential feature of the cult consisted in the lighting of the fire (*ātar*) on an open-air altar (Fig. 83), as is proved by a number of scenes in high relief from the tombs of the Achæmenid kings at Persepolis, which show the sovereign standing before the lighted altar, while Ahura-Mazdā — or, perhaps, the king's *fravashi* (tutelary spirit) — appears above it in the form of a winged genius. It is only in rare instances that we find another Indo-Iranian god, Mithra, mentioned on the Achæmenid reliefs — a divinity originally of a social character, the " god of the pact," who was later assimilated to a solar deity. Lastly, we know that the Achæmenids buried their dead. Side by side with this dynastic religion, of a fairly general character, there seems to have existed another, that of the sacerdotal sect or caste of the Magians (*Magu* or *Mōbadh*), mentioned by Herodotus. Although Herodotus says nothing about this point, it seems probable that the religion " of the Magians" referred to by him was none other than Mazdaism, the religion of Zarathustra or Zoroaster.

The date at which Zoroaster lived is uncertain. Persian scholars of today tend to place it about the seventh century B.C. Tradition has it that he was born in Media; at the age of twenty he retired from the world and at the age of thirty started his preaching, converting a prince named Vishtaspa, and making his way as far as Bactria; he was killed at the age of seventy-seven by the barbarian invaders. The *Gāthā*, or earliest of the writings forming the *Avesta*, or Zoroastrian Bible, seem to date from the actual period of the founder of the religion, the seventh century B.C., whereas the rest of the *Avesta* is apparently of later date. In the *Gāthā*, Zoroaster himself says that he came to purify religion. His teaching is loftily spiritual, being based upon what has, perhaps improperly, been called a dualistic principle. On the one hand we have Ahura-Mazdā, the principle of light and of good, conceived as the one god; on the other we have Angra Mainyu, the principle of darkness and of evil, a sort of Mazdean Satan. The former created all the good existing in the world, the latter all the evil. With Ahura-Mazdā are associated a certain number of personifications of divine qualities, which play somewhat the same part as angels do in Christianity: first there are the six *Amesha-Spenta*, or " Holy Immortals," which are personified abstractions or cardinal

virtues, such as *Vohu-Mano*, or "good thought," *Asha Vahishta*,
"superior virtue," etc. Below these superior beings come an infinite number of secondary good genii, the *Yazata*, foremost among
which we find *Ātar*, or fire, which continued to play an essential part
in the Mazdean cult; it was called the "son of Ahura-Mazdā" and
the sacred fire-altars were maintained in its honour. Among the
Yazata we may further mention *Āpo*, or water, which was no less
sacred, *Hvare*, the sun, representing in particular the power of light
and the servant of the kindly divinity *Mithra*, mentioned above, whose
own peculiar sect was one day to lead him forth to the conquest of
the Greco-Roman world; and lastly the *Fravashi*, who stood at once
for guardian angels and for the divine substance of the soul, *Vere-
thraghna* (later Bahrām), the angel of victory, etc. Over against this
army of the Good, we have the army of Evil, created by Angra
Mainyu, in which we may note the *daeva* (*dēva*) and a number of
other figures of the Indian pantheon, now degraded to the level of
demons or arch-demons, ranking with the *druj*, or ghouls, and the
pairika (*peri*) or sirens. The history of the world is that of the incessant struggle between these two principles, the duel between Good
and Evil. The Mazdeans believed in the immortality of the soul,
which, crossing the Bridge of Judgment after death, went, according
to its conduct during this life, either to the "Abode of Hymns" or to
hell, with the *druj*. This body of dogmas is completed by an optimistic theory of the ultimate destiny of things; at the end of time a sort
of Messiah was to appear, named Saoshyant, the son of Zoroaster,
who, at the side of Zoroaster — on the latter's reappearance — was to
preside over the resurrection of the dead. A flood of molten metal was
to cover the earth, thus executing the last judgment; all evil beings,
including Angra Mainyu, would be destroyed, and all the good ones
saved, thus at last marking the definitive triumph of good over evil.
We may add that, while the Achæmenid kings buried their dead, orthodox Zoroastrians exposed them, for fear of contaminating the

sacred principles of fire, earth, and water by contact with the dead body. This detail proves that, though under the Sāsānids Mazdaism subsequently became the official religion of the Persian State, under the Achæmenids it was no doubt no more than the creed of a sect or religious caste.

Moreover, no monarchy seems to have been less exclusive or more liberal than that of the Achæmenids. It is enough to recall the sense of organization, administrative genius, and religious toleration of this dynasty to indicate its character.

The administrative organization of the Persian Empire was the work of Darius I. This prince divided up his vast territories into some twenty regular governments or satrapies, each of which had at the head of it three royal officials: the satrap, who was originally in charge of none but civil affairs; the royal secretary, in charge of the chancellery; and the commander of the troops of occupation. Satraps, secretaries, and generals alike were subordinate to the envoys extraordinary, a sort of *missi dominici*, or royal commissaries, who periodically inspected the provincial administration. As we see, this organization had been inspired by a twofold principle: in the first place, by that of a centralization which was most remarkable at that time; and secondly — in the beginning, at least — by a real separation of powers intended to prevent the provincial governors from aspiring towards independence.

But this centralization in no way tended to bring about the disappearance of the various nationalities absorbed into the Achæmenid Empire. With a liberalism to which they were never false the Persians, once they had become the imperial race of the East, allowed the various subject races and already existing civilizations to go on side by side with their own. Nor was their toleration for the cults of the peoples whom they held in subjection less remarkable. The other conquering races of the East, and notably the Assyrians, had made war as much on foreign gods as on foreign peoples; Assur and Ishtar

had led captive Yahveh of Jerusalem, Baal of Tyre, Marduk of Babylon, Sushinak of Susa, and Ammon of Thebes. The Achæmenids, on
the contrary, never set themselves to make Ahura-Mazdā prevail over
the Semitic or Egyptian gods. Mazdean fanaticism, which in later
days, during the Sāsānid period, was to lead to a cleavage between
Persia and the West, was entirely foreign to them. The attitude of
the Jewish people towards them is significant; this race, which
poured forth through the mouth of its prophets nothing but impreca-
tions against its Egyptian, Assyrian, or Chaldean conquerors, as it
did in later days against its Seleucid or Roman rulers, at last found
masters after its own heart in the Achæmenids. It turned Cyrus almost into a national hero and placed Esther, a Jewess, on the throne
of the legendary Ahasuerus. And, on the whole, this verdict is that
of history. It is true that the Achæmenid monarchy, like all Oriental
monarchies, was a despotic government, too often deranged by the
whims of capricious, violent, and weak sovereigns. But these palace
dramas had no more effect upon the administration of the vast
empire than had those which stained Rome with blood under the
Cæsars. Just as Nero's mad extravagances did not prevent the provinces from enjoying peace, so the personal caprices of a Darius and
an Artaxerxes did not in the least prevent the Eastern world from
enjoying the benefits of Achæmenid organization.

A system of fixed and regular taxation took the place of the sudden and arbitrary levies extorted from the subject peoples by the
Assyrians. Communication was established between all parts of the
empire, from Asia Minor to Egypt and from Syria to Transoxiana,
by a network of highways which were carefully kept up and by a
permanent system of royal posts. There was an abrupt cessation of
those wars between race and race, people and people, city and city,
which had been the rule in the ancient world. A profound peace, the
" Achæmenid peace," similar to the " Roman peace " which was
afterwards to sway the Western world, prevailed for two centuries

throughout the whole of the East, from the Caucasus to the Arabian desert, from the Bosporus and Cyrenaica to the Jaxartes and the Indus. This was an immense advance upon previous ages and may legitimately be compared with that resulting from the establishment of the *Orbis romanus*, the " Roman world," as compared with the crumbling states of the Hellenistic age.

It is unjust to the Persians to forget their merits in this respect and to see in them no more than the protagonists of Asiatic " barbarism " against the Greeks. We must not conclude from the fact that the Persians showed themselves inferior to the Greeks in war and culture that their race and work were totally inferior; what people, whether ancient or modern, Germanic or even Latin, may not be considered barbarous by comparison with the Athenians of the fifth century? As a matter of fact, these so-called " barbarians " did not show themselves unworthy of their mission as representatives of Aryanism in the midst of the Eastern world. It may even be said that they and the Romans were the only people of antiquity capable of organizing a great empire on a durable footing — an achievement in which the Greeks never succeeded, for all their brilliant qualities. As for the Persians, it is not one of the least glories of the Aryan genius that the first result of its hegemony in the Middle East was the foundation of the Achæmenid government — a uniform, orderly government which was on the whole pacific and beneficent — in lands where the genius of the Semitic races had been powerless for hundreds and thousands of years to perpetuate anything but division, hatred, and violence.

The Medo-Persian civilization was one of the most brilliant in the East. The Greeks never wearied of eulogizing the glories of Susa and Persepolis; and the excavations of the present day, which have restored to us the " Frieze of the Archers " and the " Frieze of the Immortals," confirm this impression. At the root of this art lies the great Assyro-Babylonian tradition; the part played by Chaldeo-Assyrian influences in the genesis of Persian art was, as we shall see, so important that we can only compare it with the influence of Greek art on Roman art. From the literary point of view, we need only recall the fact that the cuneiform script was at once adopted by the Achæmenids, though with considerable simplification, which reduced the number of signs to thirty-six; thus all the Achæmenid inscriptions are written in cuneiform, whether composed in Old Persian only, or, as frequently happens, carved in three languages: Old Persian, Elamite-Anzanite, and Chaldean. As for their material civilization, the Achæmenids were so completely the heirs of the ancient monarchs of the Tigris and Euphrates in the outward trappings of royalty that they fixed their residence at Susa, on Chaldeo-Elamite territory. So that in certain respects, and setting aside moral factors, the capture of Nineveh by the Medes and of Babylon by the Persians was in some sense equivalent to a conquest of Iran by the ancient centre of Chaldeo-Assyrian civilization.

ACHÆMENID ART

YET THE ACHÆMENIDS WERE INNOVATORS IN THE WHOLE DOMAIN OF art, and first and foremost in architecture. Instead of employing the old Assyrian platforms of brick, with a mere casing of stone for the reception of bas-reliefs, they built their palaces on solid substructures of stone which may still be seen today. Moreover, they borrowed the stone column from Egypt and used it profusely. Whereas in the palaces of the Sargonids the column had been a mere ornament, it played an essential part in the Achæmenid palaces. But though the idea of these columns came from Karnak and Luxor, in the decoration of the capitals they remained Assyrian, using a motive directly traceable to the Sargonids: namely, that of the front quarters of two bulls placed back to back. On the other hand, the Achæmenid monarchy seems also to have borrowed from Egypt the idea of its rock tombs. With the exception of the little mausoleum of Cyrus at Mashhad-i Murghab, the construction of which, according to Professor Sarre, seems to have been imitated from the shape of a Persian sarcophagus (Fig. 84), all the funeral monuments of the Achæmenids are hewn half-way up a mountain-side, with a sculptured façade recalling the entrance to the tombs of Egypt

FIGURE 84
So-called Tomb of Cyrus at Pasargadæ.
— *Photo, Sevruguin, Teheran*

—except, of course, that the decoration is composed of Iranian motives, such as the sacred fire-altar and the disk of Ahura-Mazdā (Fig. 85).

A large proportion of Chaldeo-Assyrian monuments were destined for religious purposes. But in Iran the transcendental and abstract spiritualism of Mazdaism made the use of temples come to be regarded as tainted with paganism; hence architecture, unable to act as the handmaid of worship, had no object save the service of the monarchy. And this is why the two creations of Achæmenid architecture, Persepolis and Susa, are both groups of palaces.

The citadel of Persepolis has as its base a natural eminence, approached by a monumental staircase of a hundred and six steps, along both sides of which ran a bas-relief of warriors, attendants, and tributary princes, who seemed also to be mounting upwards step

FIGURE 85
Tomb of Darius, Naqsh-i Rustam.
— *Photo, Sevruguin, Teheran*

by step. This staircase, crowned by the portico of Xerxes (Fig. 87), led to a huge terrace on which stood, in a line running north-west and south-east, first the columned Hall of Xerxes, with its seventy-two columns, each more than eighty feet high (Fig. 88), then the Palace of Darius, which was of comparatively small proportions (Fig. 89), and then the much larger Palace of Xerxes, and that built by Artaxerxes III. Behind this line of buildings — that is, to the north-east

— on a second platform, raised ten feet above the other, stood the Hall of a Hundred Columns, which, according to Professor Sarre, may probably be attributed to Darius, who was no doubt inspired by the sight of the Theban colonnades. Moreover, the Achæmenid colonnades, with their stone bas-reliefs, are the only parts of Persepolis in

FIGURE 86
The staircase, Persepolis.
— *Photo, Sevruguin, Teheran*

a comparatively good state of preservation, for the parts which served as residences were built of brick in the Assyrian fashion and have entirely disappeared.[1]

The sculpture of the bas-reliefs and capitals which adorned these

[1] See E. Herzfeld: *Rapport sur l'état actuel des ruines de Persepolis* (Berlin, Teheran, 1928).

colossal groups of buildings at Persepolis and Susa bears witness that Persia was the pupil of Assyria (Fig. 90, 91). The winged bulls and bulls with men's heads which adorn the colonnade of Xerxes at Persepolis, with their faces in the round and their bodies in bas-relief, are directly imitated from the Assyrian figures of the same kind; the differences which can be noted constitute an improvement

FIGURE 87
Colonnade of Xerxes, Persepolis.
— *Photo, Sevruguin, Teheran*

on the part of the Achæmenid artists: the relief of the faces in the round is more marked, the anomaly of the five feet in the Assyrian figures is done away with, and the fan-shaped spread of the wings is particularly graceful (Fig. 92). But as a rule the imitation of Assyrian models is less direct. Thanks to the sensual cast of their genius and to their cult of power for its own sake, the Assyrians in their sculpture had remained the slaves of the material aspect of things, as their exaggerated rendering of the muscles and their meticulous reproduction of details of costume and toilet bear witness; in spite of its vigour and stupendous sense of movement, their sculpture was always, so to speak, weighed down by its excess of richness. The Persian genius, on the contrary, very rapidly tended to shake off the tyranny of the material world in order to soar upward into the sphere of pure thought and abstract speculation. In the place of the Chaldeo-Assyrian gods, so grossly sensual that the smell of the sacrifices attracted them " like flies," we have here a religion in which supernatural beings, such as the *Amesha-Spenta,* are merely personified abstractions or metaphysical qualities. Inspired as it was by such entirely different conceptions, Persian art, as Professor Sarre points out, was to give proof of a

FIGURE 88
Hall of Xerxes, Persepolis.
— *Photo, Sevruguin, Teheran*

severity of taste which was to spiritualize and lighten its forms. The difference in the treatment of drapery is striking. In Assyrian art the garment was sumptuous and heavy and clung to the body, blurring its lines in those parts which it covered, while it left whole parts of the body bare — for instance, the arms — in which, on the contrary, the play of the muscles was exaggerated. In Iranian art the garment itself, though not so floating as with their brother Scythians, was much more ample; and in like fashion the treatment of it on the bas-reliefs is deliberately broad, with a noble simplicity in the folds. When these tendencies are balanced by observation, we have works which are singularly felicitous, with a real grandeur and at the same time a restful softness of line, as in the bas-relief of the tribute of the Sacæ and Syrians on the grand staircase of the Hall of Xerxes at Persepolis (Fig. 93); works which, in the opinion of the present

FIGURE 89
Palace of Darius, Persepolis.
— *Photo, Sevruguin, Teheran*

writer, are closely allied to the Indian art of Aśoka (compare the capital at Sārnāth) and not unworthy to be compared to it. But this detachment from the material world, this austerity and systematic simplification were sometimes exaggerated to the point of excessive conventionalization and aridity. In short, the Achæmenid art of Iran (and even more so the Sāsānid) reveals the defects of its qualities. Like Romanesque art or the Chinese Buddhist art of the Wei dynasty, it has a spiritual quality, and, like these, it softened and lightened

FIGURE 91
Capital from Susa.
— *Louvre. Photo, Giraudon*

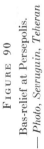

FIGURE 90
Bas-relief at Persepolis.
— *Photo, Serruguin, Teheran*

the plastic technique of the paganism which had preceded it, while at the same time emptying it of its content.

As was natural, Mazdean theology gave rise to representations of the deity. In place of the multifarious gods of Chaldeo-Assyrian sculpture, we find at Persepolis the image of none save Ahura-Mazdā (or is it the king's *fravashi*, or tutelary spirit?). It is undoubtedly derived from the figure of the god Assur, as we have seen him with his wings and disk on the standards of the Sargonids. But the Achæmenids have taken this ancient motive and created a new form out of it; with his low tiara, shaped like a cap, his wide sleeves, the graceful line of his disk with its volutes, the immense pair of outstretched wings which serves him as a background, and the treatment of his robe, whose folds repeat the lines of the feathers in his wings, the Lord of Wisdom is a worthy representative of such

FIGURE 92
Portico of Xerxes. Bull with human head.
— *Photo, Sevruguin, Teheran*

a deity as suited a more purely spiritual religion than that of our Old Testament — a spiritualism as transcendental as that of Plato. It was not till the Sāsānid period that Mazdaism was to prefer to this winged figure an equestrian Ahura-Mazdā, made in the very image of the Great King himself.

The Achæmenid king of the reliefs at Persepolis and Susa is also reminiscent of the Sargonid king, but with the same simplifications. In the first place, instead of making us spectators of every detail of the royal life, the king's poses are here reduced to four: we see him in an attitude of adoration before a fire-altar, or triumphing over his enemies in chains — for instance, Darius on the rock-carvings at

FIGURE 93

Syrian and Bactrian tributaries. Grand staircase of the Hall of Xerxes, Persepolis. — *From a cast in the British Museum. Photo, Mansell*

Behistun (Bīsutūn) — or enthroned — for instance, the same Darius on a relief in the central building at Persepolis — or striking down a monster. In all these scenes the Achæmenid, like the figure of Ahura-Mazdā described above, is wearing the *cidaris*, " a soft cap-shaped tiara, broader at the top than at the bottom." He is wearing the ample " Median robe," with long, wide sleeves, which comes down to his feet. Here again this noble simplicity produces an im-

FIGURE 94
Frieze of archers from Susa.
— *Louvre. Archives photographiques*

pression of grandeur. Standing before such works as these, we grasp the majesty of him whom even the Greeks themselves called the

Great King, and the vastness of these dominions, the most widespread that the world had yet known.

On one of the bas-reliefs at Persepolis to which we have just referred, the royal throne is supported by a whole crowd of subject

FIGURE 95
Frieze of lions from Susa.
— *Louvre. Photo, Giraudon*

peoples, each represented by its appropriate national type, costume, and name. And the inscription which accompanies this scene speaks to us like a voice from the depths of the past: " If thou dost think: ' How many different countries that King Darius possessed! ' look thou upon the image of those who uphold my throne and thou shalt know them. And this much shalt thou learn: that the lance of the

Persian penetrated afar, that the Persian waged war far away from Persia."

The enamelled revetment bricks which have been found by the de Morgan mission at Susa complete the lesson of Persepolis. The process of enamelled brickwork came from Assyria, as is proved by

FIGURE 96
Winged bull from Susa.
— *Louvre. Archives photographiques*

the fragments from Nimrud and Khorsābād representing kings, warriors, lions, bulls, birds, and trees. The Persians gave this art a more general character and drew from it some decorative combinations which are singularly pleasing to the eye in their beauty of tone and softness of line, while at the same time they produce an effect of grandeur by their nobility of conception and by the very fact that they repeat the same motives. Everybody will remember the Frieze of the Archers, the Frieze of the Lions, and that of the winged bulls in the Louvre; the archers, armed with bow, quiver, and lance and dressed, like the kings, in a long and ample tunic with wide sleeves, here wear on their heads a sort of skull-cap kept in place by a little cord, instead of the low tiara of Persepolis (Fig. 94); the lions, in spite of the vigorous treatment of the muscles and of the jaws opened in a roar, are less realistic and more decorative than those of the Sargonid reliefs (Fig. 95). The same may be said of the winged bulls of Susa, which have greater elegance but less power than those of Assyria (Fig. 96).

If we try to sum up the result of these observations, we may say that Achæmenid art strikes us as a more tranquil form of the Assyrian, with less movement and less variety than Sargonid art — as a broad, serene form of art, instinct with grandeur. In the next volume we shall see how it influenced the Maurya art of India. And we shall now see a continuation of it on the spot in the Sāsānid art of Persia.

SĀSĀNID CIVILIZATION

AFTER ITS CONQUEST BY ALEXANDER, IRAN REMAINED ENTIRELY IN the power of Hellenistic dynasties from 330 to about 250 B.C. About this date, one of the Iranian peoples in Khorāsān seized its independence: the Parthians, in Old Persian *Parthava*, later *Pahlava*, whence the name of their language, Pahlavi. This language, as we have seen, was an Iranian dialect, a form developed from Old Persian; and, whatever theories may have been advanced, the Parthians were certainly an Iranian people; even if they had an admixture of Scythian elements, as has been alleged, their Aryan character would none the less be indubitable, the Scythians themselves being no more than nomad Iranians of " Outer Iran."

The Parthian dynasty of the Arsacids, so called from its founder, Arsaces or Arshak, reigned from 250 B.C. till A.D. 224. It was in a

state of almost continual struggle with the Greek dynasty of the
Seleucids — from whom it wrested western Iran and Mesopotamia
— and afterwards with the Romans, the heirs and protectors of Hellenism in the East, who challenged the hold of the Arsacids on western Mesopotamia and Armenia. The two most famous of the Arsacids are Mithridates I (Mithradāt), the Great, who reigned
from about 174 to 136 and gave the Parthian Empire its historic
frontiers, from Marv to Babylonia; and Orodes, who in 53 B.C.
checked the invasion of the Roman triumvir Crassus at Carrhæ
(Harran).

Thus the Arsacids restored the independence of Iran and succeeded in defending it against all attacks for more than four centuries, for which reason they could justly claim to be the heirs of the
Achæmenids, whose titles of " Great King " and " King of Kings "
they revived. Yet even beneath the rule of these genuine Iranians
Iranian civilization remained, as it were, dormant, owing to the fact
that the influence of Hellenic civilization, which had conquered the
East along with Alexander the Great, was still too powerful. Great
pan-Iranian kings though they were — and there was a moment at
which their domination extended from the Syrian desert to the basin
of the Indus — and constantly at war with the Greco-Syrian *basileis*
and afterwards with the Cæsars, the Arsacids none the less continued
to be ardent friends of Hellenic culture throughout the four centuries for which their predominance lasted. The title of " philhel-
lene " is one to which they constantly lay claim on their coins; and
these coins are decidedly Hellenic, not only in their minting, but also
in their artistic inspiration — or, at least, intention — and in the
Greek characters in which their inscriptions are composed. Like their
contemporaries the Kūshān sovereigns who reigned in Bactria and
the basin of the Indus, the Arsacids " hellenized," or adopted Greek
manners, as much out of taste as because it was the fashion to do so.
It is a characteristic coincidence that when the head of Crassus, the

triumvir, was brought to him, Orodes, the greatest of them, was listening to a play of Euripides.

Yet even at the height of the Hellenistic period Aryanism, in its most uncompromising form of Zoroastrian Mazdaism, seems to have preserved one stronghold: that is, Persia proper, known to the Greeks as Persis, the modern Fārs, the ancient hereditary domain of the Achæmenids. The local princes of this province, as vassals first of the Seleucids and later of the Arsacids, have left coins bearing witness to the fervour of their Mazdaism. In the early years of the third century of our era Fārs passed into the hands of another family, having its origin in a Mazdean priestly family: the Sāsānid house, whose head, Ardashīr I, revolted against the Arsacids and killed the last of their kings (A.D. 224). In consequence of this victory, Ardashīr caused himself to be recognized as King of Kings by the whole of Iran, with the exception of Bactria, which was still occupied by the "Indo-Scythian" dynasty of the Kūshān. The capitals of the Sāsānids were Istakhr, to the north of the ancient Persepolis, in Fārs, and the double city of Ctesiphon-Seleucia (Veh Ardashīr), in Chaldca, which had already been the capital of the Arsacids.

The Sāsānid dynasty — that is, the house of Ardashīr — occupied the throne of Persia from 224 to 652 of our era. It had as its constant aim to defend the independence of Iran and Iranian culture, in the west against the Romans, and afterwards the Byzantines, and in the east against the Turco-Mongol hordes which had taken the place of the Kūshān in Transoxiana — first the Ephthalite Huns, in the fifth century, and later the T'ou-kiue Turks, in the second half of the sixth century. There were even moments when the Sāsānids aspired towards passing the frontiers of Iran proper, and once more establishing the great Achæmenid Empire of the past from the Hindu-Kush to the Mediterranean. In the west Shāpūr I (*Shāhpūr* in Pahlavi), the second of the Sāsānid monarchs, who reigned from 241 to 272, took the Roman emperor Valerian prisoner in 259, a striking victory, which was afterwards proudly commemorated in Sāsānid sculpture; he next invaded Syria, but was unable to maintain his position there. At the end of the Sāsānid period the Great King Khosrau, or Chosroes I Anūshirvān (Anūshakruwān, the " immortal-souled "), who reigned from 531 to 579, made a successful incursion into Syria, taking Antioch by a surprise attack in 540, and extended his dominion as far as the Yemen. Khosrau or Chosroes II Parvēz (Parvīz, the " victorious "), who reigned from 590 to 628, brought Syria, Palestine, Egypt, and Asia Minor temporarily under his rule in 613 and kept them for some years, and he almost succeeded in taking Constantinople, till in 628 he was actually conquered in Mesopotamia itself by the counter-offensive of the Byzantine emperor Heraclius. In the east the Sāsānids struggled with equal ardour for the defence and expansion of Aryanism. Varahrān or Bahrām II (276–293) took Seistān from the last of the Saka dynasty; while Hormuz, or Hormizd, II (303–310) seems to have exercised a certain hegemony over the Kūshān sovereign of Kābul, whose daughter he married. But at the end of the fourth century some nomads, probably of Mongol race, the Ephthalite Huns, took Transoxiana from the last of the Kūshān rulers, and afterwards, about 425, Bactria and Kābul. They next attacked the Sāsānid Empire. The Sāsānid king Bahrām V (Bahrām Gūr), who reigned from 420 to 438, repulsed them, but one of his successors, Fīrūz or Pērōz (459–484), was conquered and slain by them near Balkh in 484. At last, about 565, the Sāsānid king Khosrau I entered into an alliance against them with another people of central Asia, the T'ou-kiue, or Turks. The Ephthalites were crushed, and their dominions divided between the Sāsānids, who recovered Bactria, and the Turks, who took Sogdiana or Transoxiana. The Sāsāno-Buddhistic frescoes recently investigated by Monsieur and Madame André Godard at Bāmiān (Bāmiyān), and by Monsieur Hackin at Dukhtar-i Nūshirvān, bear witness to the expansion of the Persian Empire in Bactria at this period. After a few years, however, the

Turks, who had now become firmly rooted in Transoxiana, wrested Bactria from the Sāsānids.

Born of a restoration which was both national, religious, and monarchist, the Sāsānid Empire continued to be nationalist and pietist in sentiment so long as it lasted. The genuinely racial character of the Sāsānid monarchy is obvious in all the inscriptions and coins that have come down to us. In the formulas setting forth the king's official style, the Greek titles of *Basileus basileōn* (King of Kings) and " Friend of the Greeks " give place to the Pahlavi titles of " Servant of Auhrmazd " (the Pahlavi equivalent of Ahura-Mazdā) and " King of the Ārya." Passing over the Macedonian or Parthian usurpers, the Sāsānids claimed to be the direct successors of the Achæmenids, and a pedigree was conveniently devised connecting Ardashīr I with Darius and Xerxes. But whereas the Achæmenids had not hesitated to borrow largely, first from the Assyro-Babylonian and later from the Hellenic civilization, Ardashīr and his successors remained solely and wholly Persian. The empire of the last Darius had been a cosmopolitan one, defended by Greek and Saka peoples alike. The Sāsānid Empire was Iranian and uncompromisingly Aryan. Unlike the Greco-Roman Empire, in which all races had access to power, and which numbered Spaniards, Syrians, Africans, and Illyrians among its emperors, the Sāsānid Empire was exclusively Iranian, a certain scope at most being allowed to Aramæan or Syriac culture alongside of the national Pahlavi.

Based as it thus was upon the national sentiment, the Sāsānid monarchy was able to revive the powerful administrative machine created by Darius. The Parthian régime had been essentially feudal and consequently had incessant trouble with the hereditary satraps, who were often almost as powerful as the king. The Sāsānids were unable to abolish these feudal nobles or even entirely to deprive them of hereditary office, but they generally succeeded in securing their obedience. From the *marzbān,* or governors of the marches, and the *rād,* or governors of districts, down to the *shahrikān* and *dikhān,* or proprietors of the great territorial estates, henceforth all the nobles were obliged to respect the central power.

Mazdaism, the teaching of Zoroaster, was closely bound up with the Iranian restoration. The earliest of the Sāsānids caused a complete and definitive version of the Mazdean Bible or *Avesta* to be prepared, and it is in this form that the work has come down to us. Moreover, their religious policy seems to have been somewhat different from that of the Achæmenids. Though the latter worshipped Ahura-Mazdā, and their cult of him was practically equivalent to monotheism, they do not seem to have been, strictly speaking, Zoroastrians. Since the usurpation of the Magians on the death of Cambyses, they seem always to have distrusted this sacerdotal caste which had nearly succeeded in dethroning them. The Sāsānids, on the other hand, granted the clergy a preponderant position in the State. Alongside of the dynasty there grew up a regular Church, with its hierarchy of *Mōbadh* or Magians, under the direction of a *mōbadhān-mōbadh,* a sort of pope of Mazdaism. Supported by the nobles, the Church even became so powerful that, in the fourth century, a time came when the monarchy tried to resist it. Several kings came to grief through this policy, among them Ardashīr II (379–383), Shāpūr III (383–388), Yazdagard I (399–420), and Balāsh (484–488); the first was deposed, the next two were assassinated, and the fourth was blinded by the great nobles and Magians. A last reforming king, Kavādh or Qobād I (488–531), went so far as to give his support to the communist agitator Mazdak in opposition to the social privileges of the nobles and Magians; but he was exiled, and returned to the orthodox tradition after his restoration. On the whole, the failure of these experiments confirmed the power of the politico-religious principle on which the new State was founded: that of a close alliance between the Sāsānid monarchy and Mazdean orthodoxy.

SĀSĀNID ART

SĀSĀNID ART IS HISTORICALLY OF GREAT IMPORTANCE, AS FORMING a link between two styles of art apparently as dissimilar as the Achæmenid, based upon the Assyrian tradition, and the Muhammadan.

Sāsānid architecture is distinguished by the inauguration of a new element, the vault, which had already made its appearance at Hatra in the Parthian period under Roman influence, but now became general. In the first Sāsānid palace, that of Ardashīr I (224–242) at Fīrūzābād in Fārs, we find a vestibule adorned with a barrel-vaulted roof. There is an ovoid dome of a similar character in the palace of Sarvistān, also in Fārs. Professors Sarre and Herzfeld point out that these vaulted vestibules already contain the principle of the *eivān* (later Arabic *līwān*) of the Moslem mosques. One of the principal monuments of the Sāsānid period is the Tāq-i Kisrā, or Cupola of Khosrau, at Ctesiphon, which was really built by Shāpūr I (242–272). The central part of the edifice consisted of a vast vaulted hall, with an elliptical vault, which has recently collapsed, and served as a throne-room. Here again the great arch which remains intact reminds one of the fine vaulting of the later Persian mosques. On each side of it rose an imposing façade, half of which has remained standing, entirely faced with architectural ornaments simulating four storeys — " rows of arcading, niches, pilasters, and rounded arches " in the manner of the neighbouring country of Syria. No less important was the Qasr-i Shīrīn, erected in Persian Kurdistān by King Khosrau II (590–628), and bearing the name of this prince's favourite. It was an immense mass of buildings situated in a park of nearly three hundred acres, and including two palaces. One of these two palaces, the Qalaʻa-i chahār qapī (" Forty Gates "), included a square audience-chamber, crowned with an ellipsoidal cupola. The other and principal palace, the Imārat-i Khosrau, stands on a vast terrace supported by vaulted arches and approached by a ramp; a peristyle of twenty-four columns next led into a square throne-room with a cupola. We may compare this group of buildings with the palaces of Darius and Xerxes at Persepolis, while the arrangement of the gardens, lakes, and kiosks reminds us of the Ṣafawid palaces of Isfahān.

The analogies between this art and that of Moslem Persia would doubtless be still more striking if the Sāsānid monuments had preserved their decorations. The Tāq-i Kisrā, in particular, was certainly covered with decorations painted on stucco, none of which has come down to us. On the other hand, the materials used for the essential parts of the structure, stones and pebbles covered with a coat of plaster for the walls, and flat cut bricks for the columns, seem to have been of rather poor quality. The Sāsānid architects, like the Persian ones who succeeded them, seem quite often to have been content with buildings of a not very solid nature, each sovereign being ready to abandon the palaces of his predecessors in order to build himself new ones. The whole effect must have been obtained by the casing, the polychrome decoration of painted stucco or enamelled bricks — an ephemeral glory which, when once neglected, soon crumbles away. The disappearance of the majority of Sāsānid paintings and sculptures is all the more regrettable because in those places where the preservation of the works has been assured, either by their own nature or by their position — in the rock-carvings such as those at Naqsh-i Rustam or Tāq-i Bustān, and in the frescoes on inaccessible rocks, such as those at Dukhtar-i Nūshirvān — we find ourselves in the presence of a powerful school of art.

Naqsh-i Rustam, near Persepolis, in Fārs, has preserved some great reliefs, carved in the rock, most of which date from the reign of Shāpūr I (242–272). This prince was also responsible for the reliefs carved on the spot which bears his name — Shāpūr — to the north of Kāzrūn. One of the favourite motives treated on these rock-

hewn reliefs is that of the god Auhrmazd (Ormuzd) investing the
king with the insignia of his rank. At Naqsh-i Rustam the king represented is the founder of the dynasty, Ardashīr, who died in 242. King
and god are face to face on horseback; the two horses, which confront
each other, are exactly alike, and, save for the difference in their
attributes and head-dress, the god and the King are almost identical

FIGURE 97
Investiture of Ardashīr. Naqsh-i Rustam.
— *Photo, Sevruguin, Teheran*

too — the gesture of the two, one offering, the other accepting, the
crown, exactly corresponding (Fig. 97). This rigidly symmetrical
arrangement, in which the King is, as it were, the replica of the god,
admirably expresses the idea of " divine right," held by a dynasty
at once imperious and pietistic. The gesture with which god and
King approach each other is not like the passing contact between
Jehovah and Adam on the ceiling of the Sistine Chapel, across the

abyss which separates man from his God; it is an investiture of an absolutely feudal character, in which the human vassal lays claim to the same lineage as his celestial suzerain — a vision of undeniable power and impressive majesty, in which the ancient Sargonid motive of the king face to face with his god is ennobled by all the conceptions proper to the spiritual character of the Mazdean religion.

FIGURE 98
Humiliation of Valerian. Naqsh-i Rustam.
— *Photo, Sevruguin, Teheran*

It is true that here we have more than one reminiscence of Assyro-Achæmenid art, starting with the personal type of the royal figure itself, with the long beard and hair arranged in tiers of curls. But though, like the Achæmenid reliefs, the Sāsānid ones abstain from that overloading with detail which characterized the Assyrian ones, their modelling is more forceful than in those of Persepolis. We feel here the same impression of grandeur as we do before the Achæmenid works, and we are even conscious of a greater power in them — but of greater heaviness too. This comparative heaviness proclaims the approach of the Middle Ages. Compare, for example, the horses at Naqsh-i Rustam with those of Persepolis; instead of the light cavalry of Cyrus and Darius, we find here what are practically mounted knights loaded with coats of mail and mounted on horses like powerfully built shire horses.

Professor Sarre and Herzfeld, to whom we owe the best studies of Sāsānid art, point out that there is an investiture scene of an ab-

FIGURE 99
Capture of Valerian by Shāpūr. Cameo.
— *Bibliothèque Nationale. Photo, Giraudon*

solutely similar nature at Naqsh-i Rajab, near Persepolis, which, in spite of its dilapidated condition, seems to mark a progress in technique as compared with that of Naqsh-i Rustam. The heavy royal mantle has given place to ample garments with crisp folds, which make the figures more lifelike and elegant. The same subject is repeated again in a rock-carving on the site of Shāpūr, in which King Bahrām I (273–277) is represented receiving the investiture from the hands of Auhrmazd. Here the horses are not too close together and are so realistic and full of life that they almost remind us

FIGURE 100

Triumph of King Shāpūr I. Shāpūr.
— *Photo, Sevruguin, Teheran*

of Verrocchio. Moreover, the artist has not shown god and King both holding the crown at the same time; the god is holding it out, while the King is extending his hand in a very natural gesture to grasp it. Finally, as Professor Sarre remarks, the stuff " with its crisp folds "

FIGURE 101
Equestrian combat. Naqsh-i Rustam.
— *Photo, Sevruguin, Teheran*

indicates the noble form of the two bodies even better and more broadly than at Naqsh-i Rajab.

One of the themes which most readily inspired the Sāsānid sculptors was, as we have said above, the capture of the Emperor Valerian by King Shāpūr in 259. At Naqsh-i Rustam, Shāpūr is represented on horseback, just as in the investiture scenes, while the captive

FIGURE 102

Khosrau II hunting. Tāq-i Bustān.
— *Photo, Sevruguin, Teheran*

Cæsar bends the knee before him (Fig. 98 and 99). On the site of Shāpūr the scene is more detailed and depicts the second stage of this celebrated episode; the King of Kings, followed by his cavalry,

FIGURE 103
Khosrau II hunting. Tāq-i Bustān.
— *Photo, Sarre, Berlin*

is holding the freedman Cyriades by the hand, and presenting him to the Roman army as their leader in the presence of the kneeling Valerian (Fig. 100). Similar in style and equally full of life is

FIGURE 104

Tāq-i Bustān. Khosrau II hunting.
— *Photo, Sarre, Berlin*

another relief on the site of Shāpūr, showing the triumph of King Bahrām II (277–293) over a tribe, no doubt of Arabs; here the horses, camels, and barbarian types are delineated with a mastery worthy of the scene at Persepolis representing the tribute of the Sacæ and Syrians.

For, though we might not expect it after seeing the ponderous dignity of certain " investiture " scenes, it is the living quality of these Sāsānid reliefs that is one of their most striking characteristics. At Naqsh-i Rustam we may indicate some equestrian combats which are extraordinarily full of movement; in one of them a horseman, or, rather, a king, as yet unidentified, is transfixing a Roman horseman with his lance. The Sāsānid monarch, approaching at full gallop, has broken the Roman's weapon and is making his enemy's horse stagger under the impact, as in our mediæval tournaments. The breadth of its composition, and the concentrated vigour of its design, place this masterpiece in the same class as the best scenes of equestrian combat on the Sargonid monuments (Fig. 101).

These qualities of movement are even more clearly evident in the grottoes of Tāq-i Bustān, to the north-east of Kermanshah. The sculptures in one of these grottoes were due to Khosrau II (590–628), as is shown by a fine equestrian figure of this king on a slab in such high relief that it is almost in the round. To the left is a scene of boar-hunting in the marshes; the boars are being driven through the reeds by beaters mounted on elephants (note the resemblance between these elephants and those of the Indian art of Ajaṇṭā and Māvalipuram); the King himself is aiming his bow at the boars from a boat, followed by other boats full of musicians who are giving a concert (this motive of a concert going on while the king is hunting is to be found as late as the miniatures of the Safawid period); the huge boars falling round the royal boat, pierced through and through with arrows as they charge, are treated with a powerful realism (Fig. 102). On the other side of the same rock-carving is a deer-hunting scene,

FIGURE 105
Khosrau II hunting. Tāq-i Bustān.
— *Photo, Sarre, Berlin*

in which the monarch and his court are pursuing a flock of animals
of the deer tribe which have been started from the royal coverts; the
flight of the herd, the truth of action in all the fleeing or falling animals, seem to us in every respect worthy of the ibex hunt of Assur-

FIGURE 106
Silver platter with lion hunt of Bahrām Gūr.
— *British Museum. Photo, Mansell*

bani-pal (Fig. 103 to 105). We should not forget this scene, or the
frescoes of Dukhtar-i Nūshirvān either, when we come to the animals
of the deer tribe in the Persian miniatures. In fact, as we shall see,
Persia never lost its great artistic tradition in the representation of

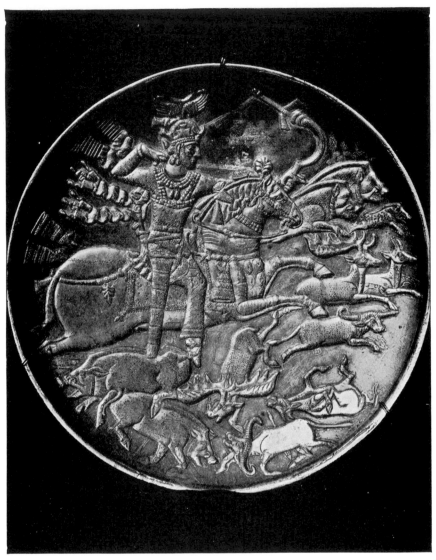

animals, which is, moreover, connected with the Maurya, Gupta, and Moslem art of India.

In the rocks carved in relief the material is sometimes recalcitrant or else worn away in course of time. But there are pieces of plate in which the art of the Sāsānids in representing animal life or heroic scenes survives unimpaired. The two silver platters, one in the Cunningham collection at the British Museum, representing a lion hunt of Bahrām Gūr (420–438), and the other in the Bibliothèque Nationale, representing Khosrau II (590–628) out hunting, are among the masterpieces of Iran. On the Bahrām Gūr platter is shown a combat between the King and a family of lions; he is shown beheading the charging lion with his right hand, and crushing one of the cubs with his left, while the lioness springs up at her spoiler, and the heavy Sāsānid charger rears to meet the charge of the beast, which is biting it in the chest. The whole group has a pathos equal to that of the most dramatic hunting-scenes of the Sargonid age (Fig. 106); for here again we certainly have a continuation of the Assyrian tradition, as the style of the charging lions alone would prove. No less fine is the figure of Khosrau II on the platter in the Bibliothèque Nationale, a galloping figure in the style of the ancient kings of Assur, who is hailing arrows into a herd of wild boars, deer, and wild goats. The rapidity of the royal huntsman's gallop is further emphasized by the streaming *kosti*, the ribbons of the mantle, and the tassels of the harness. As for the animals fleeing headlong or rolling over pierced with arrows, we find in them, as just now at Tāq-i Bustān, the realism, precision, and " power of distinguishing one type of animal from another " which the masters of Koyunjik and Khorsābād had learnt from the ancient East (Fig. 107). And this great tradition of the animal-sculptors of Mesopotamia was to persist under the régime of Islam, as is proved by a number of belated pieces of purely Sāsānid workmanship which we find at the height of the Moslem period; for instance, the fine beast of the feline tribe on a silver dish in

the Soltykov collection, now in the Bibliothèque Nationale, Paris
(Fig. 108), which we may compare with the head of a roaring lioness in the Doucet collection, sculptured in the round in black stone,

FIGURE 108
Silver platter, post-Sāsānian.
— *Bibliothèque Nationale. Photo, Giraudon*

and dated approximately by Monsieur Charles Vignier from the
fourth or fifth century of our era (Fig. 109). Similarly, when we come
to study the Moslem ceramics of Raiy, we ought never to lose sight of
the fine Sāsānid pottery in the Charles Vignier collection, with their

figures adoring fire-altars (Fig. 109 b) and their representations of animals (camels and goats).

Until recent years it was believed that no Sāsānid paintings had come down to us; but in this connexion the discoveries of the

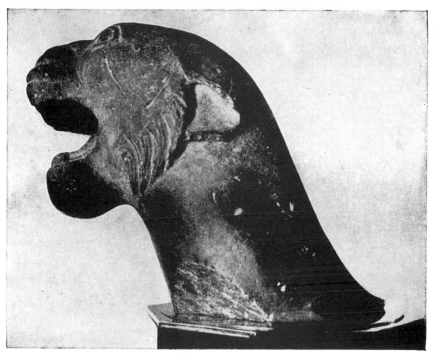

FIGURE 109
Stone head of lioness.
— Doucet collection. Photo, Laniepce

French archæological mission to Afghanistan have opened up fresh horizons to us. The great rock frescoes of Bāmiān dating from the third to the sixth centuries, which have been investigated and reproduced by Monsieur and Madame André Godard, show us, side by side with Indian or Hellenistic elements, subjects which are, properly speaking, Sāsānid (Fig. 110 and Volume III, Fig. 116). In spite

of the Buddhistic inspiration of these frescoes, one of the chief figures
represented displays all the characteristics of a Sāsānid king: the

FIGURE 109b
Sāsānian earthenware.
— *Vignier collection. Photo, Laniepce*

trimmed beard, the head-dress like a sort of tiara, surmounted by the
crescent moon and the disk of the sun, with the *kosti* floating on his
shoulders — the very type of the Bahrām Gūr and Khosrau II of the

silver platters in the Louvre and the British Museum (Fig. 111). In this connexion we may recall the fact that there was a long struggle with the Ephthalites for the region of Balkh and Bāmiān, and that it was finally annexed to the empire by Khosrau I. The frescoes of Bāmiān have a no less precious find to offer; side by side with Indian monks, Buddhas of the Gandhāra type, or a four-horse chariot of purely Roman inspiration, they contain a number of figures dressed in a long mantle with broad facings, one of them having also a narrow girdle round his waist and carrying a long sword and a lance, which are similar in every respect to the horsemen — likewise of Iranian inspiration — on the Qizil frescoes, dating from the seventh century, discovered in Chinese Turkestan by the German mission of Professors Grünwedel and Von Le Coq (Volume III, Fig. 120). The juxtaposition in the same fresco at Bāmiān of this royal type, which is absolutely that of the Shāpūrs, Bahrāms, and Khosraus, with the type which we may call " the horseman of Qizil " is proof that the paintings of Iranian tendencies, whether Buddhistic or Manichæan, which we shall find later in central Asia, from Kūcha to Turfān, dating from a period extending from the seventh to the ninth century of our era, are actually of Sāsānid inspiration — as had, indeed, been supposed before — or, better still, a provincial or outlying school of Sāsānid painting. Having established this, when we pass on to the study of central Asia we shall be better able to understand the discovery by Sir Aurel Stein at Dandān-uiliq, in Kashgaria, of an extraordinary fresco of the eighth century, representing the Buddhistic divinity Vajrapāṇi in the guise of a sort of Sāsānid king, wearing a black beard, with a tiara on his head and a green coat and boots, again quite in the style of some Bahrām or Khosrau (Volume III, Fig. 117 and 118). Before such positive proof as this, we are compelled to regard Sāsānid art as having sent forth its influence for centuries on end through Bactria and Transoxiana as far as the heart of the desert of Gobi and continued to make its influence felt there even down to a period when, in Iran proper, the Sāsānid dynasty itself had gone down before Islam.

What is more, the frescoes of Bāmiān show us that, profoundly original though it may have been, Sāsānid art was, as it were, hemmed in by classical influences. In the west, both on the rock-carvings of Naqsh-i Rustam and on the coins of the earliest kings, we may guess a certain influence from Rome, which was, however, rapidly assimilated. Similarly, in the east, in Bactria, Sāsānid art came in contact with a Hellenistic school of art, the Greco-Buddhistic art of Gandhāra, as several of the frescoes of Bāmiān bear witness. But even more interesting, in our opinion, than these influences, which are somewhat alien to the Mazdean genius, is the way in which Sāsānid art came into contact, on the same frontiers,

FIGURE 110
Fresco from Bāmiān.
— Photo, Godard

with the indigenous or Gupta art of India. We have already referred to the analogies between the technique of the animal-sculptors of Tāq-i Bustān and that of the Indian animal-painters of Ajaṇṭā and Māvalipuram. These analogies become even more striking on the rock frescoes of Dukhtar-i Nūshirvān, near Rūi, in Afghanistan, discovered by Monsieur Hackin in 1924–5 and revisited by Monsieur Barthoux in 1927. These frescoes are more specifically Sāsānid than those of Bāmiān, and, in the opinion of Monsieur Hackin, they were perhaps even ordered by Khosrau I, the conqueror of Bactria, in person, in which case they would date from about 570. As a matter of fact, the central figure represented a person wearing the head-dress surmounted by a lion's head which, according to Professor Herzfeld, was characteristic of the royal prince of the Sāsānid royal house who was governor of Bactria. There is another figure in the fresco of Dukhtar-i Nūshirvān which, in Monsieur Hackin's opinion, recalls the Shāpūr of bas-relief IV at Naqsh-i Rustam. Further, beside these royal figures, Monsieur Hackin has drawn attention to various paintings of animals — antelope, moufflon, oxen, deer, a tame lion, and an elephant — which are equally reminiscent of the Gupta animal-painters and of those of Tāq-i Bustān, or, rather, establish a connexion between the former and the latter; not to speak of female figures which are directly akin to those of Ajaṇṭā, those masterpieces of the Gupta school of painting in India.

In this connexion we may recall the affinities, dating from the very origin of these two schools of art, which have been noted between the sculpture of the Achæmenid age of Persia and the Indian (Maurya) sculpture of Sānchī. We now find the same affinities between the Gupta and post-Gupta paintings of India and the Sāsānid works of the sixth and seventh centuries which were contemporaneous with them. Perhaps we may be justified in concluding that a certain artistic contact was always maintained between India and Iran, and that there were certain subjects which the two schools had in common, notably as regards the representation of animals.

Side by side with this naturalistic aspect which constitutes an affinity between Sāsānid art and the Gupta art of India, the art of this age in Persia sometimes displays quite a different aspect: that of a heraldic art with a tendency towards decorative conventionalization.

FIGURE 111
Bowl of Khosrau II.
— *Bibliothèque Nationale. Photo, Giraudon*

This tendency, inherited from ancient Chaldeo-Assyrian decorative art and strengthened, as we have seen, by the taste of the Mazdean religion for abstraction and rigid formulas, seems to have attained its definitive form in Sāsānid Iran. It thus created a special style which it handed on to the peoples of the Caucasus, the nomad tribes of the Russian steppes, and, through them, to the northern barbarians, the Goths, the Scandinavians, and the Germans proper, as well as to the hordes of Huns and Turks towards the north-east. In their textiles and goldsmiths' work in particular we see how the Sāsānid decorators came to strip their subject of its plastic qualities and abstract from the living form designs which are purely geometrical. The museums of Europe and the sacristies of its churches are rich in Sāsānid textiles, or fabrics of Sāsānid inspiration, representing, in accordance with this fashion, fantastic monsters more or less conventionalized with a view to decorative effect: the " dragon-peacock " with the head and fore-paws of a beast of the feline tribe, and the wings and tail of a peacock " in his pride "; or horsemen mounted upon griffons or winged lions and fighting with other griffons; or wild goats or lions passant facing each other in strictly symmetrical pairs; or conventionalized beasts of the feline tribe devouring equally conventionalized beasts of the deer tribe, as in a favourite Chaldeo-Assyrian motive, which we shall find as far afield as the Hunnish textiles found by the Kozlov mission at Noin-ola in Mongolia. In this connexion, however, it is a misuse of terms to speak of Sāsānid influences on " Scytho-Sarmatian " art, for the Sāsānid dynasty did not make its appearance till the third century, at a time when the Scythians had already disappeared centuries ago and the Sarmatians were on the point of disappearing before the Goths and Huns. But what is certain — as is established by the works of Dr. Falke — is the influence exerted by the Sāsānid textiles, with their patterns of conventionalized birds, griffons, and combats between monsters, upon the textiles of central Asia from the third to the tenth century of our era (see Volume III, Fig. 88 to 101). On the other hand, this specifically Sāsānid conventionalization of animal motives will be found again, as we shall see, not only in the Moslem textiles both of Egypt and of Persia, but also in the bronze utensils, and especially the ewers in the form of birds or animals of the deer tribe, which have come down to us from the early days of Islam in regions ranging from the Caucasus to Egypt under the Fāṭimids.

From this point of view nothing could be more characteristic than the Sāsānid ewers in chased and " repoussé " copper in the Hermitage and those once forming part of the Bobrinsky collection. These noble works in the shape of lions, horses, or birds of a composite character are the direct prototypes and models of the Arab *acquamanili* (rose-water bowls for use after meals) of the Fāṭimid period, as well as of the brass household utensils of western Europe in the Middle Ages.

In fact, it is impossible to understand the arts of the Moslems unless we have grasped the enormous part played in Asia by Sāsānid art, with its double tendency, on the one hand towards the naturalistic representation of living forms, especially animals, and, on the other hand, towards decorative conventionalization and abstract geometrical designs.

CHAPTER V

Arab Civilization

PRE-ISLAMIC ARABIA AND ISLAM

IN SPITE OF THE POLITICAL EXHAUSTION CAUSED BY THE WAR BE-
tween Khosrau II and the Emperor Heraclius, the Sāsānid civilization was in its prime when the Moslem invasion took place.
For, while the Iranian King of Kings and the Byzantine Cæsar were
engaged in their protracted duel, which lasted from 610 to 628,
Muḥammad (Mahomet) (570–632) had unified Arabia and founded
Islam.

Before the coming of Muḥammad the Arabs were anything but barbarians. The Arabic language, which, with Ethiopian and Southern
Arabic, forms the southern group of Semitic tongues, is already
to be found in central Arabia as a literary language in the sixth century of our era, being used as a medium of expression by a whole
galaxy of poets. These poets, the chief of whom were Imru'l-Qais,
who died between 530 and 540, and 'Antar, who flourished during
the closing years of the sixth century, are among the greatest figures
in Oriental literature. The former was the son of a nobleman of Najd,
who, after a number of youthful adventures, lived the life of a knight-
errant. His father having been murdered by an enemy tribe, he made
it the object of his life to avenge him, after which he seems to have
entered the service of the Byzantines, among whom he died. His most
beautiful *mu'allaqa* sings his loves in a grand imagery full of

163

splendid and varied colour, which was afterwards adopted by all the classical Arab poets, but in him has the naïve charm of archaism. As for 'Antar, the second in date of the great pre-Islamic poets, he was the son of a celebrated chief and a black slave. At first he was relegated to a servile status, but by his own valour he fought his way to a place at the family hearth. He too sings in pastoral metaphors the beauty of his lady, the lovely Abla, " as gentle as a lamb "; but he

FIGURE 112
Qubbat al-Sakhra (Dome of the Rock), Jerusalem.
— *Photo, Gervais Courtellemont*

also takes as his subject combats between tribe and tribe, hereditary vendettas, and the fidelity of the camel and the horse, those companions of the nomad. He died as he had lived, on the field of battle, slain by a hostile tribe. His fame lived on in the famous *Romance of Antar* (*Sirat 'Antar*), composed between the ninth and twelfth centuries, on the basis of popular poems; the story has a fine epic swing, full of romance and colour, in which the wild, chivalrous spirit of the old Bedouins lives again.

This revelation of lofty and fiery genius in a people still in a back-ward state of rather primitive paganism, and of such lyric power and chivalry in tribes divided and subdivided to the last degree, sub-ject to no regular system of law, and living in a state of utter political anarchy, shows how unworthy of its human qualities was the in-significant role played by the Arab race in history at the opening of the seventh century. At the time when Muḥammad rose to power, pre-Islamic Arabia was full of splendid potentiali-ties, both spiritual and military.

Muḥammad was born in 570 at Mecca and be-longed to the powerful Quraish tribe, who had the trade of those parts in their hands. He was the posthu-mous son of a caravan con-tractor and started life as a camel-driver. His occu-pation was bound to bring him in touch with a variety of Arab tribes, some of

FIGURE 113
Interior of Qubbat al-Sakhra, Jerusalem.
— *Photo, Gervais Courtellemont*

which had embraced Judaism or Nestorian Christianity. These con-nexions, which could not but confirm the results of his own personal meditations, no doubt helped to decide his vocation.

At the moment when he received the " revelation " of his pro-phetic role, Muḥammad was a young, ardent, and generous man, full of enthusiasm for every noble cause and infinitely superior to his surroundings. The Arab tribes were sunk in idolatry, the nature of which is indicated by the cult of the Black Stone of the Ka'ba at Mecca; he therefore resolved to raise them to the level of monotheism, a thoroughgoing monotheism which should be quite simple and pure. They were exhausting themselves in endless civil wars, and living in a state of complete anarchy; he therefore determined to

FIGURE 114
Mosque of the Omayyads, Damascus.
— *Photo, Gervais Courtellemont*

bring them together in a great democratic and unitary state. They retained their brutal and savage customs, not far removed from barbarism; he therefore made it his task to civilize, tame, and instruct them. He would not have been of his own country and of his own age if he had not brought to the exposition of his system a certain mystical exaltation; but it was a clear and coherent system, positive, practical, and capable of immediate realization, and it was to re-

generate the Arab people and raise it to a moral level far higher
than that of its ancestors.

Having once laid down the main lines of his teaching and arrived
at the conception of the one God, Muḥammad could no longer keep
this treasury of truth to him-
self. His ardent soul led
him to preach to his nearest
relatives; but they would
have none of it, for they belonged to the pagan aristocracy of Mecca and feared
for their privileges. Muḥammad next turned to the
populace of Mecca, to the
Arabs of every tribe, and
even to strangers. His house
was full of poor men whom
he treated as friends. Rich
and poor, masters and
slaves, Christians and Jews,
he had a message for all. In
improvised speeches of impassioned eloquence he
preached to all the unity of
God and social equality,
and his words were written

FIGURE 115

Mosque of the Omayyads. Courtyard and minaret.
— *Photo, E. de Lorey*

in letters of fire upon the minds of the mobile and enthusiastic Arabs.
But the people of Mecca, and the Quraish in particular, who made
their living out of the worship of idols, resolved to put a stop to
his propaganda by killing him. He fled from the city in time and
took refuge in Medina, the inhabitants of which were the hereditary foes of the men of Mecca and hailed him as their leader. The

date of this flight, or *Hegira*, June 25, 622, marks the beginning of the Moslem calendar.

At Medina Muḥammad built the first mosque, after which, placing himself at the head of the people of that town, he set out to unify

Arabia. It was a long task and took ten years of struggle, during which the Prophet revealed himself a hero as well. He had to conquer Arabia foot by foot and tribe by tribe; and it took eight years of war to reduce Mecca. Stubbornly attached to its paganism, that city would have nothing to do with a reform which might ruin the pilgrimage to the Ka‘ba. After defeating the men of Mecca at Badr in 624, and himself being defeated by them at Uḥud (Ohod) in 625, Muḥammad at last succeeded in subduing his native town in 630. Being as politic as

FIGURE 116
Mosque of the Omayyads. Courtyard.
— *Photo, E. de Lorey*

he was generous, he destroyed the idols, but pardoned his enemies. He transformed the shrine of the Ka‘ba into a mosque, a happy act which maintained Mecca in its position as a religious metropolis, while imparting sanctity to the object of its pilgrimages.

Before the unity of the Arab nation could be attained, Muḥammad had still to subdue and convert the Jewish element at Khaibar, the pagan tribes of the Yemen, Hadramaut, 'Oman, and Najd. Once this task had been accomplished and the whole of Arabia now contained but a single people worshipping a single god, he returned to Mecca to organize the first great Moslem pilgrimage, of March 632, in which more than a hundred thousand believers are said to have taken

FIGURE 117
Interior (restored) of Mosque of the Omayyads.
— *Photo, E. de Lorey*

part. The Prophet's ideas were triumphing, but he was exhausted by twenty years of struggle and felt his end approaching. He therefore summoned his people and made known to them his last precepts: " Ye people, hearken unto my words, for I know not whether I can once more be in your midst another year. Be humane and just one unto the other. Let every man's life and property be sacred and inviolable. Let him who has received a pledge return it faithfully. Ye shall appear before your God, to whom ye shall render an account of your actions. Hearken unto the women, for they are your help-meets; ye have received them as a good thing entrusted to you by God. . . . Know that all Moslems are brothers one to another, and that you are all no more than one family of brethren. Beware of injustice. . . ." Then, raising his arms to heaven, he cried: " O God, have I said that which I had to say, and have I accomplished my mission? " And the crowd replied with one voice: " Yea, thou hast accomplished it." Upon which he said: " O God, vouchsafe to receive this my testimony," and dismissed the assembly. This scene, with its Biblical simplicity and broadly human appeal, succeeded in rallying the last few doubters to the Prophet's cause. A few days afterwards, on March 8, 632, he died, having witnessed the triumph of his work.

FIGURE 118

Monument of the Būyid period, known as the Tomb of Zobeida, Baghdād.
— *Photo, Gervais Courtellemont*

The great strength of Islam, which secured for it an amazing capacity for expansion, lay not only in the grandeur and nobility of most of its dogmas, which were far superior to the pagan-ism which they replaced, but, most of all, in the fact that it came at the right moment, into a world which was waiting for it, to peoples whose religious needs, social aspirations, and political ambitions it exactly interpreted. As a matter of fact, Islam invented nothing really new in any sphere; it did no more than carry existing tendencies into action and bring to completion, in the full light of day, an obscure process of evolution which had started several centuries before.

In the sphere of religion the teaching Muḥammad was in many respects no more than a synthesis and a simplification of previously existing doctrines — not of the crude old pagan creeds of the Arabs, which he destroyed, but of the great Oriental religions: Judaism, Christianity, and Mazdaism.

The Koran (Qor'ān), the sacred book of Islam, constantly draws its inspiration from the Bible, the Talmud, the Gospels, and even the *Avesta,* and Judaic doctrines have a large place in it. The Allah of the Koran is no more than the ancient Yahveh of Israel, the " God of Battles," a stern and abstract deity, who does not speak to the senses, but excites the imagination to the highest degree. It was from Judaism, too, that Muḥammad borrowed the sacred rules of hygiene which are indispensable in the East, the practice of frequent ablutions, circumcision, and abstention from pig's flesh, to which he added abstention from wine. He admitted the inspired character of the Pentateuch and the divine mission of Moses; and similarly he admitted the inspired character of the Gospels, the mission of Christ, and the sanctity of the Virgin. All that he rejected in Christianity was the divinity of Christ, the cult of the saints and of images, and the whole organization of the Church. On the other hand, he borrowed from it the metaphysical basis of morality, the immortality of the soul, the resurrection of the dead, the last judgment, heaven and hell. But since he was dealing with Orientals, his paradise was a veritable abode of delights. Certain of his maxims breathe a spirit like that of the Gospels and have something of the sentiment of Christian charity. He would repeat the commandment: " Love one another, and do not seek out the faults of your fellow-men "; or proclaim that: " God pardons him who repents, for He is indulgent and merciful. . . . It is not the flesh and blood of the sacrifices that rises up unto God, it is your pity that rises up unto Him. Righteousness consists in believing in God, giving to the orphan and the needy for the love of God, redeeming captives, giving alms, and being sincere. The Faithful ought to give the best of what they have gained to the poor. They are worthy of praise when they practise charity, and even more so if they do it in secret." Whether consciously or unconsciously, in addition to these Judæo-Christian influences, Muḥammad undoubtedly also admitted that of Mazdaism, which, directly or indirectly, provided him with his doctrine of angels, while it was the great duel between Ormuzd and Ahriman, quite as much, perhaps, as that between Jehovah and Satan that inspired him with the idea of the eternal struggle between Allah and Iblis.

OMAYYAD CIVILIZATION

ARABIA WAS NOW POLITICALLY UNIFIED. IN FUTURE IT HAD BUT ONE faith, ardently spiritual and absolutely monotheistic in character; one morality, that of the Koran, simple, pure, and broad; one social organization, the commonwealth based on equality, at once theocratic and patriarchal, instituted by the Prophet. And it advanced forthwith to the conquest of the East.

Muḥammad did not live to see the *Jihad*, the great war or " Holy War." It started on the morrow of his death and was carried to a successful conclusion by his successors, his " caliphs " or representatives: Abū-Bakr (622–634), 'Omar (634–644), 'Othmān (644–656), and 'Alī (656–661). As we have seen, the Byzantine Empire and that of Sāsānid Persia had issued from their prolonged duel in a state of exhaustion, and the Arabs took advantage of this to crush the former and destroy the latter. Two victories, at Ajnādain in 634 and at the Yākūsa in 636, won them the Byzantine provinces of Palestine and Syria, the conquest of which was followed between 640 and 642 by that of Egypt. Two more victories, at Qādisiya in 637 and Nehāvend in 642, next made them masters of Persia. In this upheaval, though shorn of Syria, Egypt, and soon of Africa, the Byzantine Empire at least kept possession of Asia Minor, whereas the whole of the Sāsānid Empire of Persia fell into the power of the conquerors. Thus by the end of a few years the Arab Empire extended from Africa and the Taurus to the Oxus and the Indus. In the eighth century it was even to be carried across the Oxus and wrest Transoxiana from the Turco-Iranian dynasties which acknowledged the suzerainty of China.

The first four caliphs, who reigned from 622 to 661 and under whom these vast conquests were carried out, remained faithful to the spirit of Muhammad and the traditions of their race. Arabs they were and Arabs they remained, desert sheikhs, with no courts, no luxury, and no needs, hard to themselves and to others alike, living in tents on a footing of intimacy and equality with the tribesmen. For some years the old em-

FIGURE 119
Great Mosque, Baghdād.
— *Photo, Gervais Courtellemont*

pires were governed from a nomad camp (*dwār*) by poor Bedouins. But this state of affairs could not go on. Arab rule — which stood for patriarchal simplicity, contempt for all material civilization and profane culture, and a military commonwealth — was scarcely compatible with the foundation of a stable government resting upon the old historic structure of the Middle East; and, as a matter of fact, it was not long before Aramæo-Byzantine Syria and Sāsānid Persia were victorious over their fierce conquerors, if not in the religious sense, at least in so far as culture was concerned.

FIGURE 120

Mosque of Ibn Ṭulūn, Cairo.
— *Photo, Creswell*

Syria was the first to take this peaceful revenge. After its conquest one of the most powerful of the Arab families, that of the Omayyads, belonging to the old Quraish aristocracy of Mecca, was entrusted with its government and was not slow to become acclimatized there. The reigning caliph, on the other hand — the pious 'Alī, Muḥammad's son-in-law — continued to stand for Islam in all its uncompromising orthodoxy. It could not be long before a struggle broke

FIGURE 121
Mosque of Ibn Ṭulūn.
— *Photo, Gervais Courtellemont*

out between this Bedouin of the desert and the Omayyads, who had became half-Syrianized. 'Alī was defeated, and in 660 the Omayyad Mo'awiya became caliph.

The Omayyad dynasty governed the Arab Empire from 660 to 750, with Damascus as its capital. While of course abjuring nothing of their Islamic faith, the caliphs of this house in reality turned the theocratic republic of their predecessors into a regular temporal and centralized state in the Byzantine sense of the word. Under them the

Arab Empire became in some sort a Syrian Empire. The administration was modelled upon that of Byzantium and, what is more, continued to employ a large number of Greek or Syriac officials. The Syriac Christians, in particular, exerted a considerable influence at court; one of them, Sarjūn bin Manṣūr, was Moʻawiya's principal minister. In their palace at Damascus the Omayyad caliphs named Yazīd or Walīd surrounded themselves with a luxury that scandalized the pious, while they showed signs of a liberal spirit, a taste for poetry and art, and even a dilettantism which were somewhat unexpected in these sons of the desert. Yazīd I, for example, who reigned from 680 to 683 and was passionately fond of hunting and feasting, a great connoisseur of wines, dogs, and dancing-girls, was irreligious and cultivated and reminds us more of the liberal Seleucids than of the companions of

FIGURE 122
Mosque of Ibn Ṭulūn. North-east wing.
— Photo, Creswell

the Prophet. In order to crush the opposition of the pietistic party, he either instigated or permitted the massacre at Kerbela in 680 of the family of ʻAlī, Muḥammad's son-in-law, a dramatic event big with consequences, which was to divide Islam into two hostile creeds, the dissentient Shīʻites, the avengers of the house of ʻAlī, and the Sunnites, or party of the majority, which had rallied to the new dynasty.

The Omayyads had now become regular Moslem Cæsars and wanted their court at Damascus to rival that of Constantinople. It

FIGURE 123
Bowl of Raiy ware, ninth century.
— *Louvre. Archives photographiques*

was their intention to possess palaces and mosques worthy of the Sacred Palace and St. Sophia. Hence the Greek architects whom they employed adapted Byzantine art to the exigencies of the Koranic religion and thus created Arab art.

The principal form of building produced by Arab art was naturally the mosque (*masjid*, and later *jāmi'*), the essential parts of
which were the four porticos (*riwāq* or *līwān* — Arabic for the origi-

FIGURE 124
Lustre bowl of Raiy ware, eighth or ninth century.
— *René Pottier collection*

nal Persian *eivān*) covered with a flat roof supported on columned
arcades; these four arcades surrounded a square courtyard (*ṣahn*),
in which stood the fountain for ablutions; the *līwān par excellence*,
which is on the side towards Mecca, is broader than the others and

has a greater number of aisles; it is the principal hall, the oratory intended to receive the throng of the faithful; it is often divided in
two by a grille of wooden fretwork, and in its end wall is the niche or

FIGURE 124b
Bowl of Raiy ware, eighth or ninth century.
— *Vignier collection. Photo, Laniepce*

miḥrāb marking the direction of Mecca, and the *minbar*, or preacher's
pulpit; lastly, the building is flanked by one or more towers or
minarets (*manāra*), from which the muezzin summons the faithful
to prayer. This plan, as has often been pointed out, seems to be
copied from that of the Christian basilicas of Syria; the court of the

ablutions corresponds to the atrium, the *līwān* to the narthex of a basilica — here also having the same functions as the aisle in a French
Gothic cathedral — the grille to a sort of chancel-screen, the *miḥrāb*
to " a miniature apse," and the minaret to a bell-tower. As in the By-

FIGURE 125
Plate from Susa, ninth century.
— *Louvre. Archives photographiques*

zantine churches, the decoration of the Syrian mosques consisted
chiefly of marbles, rare varieties of stone, precious metals, and
enamelled mosaics.

The chief Omayyad monuments are to be found in Damascus and

Jerusalem. The Qubbat al-Sakhra, or Dome of the Rock, at Jerusalem, wrongly called the Mosque of 'Omar, is not so much a mosque,
in the architectural sense of the word, as a sort of mausoleum or
oratory, octagonal in form and surmounted by a cupola, and is built

FIGURE 126
Enamelled faience bowl. Persian art, earlier than twelfth century.
— *Louvre. Archives photographiques*

round the sacred rock of the Biblical legend (Fig. 112, 113). It was
built about 691 by the caliph 'Abd al-Malik, who utilized Byzantine
materials, such as columns, capitals, etc. On the other hand, the
Mosque of al-Aqsa, close by, which was adapted by the same caliph,

FIGURE 127
Entrance to Mosque of al-Azhar, Cairo.
— *Photo, Gervais Courtellemont*

'Abd al-Malik, on the plan of an ancient basilica of Justinian, and the
Great Mosque, or Mosque of the Omayyads, at Damascus, built about
708 by the caliph Walīd on the site of a Christian church of the
Emperor Theodosius, follow the historic plan of a mosque described
above. The Great Mosque at Damascus, of which we reproduce some

FIGURE 128
Mosque of al-Azhar.
— *Photo, Gervais Courtellemont*

fine photographs here by courtesy of M. Eustache de Lorey (Fig.
114 to 117), is built on a rectangular plan, in which the principal
līwān, with the *miḥrāb* and *minbar*, runs along the southern, or wider,
side. It is characterized by three minarets, those of the Betrothed, of
Jesus, and of Qa'it-bey, of which the first alone is of the same date
as the original building. As in the other Syrian mosques, part of the

columns are taken from earlier buildings and are in the Byzantine style. The interior, and notably the transept, were decorated with mosaics (*fusaī-fasā*) executed by Greek artists sent for by the caliph Walīd from Constantinople. We may judge of these Omayyad mosaics in the Great Mosque at Damascus from the fragments recently brought to light by Monsieur de Lorey. We may also note those which still decorate the inside face of the arches of the outer concentric colonnade of the Qubbat al-Sakhra at Jerusalem. The mosaics are pale

FIGURE 129
Stone cenotaph of Fāṭima (1067), Damascus.
— *Photo, E. de Lorey*

blue or deep blue in tone, or brown upon gold, with decorative motives of vine-leaves trailing from vases, precious works in which we see Arab fantasy at work for the first time on an old Byzantine motive — that Arab fantasy which was later to enrich Oriental decoration with an infinite number of motives by its arabesques and Kufic script.

The civilization of Omyyad Syria became more and more brilliant every day. It seemed as though the Moslem revolution had taken place merely in order to turn Damascus into the capital of the East, when the Omayyad dynasty was swept away by a revolt starting in Persia, and with it the Syrian hegemony of Islam.

'ABBĀSID CIVILIZATION

THE RISE TO POWER OF THE OMAYYAD DYNASTY HAD BEEN REGARDED as a usurpation by the partisans of the family of 'Alī, especially after the tragic events at Kerbela. This party, who have been called the Shī'ites, had gained a numerous following not only in Arabia, but

FIGURE 130

Carved wooden cenotaph of Sukaina (about 1100), Damascus.
— *Photo, E. de Lorey*

also in Persia, which, though for a time she had bowed before the violence of the storm, was now beginning to recover herself. Though the Arabs had succeeded in imposing a new religion upon Iran, they had proved powerless to absorb the Iranian race. They had assimilated Mesopotamia, Syria, and Egypt both racially and in language,

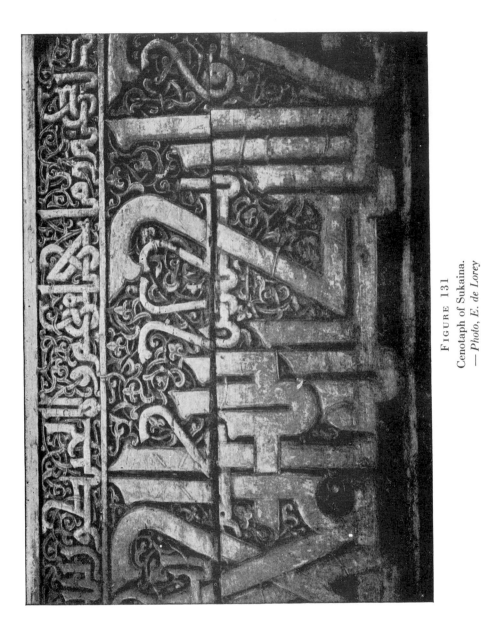

FIGURE 131
Cenotaph of Sukaina.
— *Photo, E. de Lorey*

but were unable to make any impression on the domain of Aryanism. In this region there was no interruption of linguistic continuity, for in the first document in the Persian tongue which has come down to

FIGURE 132
Bowl of Fāṭimid period with pattern in lustre, eleventh century.
— *Louvre. Archives photographiques*

us, dating from the ninth century, the language seems already to have acquired its definitive form and is a direct development of the southern Pahlavi of the Sāsānid period. Thus the conversion of Persia to Islam did not involve its absorption by Islam, as happened to the Mediterranean countries. While embracing Islam, it still remained itself, but the new Persia had gained fresh life from the elements brought to her by Islam from all parts of the world and was emancipated from her narrow nationalism, strengthened by all the energy and love of action which had found expression in the Moslem revolution, and, lastly, endowed with a more delicate, restless, and impassioned sensibility. In this respect Islam played the same part in Iran as Christianity did in the West; in their respective spheres these two Semitic religions created, one a Moslem Persia, and the other a Christian Europe, infinitely richer and more complex than Sāsānid Iran and the Greco-Roman world had been. The reason is that, by their very opposition to the national genius, these foreign cults introduced into the consciousness of the race an element of diversity, factors provocative of doubt, moral struggles, and conflicts of feeling — in other words, life and passion.

FIGURE 133

Bowl from Raqqa, tenth to twelfth centuries.
— *Louvre. Photo, Pivot*

Shī'ism was ardently espoused by the Persians and provided them with a doctrinal justification for their opposition. As we have seen, its essential feature was a sort of legitimism, which claimed the Caliphate for the family of Muḥammad and his son-in-law, 'Alī, who had been set aside by the Omayyads. In place of the caliphs in their strict sequence, the Shī'ites recognized a succession of *imāms*, or " guides," all chosen from among the descendants of 'Alī. Moreover, this Muḥammadan legitimism happened to be in harmony with Persian irredentism, for the *imām* Ḥusain, son of 'Alī, and one of the martyrs of Kerbela, was said to have married the daughter of the last of the Sāsānid kings, Yazdagard III. The passion of 'Alī and Ḥusain formed a theme which kept Persian Shī'ism perpetually at a fever heat, and this state of mind was still further heightened by the theory of the Mahdī, or " hidden guide," a sort of Moslem Messiah or Saoshyant, who was to return in triumph at the end of the world and establish the reign of God upon earth.

The political revival of Persian nationality and the religious grievances of dissident Shī'ites were turned to advantage by a princely Arab family, the 'Abbāsids, who were also related to Muḥammad, being descendants of an uncle of the Prophet. The 'Abbāsids allied themselves by marriage with the house of 'Alī and, in concert with it, stirred up the Persian

FIGURE 134
Maristān (hospital) of Nūr al-Dīn (1154), Damascus.
— *Photo, E. de Lorey*

province of Khorāsān to revolt against the Omayyads in 747. After a struggle lasting three years, they overthrew the Omayyad dynasty, and their leader, Abu'l-'Abbās, had himself recognized as caliph in 750. The *imāms* of the house of 'Alī, for whom he had pretended to be taking up arms, were set aside, and Shī'ism remained in opposition.

In spite of this abandonment of the true Shī'ite claims, the 'Abbāsid revolution marked the triumph of the Persian element in the Arab Empire. The Iranians had formed the bulk of the 'Abbāsid army, and, having gained the victory, the new dynasty summoned them to share in its power. It was they who filled the departments of state and conducted its business, as the Syrians had done under the Omayyad dynasty. The secession of Spain, whither the survivors of the Omayyad family withdrew to set up a dissident empire in 756, and later, in 969, the secession of Egypt, where another dissident caliphate — that of the Fāṭimids — was established, still further contributed towards increasing the importance of the Iranian element in the domains of the 'Abbāsids, by limiting their scope to Asia.

FIGURE 135

Mausoleum of Saladin (1193), Damascus.
— *Photo, E. de Lorey*

The " Moslem Sāsānids," as the 'Abbāsid caliphs have been called, could not take up their residence at Damascus as the Omayyads had done. They established themselves on the threshold of Iran and of the Arab world, in Babylonia, a land which had been the seat of the monarchy of the Shāpūrs and Khosraus in past ages. It was here that in 762 the second of the 'Abbāsids, al-Manṣūr, founded his new capital, Baghdād, which was destined very soon to become the first city of the East. From the very first the ascendancy of the Iranian element at Baghdād was so marked that the administration of this vast empire was entrusted to the Barmakids, a family purely Persian in race, which had also, it seems, remained quite Persian at heart. The Barmakids had the power in their hands under the caliphs al-Manṣūr (754–775), al-Mahdī (775–785), and Hārūn al-Rashīd (786–809), until, in 803, the last-mentioned, growing uneasy at their power, had one of them executed and dismissed the rest from favour. Their fall did but little to delay the triumph of the Persian element. Shortly after the death of Hārūn al-Rashīd the throne was disputed by his two sons, al-Amīn, who was supported by the Arab element, and al-Ma'mūn, whose mother was

FIGURE 136
Maristān of Qaimari (1248), Damascus.
— *Photo, E. de Lorey*

a Persian and who had the support of the Persians. In the end it was al-Ma'mūn who won the day, in 813, by the aid of his mother's fellow-countrymen; his reign, which lasted from 813 to 833, was accompanied by such a triumph of Iranian influences that for a time he even declared his adhesion to the Shī'ite doctrines.

The age of these first 'Abbāsids marks the highest point of Arab, or, rather, Arabo-Persian, civilization. The personal merit of the sovereigns had a great deal to do with this flourishing state of affairs. The most celebrated of them all, Hārūn al-Rashīd, seems to have been a prince of remarkable intelligence and subtlety, a real type of the

FIGURE 137

Mausoleum of Saif al-Dīn (1296), Damascus.
— *Photo, E. de Lorey*

great Arab nobleman of ancient descent. He was more liberal, generous, and magnificent than any other Oriental potentate and did not rest content simply to surpass the marvels of Nineveh and Babylon, Alexandria and Byzantium in the entertainments which he offered at Baghdād to the ambassadors of the whole world. This caliph of the *Arabian Nights,* who dazzled the envoys of the Empress Irene by his splendour and entered into friendly relations both with Charlemagne and with the Celestials of the T'ang dynasty, had his duties as king very much at heart.

As the fall of the Barmakids bears witness, he meant to be his own minister and enter directly into contact with his people. Like St. Louis of France, he could be seen settling the quarrels of his subjects before his own personal tribunal, and the wisdom of his judgments won him the fine title of Hārūn the Just. When night fell, he would slip into the streets of Baghdād in disguise, mingle with the cosmopolitan crowd which thronged the bazaars of the vast city, and question everybody about the sufferings, needs, and desires of the people.

The 'Abbāsid Empire was the seat of a rich material civilization. The mass of Arab tales which give us a picture of the society of those times is constantly referring to the fabulous wealth of Baghdād and the other great cities of 'Irāq. In the bazaars of the 'Abbāsid capital

FIGURE 138
Citadel of Cairo, north-eastern side (Qal'at al-Jabal), Ayyūbid period.
— *Photo, Creswell*

were amassed all the products of the East. The caravans of Iran brought to them the carpets of Samarqand, the raw silk of Māzandarān, the silken fabrics of Marv and Nishāpūr, the velvets of Tūs and Shushtar, the turquoises and lapis lazuli of Khorāsān and what is now Afghanistan, and the ceramic ware of Raiy, besides the sugar-cane and confectionary of Makrān, the fine wines and essences of Shīrāz, Yazd, and Isfahān. The caravans from Mesopotamia, Syria, and Africa brought Arabian incense, " damascened " armour, goldsmiths' work, fine harness-work, rich carpets, and gold brocades from Aleppo and Damascus, muslins from Mosul, the many-coloured glass-ware of Tyre and Beyrut, the wood-carving, ivory boxes, perfume-burners, and earthenware of al-Fustāt (Cairo). The Arab ships which plied on the Persian Gulf between Basra and the ports of the Malabar coast, touching at Sirāf and Muscat, brought back to 'Irāq the spices of the Malay Archipelago, the pearls of Cey-

FIGURE 139
Citadel of Damascus (1208).
— *Photo, E. de Lorey*

lon, the precious woods, cotton fabrics, and cinnamon of India, and the musk of Tibet, as well as the silks and satins of China. The important Arab halting-place of Sirāf on the Persian Gulf was, as it were, an outpost of Baghdād on the way to India. The voyage of Suleiman the merchant to India and China in 851, the story of Sindbad the sailor in the *Thousand and One Nights,* bear witness to the volume of sea-borne traffic between the 'Abbāsid Empire and the Far East. How considerable was the traffic by the land routes through central Asia is proved, as we shall see, by the discovery, among the pottery of Raiy, of Chinese ware of the T'ang period.

Intellectual activity was commensurate with this economic prosperity. Up to this time, Arab poetry had been merely primitive, celebrating the life of caravans, the joy of battle, the great elemental emotions of the nomad faced with the eternal spectacle of the sky and

FIGURE 140
Citadel of Aleppo, twelfth to fourteenth centuries.
— *Photo, E. de Lorey*

desert. A change came when it had to express a whole world of moral ideas hitherto unknown, the life of the new masters of the East with its refinements, the subtleties of chivalrous love, the fine distinctions of dialectic. The ancient lyric poetry of the nomad bards made way for new poetic forms, and we see the appearance of a court poetry at Baghdād which was graceful and melancholy, sportive and passionate by turns, compact of delicacy, ardour, and fantasy, a poetry as light and elegant as the decoration of the Alhambra. The

FIGURE 141

Miḥrāb of the Mausoleum of Bibars (1277), Damascus.
— *Photo, E. de Lorey*

inspiration of the great Persian poets of succeeding ages is already to be found in the 'Abbāsid poets, many of whom were, indeed, of purely Persian descent, or else of mixed Arab and Persian blood, and, while adopting the Arab language as their means of expression, had all of them remained faithful to the Iranian genius; this is true of

FIGURE 142
Mosque of Qalawun (d. 1290), Cairo.
— *Photo, Creswell*

the greatest lyric poet of this age, Abū Nuwās, who died about 810, and whose erotic and elegiac poetry reveals a sentiment both delicate and profound.

At the same time philosophic thought began to develop rapidly, the chief motive force of this movement coming from the Syriac Christians, both Nestorian and Monophysite, who continued to be

as numerous under the 'Abbāsid Empire as they had been under that
of the Sāsānids in past days. The Nestorians in particular exerted a
considerable influence by translating the leading works of the Greek
sages into Syriac, and afterwards into Arabic. Since a number of
them were sought after at the court of Baghdād and enjoyed the per-

FIGURE 143
Mosque of Ḥasan (d. 1361), Cairo (on the left).
— *Photo, Creswell*

sonal favour of the caliphs by reason of their scientific knowledge of
astronomy and medicine, their influence was able to make itself felt
openly. It was they who made the philosophy of Plato known to the
Arabs and Persians, besides that of Aristotle and the Alexandrian
school, the geometry of Euclid, and the geography of Ptolemy. The
application of philosophic speculation to the interpretation of the

Koran gave rise to the *kalām,* or dogmatic theology; two schools of this science grew up, on which Arabo-Persian dialectic was to lavish the treasures of its subtlety: that of the Mu'tazilits, whose exegesis made a parade of rationalist tendencies, and that of the Mutakallim, who were more strictly orthodox. Contrary to the customary interpretation of the Koran, many of the Mu'tazilit doctors admired the principle of free will; others stripped Allah of his comparatively anthropomorphic form, analogous to that of the Bible, and even of his metaphysical attributes, and made of him an absolute principle beyond the powers of human apprehension; some even seemed to substitute for the transcendental theism of the Koran a doctrine of divine immanence. The caliph Ma'mūn, who reigned from 813 to 833 and founded a sort of university at Baghdād, to which he summoned all the doctors to hold free disputations, openly favoured Mu'tazilism. Liberal thought had the upper hand down to the time of the caliph Mutawakkil (847–861), who gave his support to the pietistic reaction of the Mutakallim.

'ABBĀSID ART

THE 'ABBĀSID PERIOD IS OF CAPITAL IMPORTANCE FOR THE HISTORY of Arab art. Unfortunately it has to be admitted that, since the destruction of Baghdād in 1258 and the other catastrophes which have followed it, hardly anything remains of the monuments of Baghdād; the famous tomb known as that of Zobaida, who died in 831, never belonged to that princess (Fig. 118). We are more fortunate at Raqqa, on the Euphrates, where a few remains of the Palace of Hārūn al-Rashīd are left, and at Sāmarrā, a city on the Tigris, to the north of Baghdād, which from 836 to 889 for a time took the place of Baghdād as the residence of the 'Abbāsid caliphs. At Sāmarrā the ruins of the Mosque of the caliph Mutawakkil and the palace of the caliphs, the Balkuwārā, are still standing, while, so far as the rest of the site is concerned, the excavations of Professor Herzfeld's German mission and the learned works of the French archæologist H. Viollet enable us to form some idea of the architectural effect as a whole. The mosque (Fig. 119) formed " a vast rectangle enclosed by high walls, the inside of which was cased with burnt bricks, having the principal

FIGURE 144
Mosque of Ḥasan (d. 1361), Cairo.
— *Photo, Gervais Courtellemont*

hall, with its twenty-five aisles, on the south side, and three other smaller halls on the remaining sides; all these aisles, which were more than thirty-three feet in height, were supported by marble columns; the four halls opened on to a vast courtyard, the centre of which was occupied by a richly decorated fountain " (H. Viollet). As for the palace of the caliphs at Sāmarrā, Monsieur Viollet describes it as follows: " Its ruins cover a vast rectangle the side of which is more than a kilometre in length. On the western façade three arches of brick masonry are still standing. These three arches, facing the river, were used for ceremonies and public audiences, and opened on a wide view of the valley. At their feet terraces and fountains descend in broad tiers *en cascades*. Behind these are three inner courts, which give light to some rooms arranged in the form of a cross; these were the throne-rooms; next come a number of less lofty rooms, which were private apartments with luxurious baths. On the east is to be seen the plan of a large rectangular garden, surrounded by pilastered walls, in which were some waterfalls, and on which opened some little richly decorated pavilions. On the north was a vast creek, approached by a ramp honeycombed with grottoes and water-pools. And lastly, grouped behind this mass of buildings, clustered houses containing the harem, others for the accommodation of the courtiers, a small mosque, and great outbuildings for the caliph's guard and the cavalry."

Monsieur Viollet points out that this general arrangement follows the great tradition of Iranian architecture, Sāsānid influences being here combined with those of Byzantine and Syro-Coptic art. As for the internal decoration, the walls are cased with carved stucco, forming a panelled dado three feet four inches

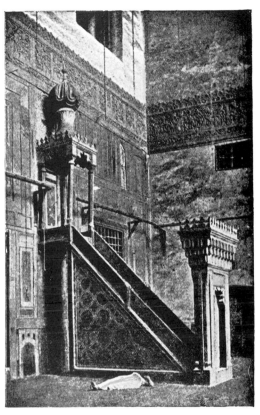

FIGURE 145
Mosque of Ḥasan. *Mihrāb* and *minbar.*
— *Photo, Gervais Courtellemont*

high, above which are a sort of trefoil arches, a form of wall-lining copied from that of the Sāsānid palaces. Similarly, at Raqqa, in the ruins of the Palace of Hārūn al-Rashīd, we find decorative motives which have come down from Sāsānid times; for instance, certain arcades,

arches, and niches which are curiously reminiscent of the Tāq-i Kisrā
at Ctesiphon. But in the art of Sāmarrā the decorative designs are
already decidedly Moslem in character, with their conventionalized
flowers forming the centre of recurring geometrical figures connected
by ribbon-work; or with their strings of beads which form a vase or a
lyre where they end or touch; or with their arabesques entwined with
grapes and vine-leaves; all of which are described in H. Viollet's
monograph.

FIGURE 146
Mausoleum of Barquq (d. 1398).
— *Photo, Creswell*

The 'Abbāsid buildings of Mesopotamia had a considerable influence, not only on later Persian art, but even on Syro-Egyptian
architecture itself. The recent works of Herzfeld, Viollet, and
André Godard have shown us how largely the Mosque of Ibn Ṭulūn
at Cairo, the first great monument of Moslem Egypt which has
come down to us, was inspired by the architecture of Sāmarrā (Fig.
120 to 122). This immense edifice was built about 876 by the governor, Ibn Ṭulūn, who since 869 had made himself practically inde-

FIGURE 147
Tomb of Barquq (d. 1398).
— *Photo, Creswell*

pendent of the Caliphate of Baghdād. It forms a rectangle some 390
feet long by some 425 feet broad and is the type *par excellence* of the
mosque with arcades. It is built entirely of brick, an astonishing
medium to find on Egyptian soil, did we not know that it was directly
imitated from Mesopotamia. Moreover, it is here that we first see

FIGURE 148
Madrasa Jaqmaqiya, Damascus (1421).
— *Photo, E. de Lorey*

the appearance of the pointed arch in these regions — a form which
also had its origin in Iran. Lastly, so far as the decorative carving is
concerned, Monsieur S. Flury has found in the Mosque of Ibn Ṭulūn
the same three motives — linear designs, deeply incised decorations,
and the vine-leaf and grape motive — that Professor Herzfeld found
at Sāmarrā. Geometrical and plant motives: here we again find these
two essential elements of what was to constitute the whole of Moslem

FIGURE 149

Mosque of Qa'it-bay (d. 1495), suburbs of Cairo.
— *Photo, Gervais Courtellemont*

decoration, which was opposed on principle to decoration based on animal forms.

The ceramic art of the first 'Abbāsid period is worthy of special attention, as is proved by a number of pieces coming from the exca-

vations at Raiy (Rhages), Zanjān, Susa, Sāmarrā, and, in Egypt, from Fustāt (Fig. 123 to 126). Many of these pieces had been assigned by the late Maurice Pézard to a date as early as the Sāsānid age; but as a matter of fact it appears that, though they show signs of Sāsānid inspiration, they are simply early Moslem work, as Monsieur Charles Vignier was the first to proclaim, and as Monsieur R. Koechlin has recently established by comparing the specimens from Susa with those from Sāmarrā, for these latter can be dated from the years during which this ephemeral capital flourished, be-

FIGURE 150
Mosque of Qa'it-bay (d. 1495).
— Photo, Creswell

tween 836 and 889. We find the same sequence of styles at Susa as at Sāmarrā: non-lustre cups, of a creamy white, decorated with a pattern of conventionalized foliage or flowers in cobalt-blue, sometimes tending towards green; cups, also in non-lustre ware, on which the pattern, whether geometrical or consisting of palmettes, is slightly in relief or else incised or modelled on a yellow and green ground; some very fine cups covered with a brilliant lustre of yellow, greenish, or reddish gold, with a pattern of conventionalized foliage, medallions, and flowers of a sumptuously decorative effect, with occasional motives of conventionalized animal forms. These are further described in R. Koechlin's *La Céramique de Sāmarrā* (Syria, 1926).

The chief centre of manufacture seems to have been at Rhages or Raiy, a town which had been famous ever since the days of the Persian Empire and maintained its importance under the various Moslem dynasties until it was destroyed in 1221. The cups and bowls from Raiy, some of non-lustre ware, with motives in relief covering the whole ground, and often with decorations in pale blue, others in lustre ware of an olive-green tinge, are remarkable for their treatment of the human figure, and especially for their motive of " the horseman with the round face," which we here reproduce from a bowl in the Nazare Agha collection. But in such pieces as these we are going beyond the 'Abbāsid period proper and have already reached the height of the Seljuk period, in

FIGURE 151
North-western *līwān* of Mosque of Qa'it-bay.
— *Photo, Creswell*

the thirteenth century. We may here mention a criterion which has
been established by the unerring experience of Monsieur Charles
Vignier for dating the pottery of Raiy; on pieces dating from
the ninth century we fre-
quently find a wreath running round the inner edge
of the plate, while on those
of the thirteenth century it
is absent.

FIGURE 152
Madrasa of al-Nāsir Muḥammad (d. 1498).
Detail of *miḥrāb.*
— *Photo, Creswell*

As we see from its pot-
tery, ʿAbbāsid Iran had
not the slightest hesitation
in representing the human
figure. This impression is
confirmed if we pass to
its paintings, as revealed
to us by the frescoes of
Sāmarrā, of which Pro-
fessors Sarre and Herzfeld
have made such a magnifi-
cent study. According to
Herr Herzfeld's conclu-
sions, the processions of
human or animal figures
which adorn the walls of
the palace of the caliphs
suggest the Greco-Levant-
ine schools which preceded them rather than the Persian miniatures
of later days. The oval shape of the feminine faces at Sāmarrā (see
the figures of naiads in Herzfeld: *Malereien von Sāmarrā*, Pl. LII,
LIV, and LXXI) reminds us to some extent of certain Levantine

figures of Buddhist inspiration from the *Viśvantara Jātaka* on the frescoes of Mirān in eastern Turkestan, dating from the third century and published by Sir Aurel Stein in *Serindia* (Volume I).

Elsewhere, in certain masculine types — for instance, in the portrait of a Christian priest reproduced by Herzfeld (*Malereien*, Pl. LXI) — we find something of that pre-Byzantine quality of Levantine art, as seen in the frescoes of Doura-Europos (Salihiya), investigated by Monsieur Franz Cumont. Lastly, we observe at Sāmarrā some representations of animals which are directly akin to the art of Mazdean Persia — processions of camels which remind us of Persepolis, or medallions of animals of the deer tribe recalling Tāq-i Bustān. Here again we seem

FIGURE 153
Mosque of Qānsūh al-Ghūrī (d. 1516).
— *Photo, Creswell*

to be dealing with " belated antiques " — or, to use the German term, *Spätantike* — antique types of a Romano-Sāsānid character surviving into the midst of the Islamic period. It was not till later that Islamic painting proper made its appearance in the miniature.

We may, however, perhaps note that the transition stage from the large-scale painting of Sāmarrā to the miniature is provided by the schools of eastern Turkestan, and notably by the Manichæan illuminations from Turfān, dating from the eighth and ninth centuries, discovered by the Von Le Coq mission, in which we already find the finish and charm of Persian miniatures, together with something of the composition and treatment of masses to be seen in the paintings of Sāmarrā. In view of the gaps in continuity in Iran proper, the necessary link has often to be provided by " Greater Iran." Moreover, even without going outside Iran itself, we may note a certain affinity between one of the frescoes of Sāmarrā, on the one hand, representing a male figure of a curiously Byzantino-Arab type, with a black beard, long, lean contours, and a suggestion of vigour (see Herzfeld: *Malereien*, Pl. LXIII), and, on the other hand, those figures of a markedly Semitic type that we notice on certain 'Abbāsid manuscripts of the school of Baghdād in the thirteenth century — for instance, the illustrations of the Dioscorides manuscript and the earliest miniatures in the Vever collection.

FIGURE 154

Fountain of the Treasure, Damascus
(thirteenth century).
— *Photo, E. de Lorey*

FIGURE 155
Mosque of Suleiman (1554), Damascus.
— *Photo, E. de Lorey*

HAMDANID SOCIETY

THE CALIPHS OF SĀMARRĀ WERE THE LAST OF THE ʿABBĀSIDS WHO
really governed their empire as a whole. After their day, when the
seat of the Caliphate had been removed to Baghdād, where it was to
remain till the catastrophe of 1258, the ʿAbbāsid dominions were
split up, if not from the point of view of religious obedience, at least
from the temporal point of view. As we shall see, Persia, while remaining beneath the normal suzerainty of the caliph, was divided up
among various Iranian dynasties. In the Arab lands properly so
called — Mesopotamia and Syria — a number of local dynasties
were likewise founded, one of the most remarkable of which was the
purely Arab (Yemenite) house of the Hamdānids, established in

western Mesopotamia and northern Syria under the form of the two emirates of Mauṣil (the modern Mosul), which lasted from 929 to 991, and of Aleppo, which lasted from 944 to 1003. The most illustrious prince of this dynasty was Saif al-Daula, emir of Aleppo from 944 to 967, a legendary hero who, while the other Moslem princes took no interest in the Holy War, spent his life in heroic combats in the attempt to protect northern Syria from the Byzantine attacks which increasingly threatened her with reconquest. During the intervals of this struggle he wrote verses, and we have a dainty poem by this paladin on the rainbow. In imitation of him his cousin and lieutenant, Abū Firās al-Hamdāni, combined military with literary glory and managed to console himself during a long captivity by composing warlike elegies, which are still famous. The court of Saif al-Daula at Aleppo became the resort of the most eminent writers of the age, such as the philosopher al-Fārābī, the founder of Arab Aristotelianism, who came from his native land of Transoxiana to seek the protection of Saif al-Daula, in whose entourage he died in 950.

Al-Mutanabbī, perhaps the greatest of Arab poets, lived for a long time at the court of Saif al-Daula. His works are characterized by a lyrical quality which is both erudite and refined — perhaps already over-refined — and reflect the complex tendencies of this noble Syro-Arabic society, the heir to three centuries of culture; on the one hand, we find a curious scepticism which enabled Mutanabbī himself to smile at his youthful pretensions to the role of prophet; on the other hand, in the midst of this well-ordered court, there survives, as it were, something of the old Bedouin epic spirit: " I am the son," he writes, " of combat and largesse, the son of the sword and the lance. The deserts and my rhymes, the camel's saddle and the mountains, stand to me in the stead of father and of ancestors." Mutanabbī had found in Saif al-Daula a hero worthy of him. In flaming metaphors he celebrates the victories of his patron over the Byzantine

FIGURE 156
Panel of faience in the Derwīshiya (1571), Damascus.
— *Photo, E. de Lorey*

legions or the other Arab emirs of the desert; or, after the triumph, the clemency of the chivalrous Hamdānid and the way in which he respected the captive princesses.

MOSLEM EGYPT: FĀṬIMID SOCIETY

LIKE THE OTHER ʿABBĀSID PROVINCES, EGYPT TOO HAD SECEDED. Twice in succession did leaders of Turkish mercenaries who had become governors of the country in the name of the caliph, Ibn Ṭulūn and Muḥammad Ikhshīd, claim the right to found a hereditary dynasty, setting up, one after the other, two practically independent dynasties, which ruled over Egypt and southern Syria; the first was that of the Ṭulūnids, which lasted from 868 to 905, and the second that of the Ikhshīds, which lasted from 935 to 969. Like the Mamelukes in later days, these earliest Turkish dynasties in Egypt distinguished themselves by their patronage of literature; we have seen how important the Mosque of Ibn Ṭulūn in Cairo is from the archæological point of view, and the relation in which it stands to the monuments at Sāmarrā. In this mosque we may also note a secondary, Syro-Byzantine influence, to be recognized in the charming motives of its capitals.

Though these Turkish governors of Egypt had made themselves independent, they had none the less always recognized the political suzerainty and pontifical authority of the ʿAbbāsid Caliphate of Baghdād. But in 969 took place a more serious secession: Egypt was conquered by the Fāṭimids, an Arab dynasty already established in Africa Minor. But, far from bowing before the spiritual authority of the Caliphate of Baghdād, the Fāṭimids had founded a dissident caliphate in Africa — a " heretical caliphate " — and had raised the standard of Shīʿism in opposition to the Sunnite orthodoxy of which the ʿAbbāsids were the representatives. The Fāṭimid al-Muʿizz having conquered Egypt and established his capital at

FIGURE 157

Panel of faience in the Derwīshiya (1571–84), Damascus.
— *Photo, E. de Lorey*

Fustāt, now become Cairo (Miṣr al-Qāhira), the Moslem East —
not to speak of Omayyad Spain — found itself still rent by schism,
torn between two opposing religious obediences: the Sunnite Caliphate of the 'Abbāsids at Baghdād, which was recognized by the
Moslems of Asia generally, and the Shī'ite Caliphate of the Fāṭimids
at Cairo, which was recognized in principle by the Moslems of Africa.

The Fāṭimids remained masters of Egypt from 969 to 1171. In
spite of the frequent disturbances caused both at Cairo and at
Baghdād by the turbulence of the Turkish mercenaries, the Fāṭimid
government was in general a beneficent one. The stable administration created by the two caliphs al-Mu'izz (969–975) and al-'Azīz
(975–996) and afterwards, at the end of the eleventh century, con-
trolled by a family of able viziers of Armenian origin secured for
Egyptian agriculture and trade a prosperity worthy of the days of
the Pharaohs or the Alexandrian age. At that time Egypt was the
great commercial emporium of the Levant, and she was to remain
so up to the time of the crusades, for the Italian merchants had got
into the habit of coming to the *fondachi* of Alexandria to obtain the
textiles and spices of India and the East Indian islands.

This prosperity was reflected in the sphere of art. Fāṭimid Egypt
became covered with buildings, some of which have come down to
our day. The earliest of these is the Mosque of al-Azhar, at Cairo,
built by the Fāṭimid general Jauhar between 970 and 972 (Fig. 127,
128). But the researches of Creswell and Flury would seem to show
that the central part alone dates from that period, the rest having
been restored, either at the end of the Fāṭimid dynasty or under the
Mamelukes (Mamlūks), or even during the period of Ottoman domination. The older parts of it, built of brick after the fashion of the
Mosque of Ibn Ṭulūn, may be distinguished from the more recent
parts, which are built of stone. What is more, from the architectural
point of view, it is thought that a Tunisian influence may be recognized
in it, to which may be due the plan with a central aisle flanked by a

double row of columns, as well as an Iranian influence, which may
be detected in the arches of the colonnade, as well as in the arched
niches between them, the pointed form of which reminded Monsieur
Saladin of Persian models. The mosque known as that of the caliph
al-Hākim (996–1020), which was really begun in 990, but the deco-

FIGURE 158
Panel of faience in the Sināniya Mosque, Damascus (1590).
— *Photo, E. de Lorey*

rations of which date from about 1012–13, during the reign of that
prince, was built on the same plan as that of Ṭulūn, and, like it, of
brick, with a cupola of brickwork — again like the mosques of
Ṭulūn and al-Azhar — supported upon an octagonal drum above
the *miḥrāb*. In the latest Fāṭimid mosques in Cairo, stone at last triumphs over brick — for instance, in the façade of the Mosque of al-
Aqmar, which was finished in 1125; together with the stone new

motives appear, such as the voussoirs forming the lintel of the entrance door, the deep niches on the façade, and the stalactite pendentives, all of which were to undergo endless development under the
Ayyūbids and the Mamelukes. On the other hand, as regards decoration properly so called, and in particular the decorative treatment of

FIGURE 159
Azem Palace, Damascus.
— *Photo, E. de Lorey*

inscriptions on stone or wooden panels, the Fāṭimid mosques can show
a few specimens which already foreshadow the glories of Mameluke
art — in particular those on the stone portal of the outer façade of
the Mosque of al-Hākim, or on the minaret of the same mosque, and
in certain pierced screens such as the round window over the entrance
of the Mosque of al-Aqmar (Fig. 129).

In this decorative stone-work we see the dawn of the tendency

towards arabesque. This style was perfected and gained in strength
and freedom in the wood-carvings of the Fāṭimid age (Fig. 130, 131),
one of the earliest of which is the door of the Mosque of al-Azhar,
dating from about 996 to 1020, now in the Arab Museum at Cairo.
The Arab Museum also contains a number of panels of carved wood

FIGURE 160
Azem Palace, Damascus.
— *Photo, E. de Lorey*

dating from the Fāṭimids, with subjects taken from living creatures,
some of which come from the palaces of those princes. These panels
represent animals of the deer tribe attacked by monsters, hares being
seized by eagles, pairs of birds face to face — old heraldic motives
borrowed from the Sāsānid textiles. We may also note the horsemen
hunting every kind of game, from lions to hares, the scenes of dancing or music, the women with camels' backs, subjects curiously

reminiscent of the painted motives on the pottery of Raiy. This lack
of scruple in reproducing subjects taken from living beings may no
doubt be explained by the Shī'ite creed of the Fāṭimid caliphs. The
affinities between their art and that of the ancient Sāsānids or of
Muḥammadan Persia should also, perhaps, be sought in their Shī'ism
—the religion of the majority of the Persian people. The same influence is evidently to be traced in the Fāṭimid bronzes, most of which
were intended for use as ewers or perfume-burners. These bronzes,
the best known of which is the griffon, forty inches high, in the Campo
Santo at Pisa, are often in the form of animals: griffons, deer, horses,
lions, hares, peacocks, etc. They are closely akin to the similar bronzes
in the Bobrinsky collection, which represent a " belated Sāsānid "
style, in that they form the transition stage between the art of ancient
Persia and the Persian art of the ninth century. Here again we can
see into what close contact with Iran Moslem Egypt had been
brought by the Shī'ism of the Fāṭimid dynasty. Moreover, a piece
of evidence connecting the two countries and their art is provided
by the bronze plaques of the little Ortuqid dynasty of northern Syria
in the twelfth century, with their patterns based on animal forms re-
minding us of Sāsānid art. We may note that these bronze animals
of the Fāṭimid period, whose shape is determined by the principle
that it should be in keeping with the use for which the object is
destined, none the less combine the various influences which have
gone to determine their style with such simplicity that they possess
an elegance, and sometimes a nobility, which cause them to rank
among the finest products of Moslem art.

The same may be said of the textiles. Many Fāṭimid fabrics made
their way into the West, no doubt as a result of the crusades, and
fine dated specimens are to be found in the Louvre, the Victoria and
Albert Museum, and the sacristies of Notre-Dame and various
churches in France. We should not forget that weaving had been, as
it were, the national art of Coptic Egypt. But Coptic textiles were

FIGURE 161
Cenotaph of Saladin, Damascus.
— *Photo, E. de Lorey*

themselves largely inspired by Sāsānid art — almost as much by the Sāsānid as by the Byzantine, as we may convince ourselves by looking at the specimens from Antinoë in the Musée Guimet; thus Sāsānid influence, whether direct or transmitted through the medium of Coptic art, seems to predominate in the Fāṭimid textiles; we find animal subjects, for preference conventionalized and in heraldic poses, such as we noted in Iran on the eve of the Arab conquest. Further, these recurring patterns of lions, eagles, griffons, and heraldic eagles — sometimes, too, of hares and birds treated in a more naturalistic spirit — are generally subordinated to a style of decoration which is, properly speaking, Moslem — interlaced patterns or running patterns of conventionalized foliage, which were to develop into the arabesque.

The ceramic art of the Fāṭimids, like their other arts, was subject to Iranian influence. We have seen how greatly Fustāt was influenced by ʿAbbāsid Sāmarrā in the days of Ibn Ṭulūn. During the Fāṭimid period Sāmarrā had fallen into neglect, and Fustāt had given way to Cairo, but this latter city continued to find inspiration for its pottery in the Persian workshops, and especially in those of Raiy. The lustre decoration of certain cups, with their motive of the hare passant surrounded by garlands of conventionalized foliage or bunches of flowers, is exactly the same at Cairo as at Raiy (Fig. 132). Here, as in Iran, the animal motives are broadly treated, especially those drawn from birds — ducks, eagles, etc.; sometimes even human figures are to be found; a basis of comparison in this respect may be furnished by a cup from Raqqa in the E. Mutiaux collection, now in the Louvre. It dates from between the tenth and the twelfth centuries and represents two female busts, the general appearance of which — as is not at all surprising — reminds us to some extent of the frescoes of Sāmarrā (Fig. 133).

SYRO-EGYPTIAN CIVILIZATION UNDER THE
AYYŪBIDS AND THE MAMELUKES

IN THE SECOND HALF OF THE ELEVENTH CENTURY THE FĀṬIMID DY-
nasty fell into a state of decadence. As we shall see, Syria proper
(the region of Damascus) was taken from it in 1076 by the Seljuk
Turks, who had already conquered Persia, and after this, Palestine
was wrested from it in 1099 by the crusades. During the struggle
with the crusades in Syria, Islam found itself abandoned to its own
resources. At last a principle of unity emerged from the Syro-Moslem
feudal régime in the shape of the Turk Nūr al-Dīn, atabeg of Mosul
and Aleppo from 1146 to 1173, who in 1154 also seized Damascus
(see Fig. 134). One of Nūr al-Dīn's lieutenants, the Kurd Salāḥ al-
Dīn Yūsuf, known to us as Saladin, who died in 1193, made himself
master of Egypt, where he put an end to the Fāṭimid dynasty and
afterwards brought the country back to the religious obedience of the
'Abbāsids in 1169; in 1174 he next took possession of Moslem Syria,
and won back Jerusalem and the greater part of Frankish Syria from
the crusaders in 1187. Beneath the government of this great man, as
valiant a warrior as he was a clever statesman, with a mind at once
pious and liberal and a generous and chivalrous character, Moslem
Syria and Egypt, in spite of their incessant struggle against the
crusades, entered upon a new era of prosperity. The Syro-Egyptian
empire created by Saladin survived after his death. Though it was
more than once divided up between various members of his house,
his dynasty, known as that of the Ayyūbids, reigned until 1250 and
produced a few princes worthy of its founder, such as Malik al-Kāmil
(1218–38), the friend of the Islamophil emperor Frederick II; it
was, indeed, under such princes as these that there was the nearest
approach to an understanding between Islam and Christianity. At
times the intelligent liberalism of the Ayyūbids, the comparative

FIGURE 162

Mausoleum of person unknown, Damascus, twelfth to fourteenth century.
— *Photo, E. de Lorey*

toleration displayed by them, and the mutual esteem which gave rise to a sort of sympathy between the Ayyūbid and Frankish knights brought about the establishment of a political *modus vivendi* and the beginnings of a moral understanding between the sultans of the house of Saladin and certain Christian princes. In many respects this was a golden age for Egypt and Syria; Cairo, Damascus, and Aleppo can

FIGURE 163
Helmets in the Mameluke style, fifteenth or sixteenth century.
— *Louvre. Archives photographiques*

still point proudly to the monuments of this great age (Fig. 135 to 138).

In 1250 the Ayyūbid dynasty was overthrown by the Mamelukes, who, as we know, were mercenaries, for the most part of Turkish or Circassian origin, purchased in the slave-markets of Moslem Russia and the Caucasus to form the personal body-guard of the Ayyūbid sultans. As soon as they had dethroned the Ayyūbid family, their leaders proclaimed themselves sultans. Their domination over Egypt and Syria lasted for more than two centuries and fell into two periods:

that of the Baḥri Mamelukes (1350–90) and that of the Burji Mamelukes (1382–1517), the latter of which came to an end in 1517
with the Ottoman conquest. The " slave kings," as the Mamelukes
have been called, did not, indeed, succeed in founding dynasties

FIGURE 164

Copper candlestick with metal inlay, and copper ewer from Mosul with metal inlay.
Ayyūbid art, thirteenth century.
— Louvre. Archives photographiques

properly so called, and as a rule the power among them fell, not to
the son of the late sultan, but to the most energetic soldier. Many of
them gave proof of a powerful personality — for instance, sultans
Bibars (1260–77) and Qalawun (1279–90), who destroyed the last
vestiges of Frankish Syria and checked the Mongol invasion. In spite

of their despotism and bloodthirsty caprices, almost all of them proved enlightened patrons of the arts. This ostentatious aristocracy of fortune, indolent yet warlike, brutal yet refined, was to leave behind it an amazing reputation in the East, not only for its military glory, but for the splendour of its luxury and the beauty of its monuments.

During the Ayyūbid period, indeed, and the Mameluke period, which was a continuation of it, Arab art rose to its highest point. The building of the Ayyūbid architects — especially those of Syria — is characterized by strength and sobriety. The materials employed are beautiful, strong, and durable. Thanks to the lasting quality of these blocks of fine stone, the simplest decorative motive assumes an infinite grace. Add to this the virile elegance of line and the powerfulness of the general conception. This Ayyūbid period, which was that of the " counter-crusades " — that is, of the great Arab age in Syria — really succeeded in endowing itself with an art of epic quality. With the Ayyūbids appeared a new architectural form, the *madrasa*, or collegiate mosque, which was cruciform in plan, this innovation being inspired by theological considerations — namely, the desire, now that the Shī'ism of the Fāṭimids had been driven out of Egypt, to assign a place in the *madrasa* to the four Sunnite or orthodox rites. At the same time the Ayyūbids restored the great monuments of past centuries, such as the Mosque of 'Amr at Cairo, the Qubbat al-Sakhra at Jerusalem, and the citadel of Damascus (Fig. 139). In this the Mamelukes followed their example, the citadel of Aleppo, for instance (Fig. 140), being rebuilt by the sultan Bibars (1260–77). But the Mamelukes also set up a number of buildings of their own. The mausoleum of Bibars is one of the most famous buildings in Damascus (Fig. 141 and 292). From 1285 onwards, Sulṭān Qalawun (1279–90) built in Cairo an architectural group consisting of a mosque, a tomb, and a hospital (Fig. 142); his mosque in particular displays " an original plan which we shall find again in the Mosque of Barquq; it consists of an oblong hall, with two columned aisles running along the sides, the ceilings of which are as lofty as those of the mosque itself." The Mosque of Sulṭān Ḥasan, which was completed in 1362, and in some respects displays Irano-

FIGURE 165
Copper tray with metal inlay. Mameluke art of fourteenth century, Damascus.
— *Photo, E. de Lorey*

Mesopotamian influence (Fig. 143 to 145), is singled out by Monsieur Saladin as the finest of those built on a cruciform plan: " In the centre it displays an open court, with the fountain for ablutions, and to the east of this courtyard opens the vast *līwān* with its pointed arches, forming the sanctuary proper; the plan is completed by the three remaining *līwāns,* and between the arms of the cross stand the colleges of the four orthodox rites, each consisting of a courtyard with a *līwān* and rooms for the students. Seen from outside, the mosque is of a grand and severe appearance, as it raises its two octagonal minarets heaven-wards, the taller of which is in three tiers and is nearly 180 feet high. The sides of the mosque are decorated externally with tall piers of plain masonry which sepa-rate the vertical tiers of the windows. Thus the architec-ture produces an unforget-table effect by the simplest of means." This impression of strength, due here to the total absence of polychromy and the supremacy of the severe grey stone, shows how the Syro-Egyptian art

FIGURE 166

Bronze lamp inlaid with silver. Mesopotamian art of thirteenth century.
— *Photo, E. de Lorey*

of the Ayyūbids and earliest Mamelukes was capable of vying in grandeur and majesty with the most imperishable of the Ottoman buildings of Constantinople.

The buildings of the Burji Mamelukes begin with the Mosque of Sulṭān Barquq (1382–98) within the city walls, which is built in the form of a cross, " with this exceptional feature, that the līwān set apart for worship is almost as broad as the courtyard itself and is divided into three aisles, rather like a Christian church " (Fig. 146 to 148). The decoration of the interior is formed of marble panels, coloured glass windows, and ceilings covered with a design of great

FIGURE 167
Panel of faience from Mausoleum of Saladin at Damascus.
— *Photo, E. de Lorey*

interlaced rosettes with a cornice of stalactites. The second Mosque
of Barquq is outside the walls and was used as his burial place. The
principal façade of this building is composed of alternating light
and dark courses; the hall containing the tombs of the Sultan and
his sons has a cupola, the inside of which is decorated with fine
stalactite pendentives of a pure and simple elegance. Here again
the traditions of vigour and virile elegance belonging to the Ayyūbid
schools of Syria are maintained unimpaired. Towards the end of the
Burji " dynasty " Mameluke art still produced works of rare elegance
and infinite delicacy in the monuments of the sultans Qa'it-bay
(1468–95), illustrated in Fig. 149 to 152, and Qānsūh al-Ghūrī
(1500–16), illustrated in Fig. 153. The memorial mosque of Qa'it-
bay, consisting of a mosque proper, a tomb, a fountain, and a *madrasa,* is also arranged on a cruciform plan. " On seeing this little
masterpiece, the first thing that strikes one is the part played in
the decorative effect by the courses of white and red. The door
itself has a granite lintel with a Greek fret of black marble inlaid
in white marble running round it; above it is a relieving arch with
alternate black and white voussoirs." Besides this symphony in two
colours, archæologists are unanimous in admiring the way in which
the graceful minaret is balanced by the cupola of the dome, that
" helmet without a visor," the outside of which is decorated with a
charming network of conventionalized foliage and rosettes. Arab
art has produced nothing in more exquisite taste than this sanctuary,
which is in some sense its own mausoleum — for a few years later,
in 1517, was to come the Ottoman Conquest. But in spite of its elegance and the sobriety by which it is still characterized, the tomb of
Qa'it-bay already reveals less vigour than the buildings previously
mentioned. In future this exquisite art enables us to perceive the
facile formulas on which it is based, by its excess of virtuosity.

None the less, the great Arab tradition in architecture was to have
a new lease of life under foreign rule, not only in Egypt, but also

in Syria, where the monuments of Damascus bear witness to its persistence, from the Mosque of Tekkiya (Fig. 155), built by Suleiman the Magnificent (1554), the Derwīshiya (Fig. 156, 157), dating from 1571, and the Sināniya (Fig. 158), dating from 1585, down to the Azem (A'zam) Palace built in the eighteenth century, now the seat of the French Institute of Moslem Archæology and Art at Damascus. We are so fortunate as to be able to reproduce here the fine photographs of these buildings given us by M. Eustache de Lorey, late director of the Institute of Damascus (Fig. 159, 160).

FIGURE 168

Fifteenth-century pottery, Bāb al-Sharqī, Damascus.
— *Damascus Museum. Photo, E. de Lorey*

The decorative ornamentation of the Ayyūbid and Mameluke monuments is in no way inferior to their architectural beauty. " In the whole of this decoration," writes Monsieur Migeon — the best of judges in such matters — " we constantly find the bud and leaf motives treated in the form of rosettes formed by garlands of conventionalized buds and flowers round a central bud. . . . Nowhere has stone been enriched by more marvellous sculptured motives, geometrical or arabesque, than in the monuments of Qa'it-bay."

The wood-carvings of the Ayyūbid and Mameluke periods emancipated themselves from the decorative formulas of Fāṭimid art.

"This," writes Monsieur Migeon again, "is the most beautiful period of this sculpture in wood in two planes, a light composition of floral or geometrical ornaments standing out in stronger relief against a decorative background in lower relief." Fāṭimid woodwork was

FIGURE 169

Plate of so-called Damascus ware, fifteenth century.
— *Koechlin collection. Photo, Giraudon*

characterized by floral decoration with a fine trellis-work and minute detail, somewhat confused and intricate. Ayyūbid art transformed and lent breadth to these subjects by placing them in the setting of its broad, strong, sober, and vigorous geometrical lines and so lending them support and relief. The cenotaph of the *imām* al-Shāfiʿi in Cairo, dating from 1178, that of Saladin at Damascus, dating from 1193, that of the emir Tālib at Cairo, dating from 1216 (part of which is now in the Victoria and Albert Museum), specimens from which are reproduced either here or in Monsieur G. Migeon's *Manuel d'art musulman, Arts plastiques et industriels* (second edition, Paris, 1927), will give an idea of this style, at once so rich, so strong, and so pure (Fig. 161 and 162). Under the Mamelukes the skill and delicacy of the foliage and rosette patterns continue to be equally amazing, but the richness is heightened by the use of coloured woods, and the virtuosity of line almost verges on preciosity. The celebrated *minbar* of Qa'it-bay (1468–96) in the Victoria and Albert Museum is perhaps the most perfect specimen of this manner. Like these wood-carvings, the ornaments cast in bronze which served to decorate the doors of the mosques bear witness to the splendour of Arab taste under the Mamelukes; it should be noted that animal motives are still met with in the chain patterns and running patterns of conventionalized foliage, which is certainly a survival of Fāṭimid licence under this orthodox rule.

Lastly, to turn to an art which is necessarily more sober and severe, the age of the Ayyūbids and the Mamelukes has left us marvellous specimens of arms, ironwork, and copper-work (Fig. 163 to 166). The copper utensils — ewers, vases, basins, trays, perfume-burners, chandeliers, cases for holding the Koran, and *kursī*, or little tables — are particularly remarkable. The beauty of the medium, the strength and grace of the shapes, are such that they can bear their rich ornamentation without becoming heavy. Moreover, in spite of the dazzling profusion of its motives, this decoration, with its powerful Kufic script, its running patterns of conventionalized foliage, its interlacing patterns, rosettes, arabesques, and occasional heraldic motives, retains a vigour and sureness of touch which make it not only a delight to the eye, but also — and this is, in our opinion, the secret of Arab decoration — a delight to the intelligence. The Mameluke mosque-

lamps, in cut, engraved, or enamelled glass, display the same characteristics and share in the same beauty. Lastly, Mameluke ceramics,
long of but doubtful identification, are now better known, thanks in
particular to the excavations of M. Eustache de Lorey at Damascus
(Bāb al-Sharqī) (Fig. 167 and 168). It found a fresh lease of life
in the Syro-Egyptian ceramics of the Ottoman age, as well as in the
graceful earthenware known as " Damascus ware," much of which
dates from the sixteenth century (Fig. 169). Such are the noble
schools which the director of the Institute of Damascus is at present
engaged in bringing to light.

Is it possible to determine which was the most important period in
this evolution of the Arab arts of the East, of which we have just
sketched a hasty outline? In our opinion, the answer cannot possibly
be in doubt. The classical Arab art of the East is represented by the
buildings of Damascus and Aleppo dating from the thirteenth century, under the Ayyūbids and their earliest Mameluke successors.
The mausoleums of Saladin, Kokburi, Saif al-Dīn, al-'Adil, and
Bibars, the *marīstān* (hospital) of Qaimari, and the Fountain of the
Treasure — to mention none but buildings at Damascus — display
essential qualities which were never again to be found to the same
extent on the territory of Islam (Fig. 135 to 137, 141, 292). There
is none of the somewhat factitious prettiness of the schools of Spain,
Egypt, or Persia about this architecture and decoration. Here everything is simple, solid, strong, and of a virile grace, and essentially
structural in character. Both as architects and as decorators the Ayyūbid masters are the only ones who understood the true value of
balance, the intrinsic worth of fine hewn stone. On their façades all
that they have done is to repeat regularly a carved keystone, or a
border as clean-cut as though carved with a sabre, or a moulding in
bold relief outlining the arch of a doorway; great unerring lines of
an amazing simplicity, at once nervous and strong, which gain an

unexpected decorative value from the severity of the beautiful material (Fig. 137 and 154). Even the honeycomb-like stalactites of the
round arches, which are like a smile on these façades, are always
sober, with none of the specious virtuosity of late Mameluke work
(Fig. 136 and 292).[1] The same rather haughty elegance, the same

FIGURE 169b

Citadel of Aleppo, detail of entrance door (thirteenth century).
— *Photo, E. de Lorey*

martial vigour, are to be seen in the Kufic inscriptions in stone, as well
as in the wood-carvings (see Fig. 130, 131, 161, 162). Compared
with these imperishable monuments of the old Damascus of the Ayyūbid period, how many of the masterpieces of neighbouring lands or
later centuries run the risk of appearing frivolous — a mixture of su-
perficiality and sham architectural effects, lacking in all permanence!

[1] See J. Rosintal: *Pendentifs, trompes et stalactites dans l'architecture orientale* (Paris:
Geuthner, 1928).

CHAPTER VI

Persian Islamic Civilization

ARABO–PERSIAN CIVILIZATION, FROM THE SĀMĀNIDS TO THE SELJUKS

W E HAVE BEEN ABLE TO FOLLOW THE EVOLUTION OF ARAB civilization from the tenth century onward, setting aside the Iranian provinces of the ancient empire of the caliphs. This omission is due to the fact that, after that period, while still belonging to the religious obedience of the " Moslem Papacy," Iran had regained control of its own destinies from the political and cultural point of view. Persian civilization had now come into existence, and we have now to give a short account of its history.

During the ninth century a great phenomenon took place in 'Abbāsid Iran: the Arab element lost its political primacy, and the Iranian element quietly gained the upper hand; while in the eleventh century, too, when the latter element yielded the hegemony to the Turks, these latter rapidly adopted Iranian customs. While clinging uncompromisingly to their own ways in Asia Minor, where they made a second Turkestan of the peninsula, in Persia they very rapidly adapted themselves to the old national culture. Thus all the dynasties, whether Iranian or Turk, which followed one after the other in Persia from the tenth to the twentieth century, contributed towards the national type of civilization.

In the ninth century the Iranian element quickly got the better of

237

the Arab. Towards 820 the Persian Ṭāhir, governor of Khorāsān, made himself independent, and he and his family kept this province till 872, at which date the Ṭāhirids were overthrown by another Per-

FIGURE 170

Cup of Raiy ware, thirteenth century.
— *Louvre. Archives photographiques*

sian family, of plebeian stock, having its origin in Seistān: the house of the Ṣaffārids, which reigned over eastern Iran till about 900. In 900 a third Persian house, of nobler lineage, that of the Sāmānids, founded by Naṣr I, overthrew the Ṣaffārids and took their place, reigning over the Iranian east in turn till 990. The princes of this new house, almost all of whom were named either Naṣr, Ismāʿīl, Aḥmad, Nūḥ, ʿAbd al-Malik or Mansūr, had their residence in Transoxiana,

FIGURE 171
Painted Raiy ware, twelfth century.
— *Nazare-Agha collection. Photo, Pivot*

at Bokhara, a land which was at that time completely Iranian. Under them the Iranian renaissance asserted itself openly, for they were but recent converts to Islam and still remembered the time when they had been Mazdeans. Once they were in power, their desire was, while

remaining true to their new faith, to restore the traditional connexion
with their country's past; and we see that they linked up their own
descent with the Sāsānid hero Bahrām Chubīn. It was under the government of this chivalrous dynasty that the history of Persian culture

FIGURE 172
Plate of Raiy ware, thirteenth century.
— *Doucet collection. Photo, Pivot*

really begins. At their court of Bokhara and in the other great cities
of their principality — at Samarqand, Balkh, Marv, and Nishāpūr
— began that reaction against the primacy of the Arabic language
which was to give birth to classical Persian literature. Rūdakī, the
first great Persian poet, who died in 954, lived at the court of the

Sāmānid Naṣr II. Shortly afterwards another Persian poet, Daqīqī, a native of Tūs, who died in 952, undertook to write an epic poem on

FIGURE 173

Painted ware, of Damascus, with reminiscences of Raiy, fifteenth century.
— *Koechlin collection, Paris*

the Iranian past, the reign of the mythical king Gushtāsp and the preaching of Zoroaster, for the Sāmānid Nūḥ I, a poem which was afterwards inserted in Firdausī's Shāh-nāma; and Firdausī himself, the Homer of Persia, who flourished from about 932 to 1021 and was, like Daqīqī, a native of Tūs, like him began his career under the government of the Sāmānids. Moreover, Sāmānid Transoxiana was a centre of philosophic studies which attracted to itself the most celebrated doctors in Islam. The greatest of Arab philosophers, Ibn-Sīnā, known to us as Avicenna, who was born near Bokhara about 980, had as his patron the Sāmānid Nūḥ II and completed his studies in that prince's library before going to live at the court of the Būyids.

While the Sāmānids were reigning over eastern Iran, another Iranian dynasty, that of the Būyids, had made itself master of western Persia, which it divided up among its members. From 935 to 1055 the three branches of the Būyid family reigned in this way, one over 'Irāq-i 'Arabī, another over Fārs, and a third over 'Irāq-i 'Ajamī. The Būyids, too, claimed to be descended from the national dynasty of the Sāsānids, and also, like all the Persians, professed Shī'ism. In 945 a member of their house, known by the name of Mu'izz al-Daula, entered Baghdād and forced the Caliph to appoint him *amīr al-umarā* ("Emir of the Emirs"), a position corresponding to that of the Merovingian mayors of the palace. As a matter of fact, from that day till 1055, the Būyid "emirs of the emirs" arrogated all authority to themselves in the name of the 'Abbāsids, whom they had reduced to impotence. The most celebrated of them was 'Aḍod al-Daula (944–982), who reorganized the whole of the Būyid domains on a uniform plan and rivalled his contemporaries, the Sāmānid princes, as a patron of the arts. Thus he set up various buildings in Baghdād and caused great public works to be carried out in Fārs, such as the Band-Amīr, or dam, across the Kur near Shīrāz. His glories were sung by the great Arab poet al-Mutannabī, who spent some time in his dominions, at Shīrāz. He was the first of the Moslem princes to induce the caliph to grant him the titles of sultan and king (*malik*) and afterwards that of king of kings (*malik al mulūk* and *Shāhinshāh*), which amounted to reviving the title — and almost the reality — of the

FIGURE 174

Wall-tiles of Raiy ware, star and cross shapes (thirteenth century).
— *Louvre. Archives photographiques*

ancient Sāsānid monarchy under the ægis of the 'Abbāsid Caliphate, which had now become a mere spiritual papacy. We shall find other Būyid princes, lords of Raiy, Hamadān, and Isfahān, among the patrons and friends of the philosopher Avicenna.

In the eleventh century the two Iranian dynasties of eastern Iran and western Persia were overthrown, one after the other, by the

FIGURE 175
Ivory casket, Moresque art of Spain, with Persian inspiration.
— *Louvre. Photo, Giraudon*

Turkish invasions. The Turkish element, which originally came from central Asia — the region which is now Chinese Turkestan and a part of what is now Mongolia — had filtered through into the Moslem world from the ninth century onward by a process of peaceful penetration, in the guise of mercenaries in the service of the Arabo-Iranian dynasties, just as the Germani had first been admitted into the Roman Empire of the fourth century as auxiliaries and *fœderati*.

As at Rome, this sporadic and pacific immigration was soon succeeded by the invasion of armed bands.

The first Turkish dynasty to be set up in Iran was that of the
Ghaznavids, who had originally been mercenaries in the pay of the
Sāmānid princes of Iran, but had fallen out with their suzerain and
departed, towards 960, to settle at Ghazna, in Afghanistan, from

FIGURE 176
Persian art, thirteenth or fourteenth century.
— *Doucet collection. Photo, Laniepce*

which they took their name. About 995 they forced the last of the
Sāmānids to cede them a part of Khorāsān. Shortly afterwards their
leader Maḥmūd (999–1030) stamped out the Sāmānid dynasty, some
of whose possessions (Khorāsān and Transoxiana) passed into his
hands; he further conquered the other Iranian dynasty, that of the
Būyids, and deprived it of 'Irāq-i 'Ajamī; and finally he turned towards India and took the Punjāb from a number of Indian rajahs.

Thus Maḥmūd the Ghaznavid was the earliest of the Turko-Moslem conquerors. He was also the first Turkish chief to bear the title of *sulṭān*, which was conferred upon him by the Caliph of Baghdād.

FIGURE 177
Miniature, possibly thirteenth-century Persian or Transoxianian Mongol
of the fourteenth century.
— *Vever collection. Photo, Laniepce*

Moreover, this Turk, who was a most orthodox Sunnite Moslem, took his position as patron of Arabo-Persian civilization very seriously. The most famous of the Persian poets stayed at his court —

'Unṣurī, Minūchihrī, and Firdausī. The greatest of them,
Firdausī, even dedicated to
him his *Shāh-nāma,* which he
finished in 1010; and the fact
that they ultimately quarrelled
should not make us forget the
poet's long period of favour.
At any rate, it is curious to
note that the Iranian national
epic was composed under a
Turkish dynasty; there could
be no better illustration of the
continuity of Persian culture
throughout all the political
vicissitudes of the country.

In 1040 the Ghaznavids
were driven out of eastern Iran
by another Turkish house, that
of the Seljuks. In 1055 the
Seljuk leader Tughrilbeg
(Toghrul Beg), who died in
1063, next dethroned the
Iranian dynasty of the Būyids,
which had established itself at
Baghdād side by side with the
'Abbāsid caliph and was still
reigning over western Persia.
He took the place which the
Būyids had occupied at the

FIGURE 178

Miniature from a *Treatise on Automata,*
early thirteenth century.
— *Vever collection. Photo, Pivot*

side of the Caliph, who recognized him as his temporal vicar, with
the Persian titles of sultan and king of kings (*shāhinshāh*). The

second Seljuk sultan, Alp Arslan (1063–72), crushed the Byzantines at Malāzqerd in Armenia, a decisive victory which delivered

FIGURE 179
Miniature. Probably Persian, about thirteenth century.
— *Vever collection. Photo, Pivot*

Armenia into the hands of the Seljuks and threw open Asia Minor to them. Under the third sultan of this race, Malik-shāh (1072–92), the Seljuk Empire reached its apogee. At that time it included the whole of Iran, Mesopotamia, Syria, and Asia Minor. From the religious point of view, the Seljuk conquest marked the victory of the Sunnite element over the Shī'ites, who had enjoyed the patronage of the Būyids; for the new dynasty were orthodox Moslems. It would be a mistake to suppose that the accession of this Turkish house marked any decline in the sphere of politics or culture. Not only did the Seljuks adapt themselves very rapidly to the Arabo-Persian civilization, but they constituted themselves its faithful defenders. The government of Malik-shāh, under the direction of his famous vizier Niẓām al-Mulk, was beneficent and enlightened. Niẓām al-Mulk, who was himself the author of a political treatise, the *Siyāsatnāma,* was the patron of all the great writers of his time, such as the Persian poet 'Omar Khaiyām ('Umar-i Khaiyām) and the philosopher al-Ghazālī,

FIGURE 180
Tomb of Oljaitu at Sulṭāniya (1320).
— *Photo, Sevruguin*

and created a university at the Niẓāmīya *madrasa* in Baghdād, which exerted a considerable influence on Arabo-Persian literature.

After the death of Malik-shāh, in 1092, his empire was partitioned between various branches of the Seljuk house, the two chief of which were those of Persia and of Asia Minor. The sultanate of Persia remained in the hands of the sons of Malik-shāh. The chief of these sultans was Sanjar (or Sinjar), 1117–57), a chivalrous prince who spent his life waging war in Transoxiana in order to defend Iran against fresh Turko-Mongol invasions. Ultimately, however, in 1194, the Seljuks of Persia were overthrown by another Turkish dynasty, which was, like themselves, Moslem in religion and had adopted

FIGURE 181

Persian art, thirteenth or fourteenth century.
— *Doucet collection. Photo, Laniepce*

Iranian customs — that of the shahs of Khwārizm (now Khiva), who ruled over Iran from 1194 till the great Mongol invasion of 1220, and in general carried on the work of their predecessors. The memory of the glorious age of the Seljuks is still kept alive at Raiy, or Rhages,

FIGURE 182

The Great Khan Mangū and his family. Miniature from a manuscript of
Rashīd al-Dīn.

— *Bibliothèque Nationale. Archives photographiques*

near the capital of modern Persia, by the famous round tower with pointed crenellations, which escaped destruction by the Mongols, and, even if it does not go back to Toghrilbeg himself, as tradition would have it, seems, none the less, in accordance with Professor Sarre's opinion, to date from the twelfth or thirteenth century.

Another branch of the Seljuks which we must not omit to mention is that of Asia Minor. This Seljuk sultanate of Asia Minor (or, in Turkish, " Rūm "), founded by younger branches of the dynasty, lasted longer than the others, from 1077 to 1302, with Konia (Qōniya) as its capital. Its historical importance should not be under-estimated. Ethnographically, it had the effect of dehellenizing Asia Minor and turning that land, which had for so long been Byzantine, into a territory as thoroughly Turanian as their native Turkestan. In art, and even in literature, it to a large extent opened up the " new Turkey " thus created to Iranian influences. At the court of Konia, in fact, Persian culture reigned supreme, as is proved by the very names of the sultans — Kaikhosrau, Kaikā'ūs, Kaiqubād — which were borrowed from Iranian epic; and also by the story of the great Persian mystic poet Jalāl al-Dīn Rūmī (1207–73), whose family came from Persia and settled at Konia under the protection of the Seljuks, where he founded the famous order of the *Mavlavī*, or dancing dervishes.

PERSIAN LITERATURE FROM THE TENTH TO THE THIRTEENTH CENTURIES

HENCE, IN SPITE OF THE TURKISH ORIGIN OF THE REIGNING DYNASTIES, the Ghaznavid, Seljuk, and Khwārizmian period is a great period in Persian literature and art. Thus the memory of the Ghaznavid house, for instance, is indissolubly bound up with that of the poet Firdausī.

Firdausī, born about 932 in a suburb of Tūs in Khorāsān, incorporated the heroic legends of pre-Islamic Iran in an enormous poem

FIGURE 183

The Khan Kaikātū. Miniature from a manuscript of Rashīd al-Dīn.
— *Bibliothèque Nationale. Archives photographiques*

of sixty thousand verses, the *Shāh-nāma*, or *Book of the Kings*, which
he completed in 1010 and dedicated to his patron, the Sultan
Maḥmūd of Ghazna, at whose court he lived. Having fallen out with
Maḥmūd, he left Ghazna and made his way to western Persia, the
territory of the Būyids. In 1020–1 he returned to Tūs, where he died.

FIGURE 184
Tomb of Timur (d. 1405), Samarqand.
— *Photo, Henri Viollet*

The Iranian epic to
which the genius of Fir-
dausī gave its definitive
form had already been
brought together about
650, at the end of the
Sāsānid period, by a
learned Persian (the
" Danishwar ") in a work
written in Pahlavi, but
now lost, called the
Khudāy nāma. It was the
epic content of this work,
half historic, half legendary, that Firdausī elabo-
rated in modern Persian.
Hence, in spite of the
conversion of Persia to
Islam, we find in the Moslem poet the whole of the
Iranian legend as it was current in the age of the Sāsānids.

We cannot attempt to give an account here of the contents of the
Shāh-nāma. Several of its most famous episodes will be alluded to
below, in connexion with the representations of them in Persian
miniature. We will confine ourselves to mentioning that the poem
opens with the story of Gayōmarth, the first man, and of the fabulous
dynasty of the Pīshdādiān kings: Hūshang, Tahmurat, and Jamshīd,

inventors of the arts and of civilization. The antagonism between two of the sons of Jamshīd, Īraj, the ancestor of the Iranians, and Tūr, the ancestor of the Turanians, was the beginning of the secular rivalry between Iran and Turan — that is, the Persian world and the Scythian world. Īraj having been put to death by Tūr, Minūchihrī, a descendant of his race, avenged him by shedding the blood of Tūr, but the struggle continued to be waged against the new king of Turan, Afrāsiyāb.

FIGURE 185
Tomb of Timur.
— *Photo, Le Brecq*

And at this point the hero *par excellence* of the Iranian epic, Rustam, who is at once the Hercules and the Roland of Persia, makes his appearance in Firdausī's poem. He was connected by legend with eastern Iran; his father, Zāl, who had once been exposed, like Cyrus in Herodotus, and saved by the fabulous bird Sīmurgh, was king of Seistān, while his mother was the daughter of the King of Kābul. The Pīshdādiān family having died out, Rustam established on the throne of Persia the dynasty of the Kaiyānids, which would correspond to the historic house of the Achæmenids, but is

FIGURE 186
Madrasa of the Shīr-dar, Samarqand.
— *Photo, Le Brecq*

here represented by the mythical kings Kaiqubād, Kaikā'ūs, Kaikhosrau, Luhrāsp, Gushtāsp, Isfandiyār, Bahman, Queen Humāy, and Dārāb, under whom the struggle between Iran and Turan was still carried on, distinguished, on the Iranian side, by the exploits of Rustam. One of the finest episodes in it is the duel between Rustam and his own son Sohrāb, the fruit of a passing love-affair of the hero's with a Turanian princess; having grown to man's estate, Sohrāb meets his father, and, having failed to recognize him, challenges him to combat and receives a mortal wound; one of the most moving scenes in the epic is that in which the recognition between father and son at last takes place a few moments before the latter's death. Another famous episode is the story of the Iranian cavalier Bījan (Bīzhan), who, while out hunting, meets the daughter of the King of Turan and, seduced by her,

FIGURE 187
The Shīr-dar, Samarqand.
— *Photo, Le Brecq*

allows himself to be captured by the enemy and thrown into a pit, from which he is delivered by Rustam. Thanks to Rustam's intervention, Kaikhosrau, the king of Persia, at last gains a decisive victory over the Turanians, and their king, Afrāsiyāb, is taken prisoner and put to death. A third episode, which often provides a subject for miniatures, is the story of Prince Isfandiyār (Isfendiar), son of King Gushtāsp, who in turn wins fame by repulsing the Turanians; but Isfandiyār, desiring to measure himself with Rustam, is slain by the hero, who is still under the protection of the fabulous bird Sīmurgh. As for the invincible Rustam, he was in turn to perish through the treachery of his half-brother Shaghād and the King of Kābul, who caused him and his faithful horse, Rakhsh, to fall into a pit full of sharp sword-blades.

FIGURE 188
Madrasa Khanum, Samarqand.
— *Photo, Henri Viollet*

The *Shāh-nāma* next takes as its subject the story of Alexander the Great (Iskandar), who is here represented as an Achæmenid prince, the " son of Dārāb" (one of the kings named Darius) and a Macedonian princess. Iskandar is in exile in his mother's country, but arrives to claim his throne, conquers his half-brother Dārā (Darius

Codoman), and becomes lawful king of Persia. The *Shāh-nāma* says nothing about the Arsacids, but commemorates the history of the Sāsānids, several of whom had already become legendary heroes — for instance, Bahrām Gūr, the lover of the princesses of the Seven Climates, Khosrau Anūshirvān, and Khosrau Parvīz, the lover of the beautiful Shīrīn.

Such is this vast epic, which contains striking beauties, as well as some tedious passages, and a knowledge of which is indispensable for the understanding of the later lyric poetry of Persia, and even of its painting.

Seljuk Persia gave birth to two great writers: the philosopher Ghazālī, who wrote in Arabic, and the poet 'Omar Khaiyām, who wrote in Persian. Ghazālī (1058–1112), who, like Firdausī, was a native of Tūs, studied at Nishāpūr, and afterwards taught at the Niẓāmīya *madrasa* at Baghdād under the patronage of the Seljuk vizier Niẓām al-Mulk; but he soon renounced the life of the world, and henceforth, with the exception of a fresh period of teaching at Nishāpūr, lived in a pious and studious retreat until his death, which took place at Tūs in 1112. This retreat marked a new tendency of his thought. He had originally been a disciple of the Arab philosophers, all of whom were to a greater or lesser extent the heirs of Avicenna — that is, of Aristotelianism — but, the study of the Greek masters having shown him that intellectualist systems are mutually destructive, he became convinced of their vanity, and fell back upon religious experience, evolving the theory of Ṣūfism — that is, Moslem mysticism. Thus his philosophic scepticism was accompanied by a deep religious sentiment, which makes this philosopher the precursor of the great Persian mystic poets.

His contemporary 'Omar Khaiyām, who was born at Nishāpūr about 1040, was an astronomer as well as a poet and was for some time director of the observatory at Marv. Like Ghazālī, he enjoyed the patronage of the vizier Niẓām al-Mulk, after whose death he

FIGURE 189

Blue Mosque, Tabrīz.

— *Photo, Sevruguin*

FIGURE 190

Khosrau and Shīrīn. Timurid school of Persia, early fifteenth century.
— *Vever collection. Photo, Pivot*

FIGURE 191

Arrival of Humāy at the court of the Emperor of China.
Timurid art, school of Herāt, about 1430.
— *Musée des Arts Décoratifs, Paris. Photo, Giraudon*

returned to Nishāpūr, where he died about 1123 (the date is uncertain). Like Ghazālī, Khaiyām broke away from the intellectualism of his masters, but he ended, not in mysticism, but in scepticism — and in the first place religious scepticism: " The whole of the human race is doomed to heaven or hell. But who ever went to hell? Who ever returned from heaven? " But his scepticism is also philosophical: " Nobody can pass beyond the curtain which hides the Riddle. Nobody knows what lives beneath appearances." — " Drink, for thou shalt sleep long beneath the clay, with none near thee, whether friend, comrade, or woman. Watch lest thou tell this secret to anyone: tulips once faded shall never flower again." — " None of those who have questioned the dark mystery has taken a single step outside the circle of shadow." This bitter wisdom is the source of a deep disillusionment: " My coming to life was of no profit to the celestial sphere, and my departure will diminish neither its beauty nor its grandeur. My two ears have never heard any man tell the reason of this coming or of this going." — " We are pawns in the game played by Heaven. We serve as its pastime on the chessboard of Being. After which we are returned one by one into the box of nothingness."

This disillusionment finds expression in poignant poetry, for in Khaiyām intellectual nihilism comes into conflict with a quivering sensibility: " What use is our coming? What use our going? Where is the chain which forms the warp of our life? How many a delicate body does the world shatter! Whither has their smoke departed? " Even the Bacchic songs which form Khaiyām's principal theme conceal with difficulty a poignant and deeply human anguish: " Drink wine, for such is the treasure left thee from the days of thy youth, the season of roses, wine, and boon companions. Be happy for an instant: this instant is thy life." — " Seat thyself upon the sward, my idol: ere long this sward shall spring from my dust and from thine." And finally comes the moral of a melancholy wisdom, consoled only by the ephemeral beauty of things: " The springtime softly fans the

FIGURE 192

Timurid art, school of Herāt, about 1440 (?).
— *Vever collection. Photo, Laniepce*

face of the rose. How sweet is a beloved face in the shade of the garden! Nothing that thou canst tell me of the past has any charm for me. . . . Enjoy today, speak not of yesterday! "

The Khwārizmian period produced four great Persian poets — Niẓāmī, 'Aṭṭār, Sa'dī, and Jalāl al-Dīn Rūmī. Niẓāmī, a native of the region of Qum, died in 1201; he treated the great romantic themes of Arabo-Persian poetry, especially the touching legend of Majnūn and Lailā, the Arab Romeo and Juliet, separated by the rivalry of their tribes; Lailā having been married against her will to another suitor, Majnūn retires in despair to the desert. When she becomes a widow, Lailā at last rejoins Majnūn, but before long dies, her lover following her to the tomb. Niẓāmī also wrote a poem on the legend of the fair Shīrīn, who inspired a passion both in King Khosrau Parvīz and in the architect Farhād, the latter of whom, thinking her to be dead, killed himself in despair.

FIGURE 193
Timurid art.
— Demotte collection. Photo, Laniepce

'Aṭṭār, who was born at Nishāpūr and died about 1230, is a Ṣūfi poet whose mysticism clothes itself in the most poetical imagery in the curious poem of the " Language of the Birds," in which we see the world of birds — that is, of souls — led by the hoopoe, set off in search of God, who is symbolized by the fabulous Sīmurgh. The ultimate end of the journey is a mystic annihilation in God, conceived, apparently, as the Universal Essence, to quote the words of the

hoopoe: " The Being whom I announce to you does not exist in isola-
tion, the whole world is this Being. Existence or nothingness, it is
still this Being." And elsewhere: " There, in presence of a single ray
of the spiritual Sun, thou dost see the disappearance of the thousand

FIGURE 194
Apocalypse of Muḥammad, school of Herāt, 1436.
— *Bibliothèque Nationale. Archives photographiques*

shadows which surround thee. . . . When the Ocean of space ceases
to toss its waves, the figures formed on their surface disappear. . . .
He whose heart is lost in that Ocean is lost in it for ever and dwells
at rest."

Saʿdī, the greatest of the Persian poets, was born at Shīrāz about

FIGURE 195

Apocalypse of Muḥammad, school of Herāt, 1436.
— *Bibliothèque Nationale. Archives photographiques*

1184, according to some authors, or about 1193, according to others. He began his studies at the Niẓāmīya *madrasa* in Baghdād, made a number of journeys to Syria, Arabia, and Asia Minor, and died at Shīrāz about 1282 or 1292. His chief works are the *Bustān* (*The*

FIGURE 196
Apocalypse of Muḥammad, school of Herāt, 1436.
— *Bibliothèque Nationale. Archives photographiques*

Garden), written in 1257, and the *Gulistān* (*The Rose-garden*), written in 1258, as well as a *dīwān*, or collection of odes. His doctrine, like that of ʿAṭṭār, is the mysticism of the Ṣūfis, but, unlike his predecessor, he has the temperament not so much of a true mystic as of a moralist, though Ṣūfism furnishes him with admirable themes

for his poetry. His moralizings are smiling, moderate, and profoundly human, by turns optimistic without exaggeration and melancholy without despair, and remind us of Horace. At once a *bon vivant,*

FIGURE 197
Apocalypse of Muḥammad, school of Herāt, 1436.
— *Bibliothèque Nationale. Archives photographiques*

an honest man, and a man of God — not to speak of an exquisite
poet — he is the noblest figure of what we may call Persian
humanism.

Sa'dī himself tells us how the idea of writing the *Gulistān* came to him: "We were taking a walk. It was in the springtime. A gentle

FIGURE 198
Persian art, fifteenth century.
— *Vever collection. Photo, Pivot*

warmth was diffused through the air, and the reign of the rose was beginning. The trees wore a garment of leaves like the festal garb of those who are happy. It was the first evening of the Jalālian month. A nightingale was singing in a cypress-tree, and pearls of dew trembled on a crimson rose like drops of sweat on the cheeks of a blushing girl. That night I led my friend into my garden. Of a truth you know no garden more delightful. One would have said that diamond dust had been scattered upon the ground, and that the necklace of the Pleiads hung from every vine-leaf. The limpid waters of the brook rippled by. The birds sang sweetly, and a great silence reverberated in my heart. . . . In the morning I saw that my friend had filled the skirt of his robe with roses, basil, hyacinth, and amaranth. He meant to bear this perfumed burden to the city. I said to him: ' The garden rose is a thing of a day, the promises of the flowers are sometimes vain.' ' What shall I do? ' he answered. I replied: ' I mean to compose the book of *The Garden of Roses* for the delight of men's minds. And the autumn wind shall not wither the leaves of its trees, nor shall the sudden whirlwind overthrow such pleasures as the spring shall bring us.' "

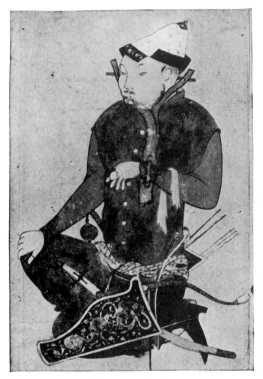

FIGURE 199

Portrait of a captive or wounded prince (?), attributed to Bihzād, school of Herāt, end of fifteenth century.
— *J. D. collection. Photo, Laniepce*

It is impossible to analyse the work of Sa'dī, the whole character of which consists in subtle shades and delicate observation. We will

FIGURE 200

Portrait of the same prince (?), said to be Murad Aq-Qoyunlu, attributed to Bihzād.
— *Koechlin collection. Phoio, Pivot*

merely cite a few examples of his manner; for instance, the following perfect masterpiece: " To meet one day in the plain — thou and I; to leave the city together — thou and I. Thou knowest how good it would be together — thou and I, when nobody was present but only — thou and I " (*Quatrains*). Or this dainty picture, ending in a touch of irony: " Never had I known moments more delicious. That night I clasped my lady to my breast and gazed into her eyes swimming with sleep. . . . I said to her: ' Beloved, my slender cypress-tree, now is not the time to sleep. Sing, my nightingale! Let thy mouth open as unfolds the rosebud. Sleep no more, turmoil of my heart! Let thy lips offer me the philtre of thy love.' . . . And my lady looked upon me and murmured low: 'Turmoil of thy heart? Yet dost thou wake me? ' " Or again: " Thy

FIGURE 201
Seated dervish, attributed to Bihzād.
— *J. D. collection. Photo, Laniepce*

lady has repeated all this time that she has never belonged to another. She has related the story of her life and told over the names of those who can confirm what she has said. . . . And thou dost smile, for thou knowest that she has belonged to another and that she lies. But what matter? Are her lips the less warm beneath thy lips? Are her shoulders less soft beneath thy caress? " (*Bustān*). Underlying this smiling wisdom is a voluptuous melancholy which again reminds us of Horace: " The age of sport and pleasures is no more for me. . . . I too have been young; the rose was less fresh than my face, the crystal less brilliant, ebon curls fell down upon my neck, a silken tunic was a burden too heavy for my delicate limbs . . ." (*Bustān*). But there is more in Sa'dī than an Epicureanism by turns gay and melancholy. In him emotion finds accents which are unmistakable. Witness the following short elegy on a separation: " They say the breeze of May is sweet, even as the perfume of the rose, the song of the nightingale in the rose-garden, the green plain, and

FIGURE 202

Turkish prince reading, at one time attributed to Bihzād.

— *J. D. collection. Photo, Giraudon*

the blue sky. O thou who knowest not, all these are only sweet when one's lady is there." Or later: " I said: ' I shall have strength on the day of separation.' But when the day came, my strength failed me " (*Quatrains*). And we may end with these verses, in which all the tenderness of the Persian sage's heart finds expression: " Torment not the ant as she drags along her grain of wheat, for she lives, and life is sweet."

Jalāl al-Dīn Rūmī (1207–73), the greatest of the Persian mystics and the author of the *Mathnawī*, was a native of Balkh. About 1226 his family settled in Konia, the capital of the Seljuk sultans in Asia Minor, who were the poet's patrons. Rūmī spent his life at Konia, where he founded the religious order of the *Mavlavī* dervishes, and where his tomb still stands.

Rūmī's poetical works are inspired by the mysticism of the Ṣūfis, of whom he was one of the chief representatives. It is a most curious mysticism, which at times approximates to the theistic type of the Christians, at times to the pantheistic yogism of the Indians, but is always consumed with love of God, regarded as the Beloved: " What are words to me? " (said God to the faithful believer). " It is a burning heart that I require; set hearts on fire with love; then take no heed either for thought or for expression." In another passage the believer cries, in a mystic delirium which amounts to absolute annihilation of human personality in the Godhead: " I die as a stone and I become a plant, I die as a plant and am raised to the level of an animal, I die as an animal and am reborn as man; when I die as man, I shall live again as an angel. I shall go even beyond the angels and become a thing that no man has ever seen, and then I shall be nothingness, nothingness! " By a phenomenon rare in Islam, this fusion with God leads to a sort of intimate communion with nature, in the Hindu fashion: " I am the sun-dust, I am the sun's orb, I am the glow of dawn, I am the breath of evening. . . ." In fact, Rūmī sees so clear a manifestation of God in nature that, as the Baron Carra de Vaux observes, we might almost believe at times that he saw God Himself in it: " The universe," cries the Ṣūfi poet, " is the form of the Universal Intelligence." It is no doubt in this sense that Rūmī represents God as saying: " I am this world and the world to come . . . ; I am man, I am the genie and the pearl of the Ocean of Being, I am the mountain and the plain, the jewel and the Ocean."

THE ORIGINS OF PERSIAN PAINTING

THE PERSIAN ART OF THE SELJUK AND KHWĀRIZMIAN PERIODS WAS worthy of the literature of these ages.

It was during the twelfth and thirteenth centuries that the use of lustre decoration reached its highest point in the ceramics of Raiy (Rhages), contemporaneously, moreover, with the technique of painted or incised ornament. What here interests us in this ware is not so much the changing beauty of the metallic lustre on certain specimens, " with its gleam of greenish gold on a ground of creamy white," as the design in itself, with its human figures, in which the face, with its characteristic roundness, heralds the types prevalent in the earliest Iranian miniatures (Fig. 170). The figures on the Raiy ware may be compared with the exactly similar types in the minia- tures reproduced by Sir Thomas Arnold in his *Islamic Book* — for instance, Plate 43. Soon, especially on the polychrome specimens, the figures even ceased to be regarded as a mere decorative motive and came to be arranged in regular scenes: *dīwān* scenes (that is, royal audiences), hunting-scenes, horsemen playing polo, princely repasts (Fig. 171 and 172); side by side with the representation of the human figure, the art of representing animal forms was to de- velop, not only in the horse, which is inseparable from its rider, but in drawings, for the most part remarkable in their realism, of lions, bears, camels, buffalo, animals of the deer tribe, hares, and birds (Fig. 173). Thus during the thirteenth century Persian painting be- gan to find more confident expression on the bowls, vases, and wall- tiles of the artists of Raiy and at the same time in the miniatures of manuscripts (Fig. 174 to 176).

As a matter of fact, we are here dealing with traditions which had

FIGURE 203

Sanjar listening to a petition. Transoxianian art. Manuscript
dated 1538.

— *Bibliothèque Nationale. Archives photographiques*

never disappeared from the soil of Iran. The earliest Persian paintings are in no way different from the Manichæan illuminations and miniatures of the eighth century.

Manichæism, as we know, was a curious mixed religion, half Mazdean, half Christian, founded in the Sāsānid Empire in the middle of the third century of our era by the Persian Mānī, who was born at Ctesiphon about 214 and martyred by King Bahrām I as a heretic in 275. Now, the whole of Moslem tradition agrees that Mānī was a celebrated painter (he is referred to by Firdausī as " Mānī the Painter "), the illustration of the Manichæan scriptures being recommended by this sect as the best form of propaganda. This tradition is fully confirmed by the finds of the German missions of Grünwedel and Von Le Coq in the region of Turfān. Here, in the middle of the desert of Gobi, in the heart of what is now Chinese Turkestan — the seat

FIGURE 204

Concert in a garden. Turkish art, eighteenth century (?).

— *Louvre. Photo, Pivot*

between 760 and 840 of the Uigur Empire, a state Turkish in race and Manichæan in religion — Professors Grünwedel and Von Le Coq have discovered a large number of frescoes and illuminated manuscripts (now in the Museum für Völkerkunde in Berlin), representing

FIGURE 205

Plaque decorated with conventionalized foliage in green enamel. Samarqand.
— *Photo, Giraudon*

FIGURE 206

Masjid-i Shāh, Isfahān (about 1612).
— *Photo, Sevruguin*

FIGURE 208
Masjid-i Shāh. Porch.
— Photo, Sevruguin

FIGURE 207
Masjid-i Shāh, Isfahān. Entrance to the sanctuary.
— Photo, Gervais Courtellemont

FIGURE 209

Masjid-i Shāh, Isfahān. Inner *eivān*, at side.

— *Photo, Gervais Courtellemont*

figures of Uigur princes and princesses, donors of both sexes, and Manichæan monks, of which the last-named are certainly in part Iranian (see Volume III of the present work, Fig. 124 to 129). In spite of the inscriptions, which are in the Uigur form of Turkish, the impression produced by these works is purely Iranian. In some respects the floral motives and conventionalized foliage already foreshadow the Persian miniatures of the Mongol period (see Volume III, Fig. 130). The figures sometimes have round young faces, exactly

FIGURE 210
Maidān-i Shāh and Ala Qapy, Isfahān.
— *Photo, Gervais Courtellemont*

like those which were to appear in the Persian miniatures of the fourteenth century (see Volume III, Fig. 125); sometimes, on the contrary — as in the portraits of the Uigur princes — there are faces with black beards, more pronouncedly oval, in spite of their central-Asiatic roundness, which this time remind one, not of the Timurid miniatures, but of the frescoes of Sāmarrā or of the Mesopotamian painting of the thirteenth century (see Volume III, Fig. 126).

There is nothing surprising in this. The Sāmarrā paintings discovered by Professor Herzfeld are exactly contemporaneous with these groups of Manichæo-Uigur donors and monks discovered by Von Le Coq at Turfān; while the Irano-Buddhistic frescoes, dating from the eighth century, found by Sir Aurel Stein at Dandān-uiliq near Khotan are also contemporaneous with the 'Abbāsid frescoes of Sāmarrā. The Vajrapāṇi of Dandān-uiliq, with its reminiscences of

FIGURE 211
Mosque of Jum'a, Isfahān.
— Photo, Gervais Courtellemont

the Sāsānid style (see Volume III, Fig. 117 of this work), has also many affinities with the human figures in the earliest 'Abbāsid miniatures of the school of Baghdād, in the thirteenth century, of which we shall speak below. And we are reminded of these same 'Abbāsid miniatures (and especially of those of the manuscripts in the Schefer collection) by the figures mounted on horse and camel on the wooden panels at Dandān-uiliq reproduced by Sir Aurel Stein in his *Ancient Khotan* (see Volume III, Fig. 118 of this work). Lastly, the whole of Persian painting — its models, its ideals, and its technique — is recalled to our minds as we look at the graceful horsemen and beautiful pages discovered by Grünwedel and Von Le Coq at Qizil near Kūcha, in the so-called " Grotto of the Painters " and " Grotto of the Hippocamps " (see Volume III, Fig. 120 and 121).

These mounted figures at Qizil serve as a link between certain of

those in the fifth century Sāsānid frescoes at Bāmiān, reproduced by
Madame André Godard, and the fine gentlemen beloved of Persian
classical miniature (see Volume III, Fig. 116 and 119). In spite of
the distance in time, the painter who has left us a portrait of himself
in the " Grotto of the Painters " at Qizil (see Volume III, Fig. 120)

FIGURE 212
Royal Palace and Gate of Ala Qapy, on the Maidān-i Shāh, Isfahān.
— *Photo, Sevruguin*

may be hailed as the first Iranian artist of whom we have any authen-
tic knowledge (see Volume III, Fig. 121 to 123).

But we are here dealing with Outer Iran, the part which had remained Buddhist and Manichæan, and escaped first from Sāsānid
orthodoxy and afterwards from conversion to Islam. The first great
school which has come down to us from the Moslem Iran of the

caliphs is the strictly 'Abbāsid school of Mesopotamia of the twelfth and thirteenth centuries (Fig. 177 and 179). It must be admitted that this school is not so much Persian as strictly Arab and Byzantine in inspiration. The influence of Byzantine technique is evident here.[1] Moreover, the figures are in general of a pronouncedly Semitic type,

FIGURE 213
Chihil-Sutūn, Isfahān (about 1693).
— *Photo, Sevruguin*

with aquiline noses, oval faces framed in black beards, vigorous poses, and nervous gestures, expressive of a fierceness as Semitic as the types themselves and with none of the mannered grace and over-refined charm of later Persian art. They have something of the hardness and angular character of Byzantine figures, but without their

[1] Sir Thomas Arnold: *Painting in Islam* (Oxford University Press, 1929), Pl. VIII and IX ("Examples of similar types in Christian and Muslim MSS.").

hieratic quality. On the contrary, they have an originality, a fire, and a freedom in the grouping which remind one of the school of Giotto. The chief masters of this school seem to have been as follows: (1) Abd-Allāh ibn-Faḍl, who in 1222 painted the miniatures illustrating a *Pharmacology of Dioscorides*, formerly in the F. M. Martin collection; (2) the unknown master who about 1230 illustrated the

FIGURE 214
The Chihil-Sutūn.
— *Photo, Henri Viollet*

Maqāmāt of al-Ḥarīrī, now in the Asiatic Museum at Leningrad; (3) Yaḥyā ibn-Maḥmūd of Wāsiṭ, who about 1237 illustrated another manuscript of the *Maqāmāt* of al-Ḥarīrī, now in the Bibliothèque Nationale (*fonds Schefer*). In the two last-named manuscripts we may note groups representing crowds which have, as we remarked just now, an intensity of expression, a vigorous mimicry, and power of reproducing personality which, in our opinion, Persian miniature-painting was never, perhaps, to exhibit again to the same degree.

On the other hand, the caravans mounted on camels, the wedding processions, the groups of standard-bearers mounted on horses or mules (see the *fonds Schefer* manuscript), display a realism in the painting of animals which is equally striking. Just as the Assyrian sculptors created the type of the lion once and for all, just as the

FIGURE 215
Another view of the Chihil-Sutūn.
— *Photo, Gervais Courtellemont*

sculptors of Sāñchī created the type of the elephant for the whole of Indian art after them, so Yaḥyā ibn-Maḥmūd of Wāsiṭ and his imitators definitively created the type — graceful, though with a touch of caricature — of the Arabian camel, whether used as a beast of burden, a luxury of the rich, or for use in war. Fourth among the great 'Abbāsid painters we may mention the artist who lived at the beginning of the thirteenth century and illustrated a *Treatise on Automata* by Badī' al-Zamān al-Jazarī, one folio of which, representing a cup-bearer, at present in the Vever collection, may be said to have a certain resemblance to some of the paintings at Dandānuiliq mentioned above (Fig. 178). Lastly, we may mention a page in the Vever collection, which we reproduce as Fig. 179, representing a woman fainting in the arms of an old man, attended by three other persons in attitudes of distress, a perfect Moslem *Pietà* of intense pathos. A number of specimens of this powerful Arabo-Persian school of Baghdād, which reached its highest point in the thirteenth century, but which continued to exist well on into the fourteenth century, under the rule of the Mongols, may be found in Sir Thomas Arnold's two

FIGURE 216
The Chār-Bāgh, Isfahān.
— *Photo, Henri Viollet*

splendidly illustrated volumes which have recently appeared: *Painting in Islam,* Plates XVIII, XIX, etc., and *Islamic Book,* Pl. 33 and following.

In the presence of such works as these, the rarity of which we cannot but deplore, it is impossible to doubt the capacity of the Arab genius for the pictorial art. Unfortunately, in lands of genuinely Arab race this capacity was rendered sterile, not, as has been said, by the prohibition of the Koran (which is by no means as categorical as is sometimes alleged), but by the religious scruples of later days. Moslem painting was to reach its full

FIGURE 217
Palace of Ashraf.
— *Photo, Sevruguin*

FIGURE 218
Bridge of Bābā Rokn al-Dīn, Isfahān.
— *Photo, Sevruguin*

development on Iranian territory in the Mongol, Timurid, and Ṣafa-wid periods.

Side by side with this 'Abbāsid school of painting, to which we shall give the name of the school of Baghdād, and which is evidently inspired by Byzantine art, we should mention another school belong-ing to the same period, but peculiar to eastern Iran, which seems, on the other hand, to have been, to a certain extent, remotely affected by Chinese influence. Monsieur Sakisian has discovered, in particular, in the Yildiz Library at Constantinople, a collection of the *Fables of Bidpay*, a native of Khorāsān, probably dating from the twelfth cen-tury, the Seljuk period, " in which the realistic treatment of the ani-mals, painted in flat tints, shows a certain familiarity with Chinese technique, side by side with the old Achæmeno-Sāsānid tradition of naturalistic representation of animals. As Monsieur Koechlin points out in the *Revue de l'art* (September–October 1930, page 230), " at that time Persian painting had not as yet quite found its right way and had not arrived at any unity of style. It was not long, how-ever, before the foreign elements were absorbed, and unity was es-tablished within the school, a unity even stronger than might have been supposed."

Is it possible to speak of Moslem sculpture as well at this period? Certainly it is, if we think of the reliefs at Konia, going back to the fine period of the Seljuk sultanate of Rūm in the thirteenth century. As Professor Sarre has pointed out, the few fragments of this art pre-served in the Museum at Konia — winged genii supporting a globe, galloping horsemen cleaving lions and dragons in two, winged lions pursuing antelopes — are directly reminiscent of the great Sāsānid reliefs mentioned above, or of certain textiles and specimens of gold-smiths' work which are likewise Sāsānid — a curious piece of evi-dence as to the persistence of ancient Persian decorative motives in the heart of mediæval Anatolia under Turkish rule. In other Seljuk buildings of Anatolia, at Cæsarea, Nigdeh, Sivas, etc., we also find

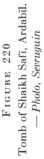

Figure 220
Tomb of Shaikh Safī, Ardabīl.
— *Photo, Sevruguin*

Figure 219
Mausoleum of Shaikh Safī al-Dīn, Ardabīl.
— *Photo, Sevruguin*

lions' heads used as gargoyles, and heads of dogs, horses, ducks, dragons, or birds with human heads decorating the stones of an arch. We are therefore faced here with a general tradition: the Seljuk art of Anatolia is a Persian art.

FIGURE 221
General view of Shīrāz.
— *Photo, Henri Viollet*

MONGOL PERSIA: THE IL-KHĀNS AND THE TIMURIDS

AT THE BEGINNING OF THE THIRTEENTH CENTURY THE WHOLE OF Iran — with the exception of the little temporal domain of the 'Abbāsid caliphs, which was confined to Baghdād and 'Irāq-i 'Arabī — was governed by the dynasty of the shahs of Khwārizm — that is, what is now the district of Khiva — a dynasty Turkish in race and

Moslem in religion, with a culture that was already strongly influenced by that of Iran. But in 1220 the Mongolian storm burst upon it, and in a few months' time the Khwārizmian Empire was destroyed by the armies of Jenghiz-Khan, which conquered Transoxiana and eastern Iran in 1220 and 1221, reducing them to a state of appalling devastation. The Mongols were later to show themselves humane and even liberal masters of Persia; but these first invaders were still barbarians, utterly ignorant of the Arabo-Persian civilization, so that for the moment their irruption was one of the worst cataclysms in the history of Iran. At first it was at any rate confined to eastern Iran, for the provinces of the southwest, such as Fārs and the 'Abbāsid territory of Baghdād, escaped the catastrophe. Between 1224 and 1231, it is true, the heir of the shahs of

FIGURE 222
View of Shīrāz.
— *Photo, Henri Viollet*

Khwārizm, the romantic figure of Jalāl al-Dīn Mangburni, whose story, as related by Nasawī, is the most extraordinary tale of adventure, tried for a time to restore the kingdom of his fathers from Isfahān to Tabrīz. But this ephemeral restoration went down before

FIGURE 226

Apocalypse of Muḥammad, illustrated by Aghā Mīrak (1539).
— *British Museum*

FIGURE 227

Bahrām Gūr and his women. Attributed to Aghā Mīrak (1524).
— *F. R. Martin collection. From F. R. Martin, Pl. 98*

a fresh Mongol invasion in 1231, which this time submerged the whole of Persia, with the exception of the 'Abbāsid domain of Baghdād. At last, in 1258, came the *coup de grâce*. The Mongol khan Hulagu, who had been entrusted with the government of Persia by his brother the Great Khan, took Baghdād, put the last Caliph to death, and destroyed the Caliphate. The whole of Iran was now Mongol.

The Mongols of 1258, however, were not the same as those of 1221. In the mean time they had come into contact with countries possessing ancient civilizations, China on the east and Persia on the west, and had themselves become civilized. Apanages were founded for the successors of Jenghiz-Khan in the heart of the Mongol Empire, which followed the lines of the ancient monarchies sprung from the soil, and developed by the force of events into separate states. As early as 1227 Chaghatai (Jaghatai), one of the sons of Jenghiz-Khan, had founded a local khanate in Transoxiana and eastern Turkestan, which soon became assimilated to its Turkish surroundings and was converted to Islam. In like fashion, when Hulagu, the descendant of Jenghiz-Khan, had conquered Baghdād, he founded a dynasty of his own in Persia, that of the Il-khāns, as they were called, which reigned over that land from 1256 to about 1336 and had as its centre the region of Tabrīz in Āzarbaijān. His rule was happy in its effects. It brought Persia the benefits of a uniform government which was at once firm and liberal. Statesmen such as the Jewish minister Sa'd al-Daula, who died in 1291, and the historian Rashīd al-Dīn, who died in 1318, are among the best administrators that Iran has ever known. It should be noted in particular that, though the Mongol régime was founded by the sword, its characteristic feature, both then and later, was a remarkable racial and religious toleration, due to the fact that, though established on Moslem territory, the first of the Il-Khāns, such as Hulagu (1256–65), Abagha (1265–81), and Arghun (1284–91), continued, so far as they were personally con-

cerned, to be Buddhists, with a decided leaning towards Nestorian-
ism, in accordance with the traditions of the ancient Mongols. Moreover, out of opposition to their natural enemies, the Mamelukes of
Egypt, their policy was to court an alliance with Christendom, from
the Latin West and Byzantium to the Armenian element in Asia
Minor. This attitude was maintained by their successors, even by
those who, more from motives of policy than from religious zeal,
had embraced the creed of their subjects. The Mongol khans who
were converted to Islam, such as Ghazan (1295–1304) and Oljaitu
(1304–16), showed themselves in general faithful to the eclectic and
liberal traditions of their predecessors. Like the latter, they attached
importance to remaining in touch with their cousins of the elder line,
descended from Jenghiz-Khan, the Buddhist Great Khans of China.
Thus the period of the Mongol dynasty of the Il-khāns in Persia was
characterized in the first place by a Chinese influence which made
itself deeply felt in the sphere of art.

There are too few traces of the period of the Il-khāns left to us for
it to be possible to base any theory upon them. We need only note the
tomb of Hulagu's daughter at Marāgha, dating from 1260, and the
tomb of Oljaitu at Sulṭāniya, dating from 1316; the former consists
of a tower, decorated with enamelled tile-work mosaic, which was
once surmounted by a pyramid with an octagonal base; the latter
is an octagonal structure crowned by a cupola and completely lined
inside with glazed or enamelled tiles or bricks set in a mosaic pattern. It has been suggested that the former of these monuments is
intended to represent a vast tent, a type possibly copied from the customs of Mongol life. As for the latter, it represents " the first example of ceramic decoration applied on a large scale," so that the
palaces of the Ṣafawid dynasty are already foreshadowed by this
monument (Fig. 180), built while the supremacy of the house of
Jenghiz-Khan was at its height.

FIGURE 228

The poet in a blossoming tree. School of Aghā Mīrak.
— *Vever collection. Photo, Giraudon*

FIGURE 229

Portrait of Shāh Tahmāsp, by Sulṭān Muḥammad, about 1530–40.
— *Vever collection. Photo, Laniepce*

But the apogee of the Mongol period is marked above all by the marvellous cathedral mosque of Varāmīn, to the south of Teheran and Raiy (Fig. 282). Built in 1322 under the last of the Hulagid Il-Khāns, this mosque underwent considerable restoration, it is true, during the Timurid period. But for this reason it displays even more successfully the logical and historical continuity of Persian tradition, with its architectural simplicity and the purity of its lofty dome, across the centre of which extends a magnificent rosette-shaped ornament of mosaic. We may also draw attention to the stalactite decoration of the great porch with its pointed arch, consisting of a honeycomb vaulting of brick, or, again, inside the mosque, to the sanctuary (mihrāb), facing the entrance door, with its pointed niche, the lacework arch of which rests upon a delightful little frieze supporting a rich Kufic inscription. And, lastly, on the façade there is an exquisite facing of faience in two shades of blue, which will soon, alas! have disappeared. On the other hand, it would be a profitable study for an archæologist to compare the plaster decoration of this building with that of the façade and sanctuary of the old mosque at Hamadān (Fig. 291).

As regards painting, our information is more abundant. From the first, Chinese influence can be noted in it; but in Persia, as we may remember, this Chinese influence was met by an already well-established native tradition. As a matter of fact the school of Baghdād, whose achievements we have seen in thirteenth-century 'Irāq, continued to make its presence felt as far as the heart of Transoxiana under the Mongols. We have proof of this both in the library of the Royal Asiatic Society and in that of the University of Edinburgh, in the shape of the miniatures in a manuscript of Rashīd al-Dīn, dated 1310 and illuminated by a certain Muḥammad ibn Maḥmūd of Baghdād, which comes from Transoxiana in the days of Jaghatai. Two pages of this fine work, one representing Ḥamza and 'Alī on horseback, the other Muḥammad the Prophet besieging the city of the

FIGURE 230

Bahrām Gūr hunting. Manuscript signed by Sulṭān Muḥammad, about 1540.
— *British Museum*

Banū Nadīr, are in the great 'Abbāsid tradition of the thirteenth century, vigorous and sober in execution, with figures of an Arab
type mounted on tall
chargers of the Transoxi-
anian breed, which are
quite different from the
little Mongol ponies. A
number of reproductions
are to be found in Sir
Thomas Arnold's and
Adolf Grohmann's *The
Islamic Book* (1929), Pl.
36 to 41. In the same work
(Pl. 42 to 47) are repro-
ductions of a Harīrī
(Maqāmāt) in the National
Library, Vienna, dated
1334, which is in the same
style. As these various reproductions will prove, we
still have here the Arabo-
Persian school of Baghdād,
with its strongly Semitic
types and Byzantine tend-
encies, lasting on well into
the fourteenth century.
The pages from the "Life
of Moses" in the Univer-
sity Library, Edinburgh,
are of an equally pro-
nounced 'Abbāsid character; yet many subjects in this same
manuscript, such as the bodhi-tree (tree of Illumination) and

FIGURE 231

Young man reading, by Shaikh Muḥammad.
— *Koechlin collection. Archives photographiques*

the "mountains of India and their inhabitants," are already treated entirely in the Chinese manner; on other pages there is a scene from the court of 'Ala al-Dīn, sultan of Delhi, in which both the Sultan and his vizier display the thoroughly Semitic vigour of the 'Abbāsid school, while opposite them we note some figures of young people which are already of a Chinese type. Lastly, still in the same manuscript, we have a battle scene from the *Mahābhārata*, which is obviously wholly Sino-Mongolian in character. We once more find proof of this curious blend of influences in a miniature of a *Shāh-nāma* in the Vever collection, also coming from Transoxiana in the first quarter of the fourteenth century — that is, under the rule of the Jaghatai branch of the house of Jenghiz-Khan. On one page of this *Shāh-nāma*, representing a horseman against a background of mountains, the horse — a tall, lean horse of the Sogdiana breed — the rider,

FIGURE 232
Couple in a garden, by Ustād Muḥammad, about 1530.
— *Formerly in the Goloubew collection.
Photo, Goloubew*

whose profile is still quite of the Arabo-Persian type, the firm and vigorous decoration, the intentional hardness of execution, and the absence of all over-refined prettiness, all indicate survivals of the 'Abbāsid tradition, while a group of figures on the right shows both Chinese workmanship and Chinese types (see Fig. 181).

In the Rashīd al-Dīn of the Bibliothèque Nationale the Sino-Mongolian influence asserts itself still more directly and undeniably. This famous manuscript, upon which Monsieur Blochet has written a masterly study, was written and illustrated, according to the researches of this scholar, at Tabrīz between 1310 and 1315, while the historian Rashīd al-Dīn was still living. In the pictures of the Great Khan Ogodai receiving ambassadors, the Great Khan Mangu and his women, and the nine sons of the Khan Tului, Chinese influence reigns unchallenged and, it may be said, in its native state. It is, indeed, quite natural that the artistic formulas of the Far East should have been meticulously adhered to in these portraits of the house of Jenghiz-Khan. Thus the types are frankly Mongol and the workmanship wholly Chinese. There could be no better proof of the persistent taste of the Il-Khān dynasty for the manners and traditions of China, from which they drew their origin (Fig. 182 and 183). We may also note the figures of an absolutely Sino-Mongol type representing the court of Sultān Sanjar in the Dīwān of Mu'izzī in the India Office Library, reproduced in Sir Thomas Arnold's The Islamic Book (Pl. 42). The same characteristics are to be found in certain pages of a Shāh-nāma of the same period, the first quarter of the fourteenth century, bequeathed to the Louvre by Monsieur Marteau. The cavalry charge depicted on them, representing an actual episode in the Khubilaid wars, may be compared with the Japanese scenes of charging cavalry in the famous Heiji monogotari, illustrated by Sumeyoshi Keion in the thirteenth century. But from this time onward the fusion of the imported Chinese elements with the indigenous Persian ones was on the way to a harmonious consummation, as is shown, for instance, by the page of the

FIGURE 233

Gayōmarth takes up his residence in the mountains.
— *From a manuscript of the* Shāh-nāma *in the possession of M. André Godard.*
— *Photo, Laniepce*

FIGURE 234

Minūchihrī vanquishing Tūr.
— *Godard* Shāh-nāma. *Photo, Laniepce*

FIGURE 235

Nuptials of Zāl and Rudaba, parents of Rustam.
— *Godard* Shāh-nāma. *Photo, Laniepce*

Bibliothèque Nationale manuscript of Rashīd al-Dīn representing the siege of Baghdād by the Khan Hulagu.

The house of Hulagu, or the dynasty of the Il-Khāns, disappeared in 1335 before the growth of feudalism, and Persia was divided up

FIGURE 236

Kai Kawūs, borne up by eagles, starts out to conquer the heavens.

— *Godard* Shāh-nāma. *Photo, Laniepce*

between a fairly considerable number of local dynasties. The chief of these secondary dynasties were the following: (1) the Mongol house of the Jalayirids at Baghdād (1336–1411); (2) the Arabo-Persian house of the Muẓaffarids at Isfahān and in Fārs (1313–93); (3) the Afghan house of the Kart (or Kurt) at Herāt, in Khorāsān (1245–1383). The most remarkable of them was that of the Muẓaffarids, two representatives of which, Shāh Shujā' (1357–1384) and Shāh Manṣūr (1387–93),

distinguished themselves by their patronage of the great Persian poet Ḥāfiẓ, who was born about 1320 and died in 1389. At the end of the fourteenth century these little provincial kingdoms, the fragments of the Il-Khān dynasty, were destroyed one after the other by the Turkish conqueror Timur-lang, known to us as Tamerlane.

Timur was born in Transoxiana in 1336, of a great Turkish family in that region allied to the house of Jenghiz-Khan. He devoted the first years of his reign to making himself master of his native land by driving out the last of the Mongol khans of the family of Jaghatai and eliminating his local competitors. Having become king of Transoxiana in 1369, with Samarqand as his capital, Timur wrested Persia from the dynasties that shared it between them. He took Khorāsān from the Kart in 1383, Fārs from the Muẓaffarids in 1393, and Baghdād from the Jalayirids in 1393, thus restoring the unity of Iran for his own benefit. He next carried his arms into Russia, where he advanced as far as Moscow in 1396, into India, where he occupied Delhi in 1398, and into Asia Minor, where in 1402 he defeated the Ottoman sultan Bāyazīd at Angora. All these conquests were accompanied by acts of indescribable savagery and by ravages and massacres worthy of the earliest Mongols. These cruelties were all the more inexcusable in Timur's day, for he was a most pious Moslem, and all his wars — whether in Persia, Russia, India, or Asia Minor — had been waged against other Moslems. Yet this fierce warrior had another side; he was an enlightened prince, a friend of the arts, and a patron of learned men and poets. Legend will have it that at the capture of Shīrāz he pardoned the poet Ḥāfiẓ for a jest. In his beloved Transoxiana he gave himself up entirely to the arts of peace. If he sacked Shīrāz, Baghdād, Damascus, and Delhi, it was in order to adorn his capital, one of the wonders of which is his tomb, the Gūr Amīr (Fig. 184, 185).

On the death of Timur in 1405, after a confused period of struggles between his numerous heirs, his fourth son, Shāh Rukh, succeeded in making the various members of his family recognize his authority, and in his turn reigned over Transoxiana and Persia from 1405 to 1445. This prince, who established his capital at Herāt, was the greatest of the Timurid sovereigns. Generous and humane, a friend of peace, yet, when occasion called for it, a skilful leader in war, he was a patron of learned men, poets, and artists, whom he

FIGURE 238

Bijan, conqueror of the Turanians.
— *Godard* Shāh-nāma. *Photo, Laniepce*

FIGURE 239

Rustam drawing up Bījan from the pit into which he had been thrown by the Turanians.
— *Godard* Shāh-nāma. *Photo, Laniepce*

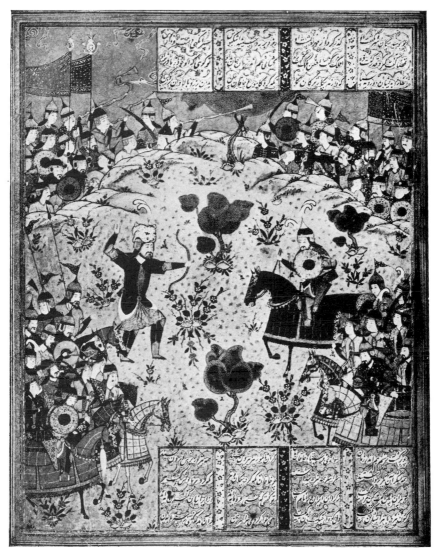

FIGURE 240

Rustam victorious over the Turanians.
— *Godard* Shāh-nāma. *Photo, Laniepce*

attracted in crowds to Herāt, where he had founded a magnificent library. His son Ulugh Beg, whom he had established as governor in Transoxiana and who was to succeed him on the throne from 1447 to 1449, imitated his example by showing special favour to the study of astronomy. Ulugh Beg was also a poet, and his court at Samarqand rivalled Herāt as a literary centre. At this time the " Timurid Renaissance," as the artistic and literary movement in the fifteenth century was called, was in full swing in these two cities. In art, as we shall see later, it was characterized by a marvellous wealth of pictures displaying both Persian and Chinese influences; and, from the literary point of view, by a remarkable development of Persian literature, and also by the birth of a whole Turkish literature, obviously inspired by the great Persian models, but written in the Jaghatai tongue — that is, the Turkish dialect proper to Transoxiana. This high culture was maintained under the Timurids Abū Saʿīd (1452–69), and Ḥusain Bāiqarā (1469–1506), who reigned at Herāt in the second half of the fifteenth century. The political power of these two princes now extended no farther than eastern Iran, for western Persia had just fallen into the hands of the two Turkoman tribes of the Qara-Qoyunlu (or Turkomans of the Black Sheep) and the Aq-Qoyunlu (or Turkomans of the White Sheep), and Abū Saʿīd perished in the attempt to recover this region. Ḥusain Bāiqarā gave up the attempt to recover the west and contented himself with reigning over the Iranian east. He chose as his minister the great Turkish poet, historian, and moralist Mīr ʿAlī Shīr Navāʾī (1440–1501), who remains the greatest name of the Timurid Renaissance so far as the Jaghatai language is concerned. Mīr ʿAlī Shīr and Ḥusain Bāiqarā attracted the most celebrated writers of the age to Herāt, notably the poet Jāmī and the two historians Mīr Khwānd and Khwāndamīr. It was at the request of ʿAlī Shīr that Mīr Khwānd, who died in 1498, composed his Persian universal history, the *Rauḍat al-safāʾ*. It was also for ʿAlī Shīr that Khwāndamīr, the grandson of Mīr Khwānd,

who lived from 1475 to about 1535, composed his first work, just as
at the end of his life he was to finish his *Habīb al-siyar* at the court of
the Timurid sovereigns in India, Bābur, and Humāyūn. Finally,
Ḥusain Bāiqarā was the patron of the chief artists of his day, such
as the painter Bihzād and the calligrapher Sulṭān 'Alī of Mashhad.

The Timurids were driven out of Transoxiana and eastern Iran
between 1500 and 1501 by the Mongol dynasty of the Shaibānids,
who were descended from the family of Jenghiz-Khan. Muḥammad
Shaibāni compelled Bābur, the last of the Timurids, to take refuge in
India — where he was to lay the foundations of the " Mughal "
Empire — and set up a fresh domination in Transoxiana, that of the
Üzbegs. The empire of the Üzbegs, which had Bokhārā and Samarqand as its capitals, remained in the power of the dynasty of the
Shaibānids from 1500 to 1599. This dynasty, which was profoundly
Turkish in culture, though very Moslem in religion, kept up the
great Timurid tradition, especially in Jaghatai literature and painting. The decadence of Transoxianian culture did not finally set in
till the Shaibānids had been replaced by other Turkish dynasties
at Bokhārā.

Timurid architecture is represented in the first place by the monuments of Samarqand, Timur's capital (Fig. 184 to 188). We may
mention the mosque set up in memory of Timur's sister, who died
in 1371, the Mosque of Shāh-Zinda (1392–1434), and the famous
Gūr Amīr, or Mausoleum of Timur, dating from 1484. The most
characteristic point about the first two of these buildings is the
preponderant part played in them by enamelled decoration. There
is a material reason for this: Transoxiana, possessing no stone-
quarries, was forced to use brick. There was also a reason of taste:
the luxury of the Turkish tribes of central Asia consisted chiefly
of carpets of many colours, and they liked to have the polychrome effect of these carpets reflected in the ceramic decoration
of their architecture. Thus in such monuments as the Mosque of

FIGURE 241

Rustam listening to the last words of his son Sohrāb.
— *Godard* Shāh-nāma. *Photo, Laniepce*

FIGURE 242

Death of Rustam.

— *Godard* Shāh-nāma. *Photo, Laniepce*

FIGURE 243
Shāpūr playing at ball before Ardashīr.
— *Godard* Shāh-nāma. *Photo, Laniepce*

FIGURE 244

Bahrām Gūr slaying the lions.
— *Godard* Shāh-nāma. *Photo, Laniepce*

Timur's sister and the Mosque of Shāh-Zinda the architecture is merely a pretext for the effects of the enamelled mosaic, the dominant note of which is a turquoise-blue, which alternated harmoniously with the pale pink of the brick. As to the Gūr Amīr, the essential feature of it is a hall in the form of a cross, contained within an octagon and surmounted by an enormous bulbous dome. This dome is decorated externally with semi-cylindrical ribs in enamelled brickwork, while the drum which supports it is decorated with a band of inscriptions in Kufic script, also in enamelled bricks. We have to thank the courtesy of Messieurs Henri Viollet and Le Brecq for the photographs of this monument which we give here.

With this group of the Timurid period may be associated the Blue Mosque of Tabrīz, built between 1437 and 1468 by Jahān Shāh, of the ephemeral Turkoman dynasty of the Qarā-Qoyunlu, which succeeded the Timurids in western Persia. It too is decorated with faience mosaics of great beauty, in which the range of colour, as noted by Dieulafoy and Sarre, " varies from pale to dark blue, with tones of dull green, leaf-brown, and black, sometimes, even, enhanced with arabesques of gold " (Fig. 189).

The Timurid period (1369–1500), together with the Shaibānid period, which was a continuation of it (1500–1600), was one of the greatest periods of Persian painting both in Iran and in Transoxiana. It is now that we come to a harmonious fusion of Chinese and 'Abbāsid influences in the schools of Herāt and Samarqand, together with one which was, strictly speaking, Persian and which in the end assimilated the other two.

These two currents of Iranian and Chinese influence are also found in juxtaposition, though without any fusion between them, in certain paintings of the second half of the fifteenth century from Khorāsān, which were once in the Goloubew collection, but are now in the Vever collection and the Boston Museum. On a piece of Chinese silk, on which was already painted a branch of a tree, with a bird of purely Ming workmanship, were subsequently painted the Iranian lovers Khosrau and Shīrīn, in Persian costumes, but with Chinese faces, in such a way that critics cannot tell whether we have here a Persian painter working in the Chinese manner, or a Chinese artist working in the Persian manner (Fig. 190). The same character is to be found in a miniature belonging to a manuscript of Khwājū Kirmānī in the possession of the Musée des Arts Décoratifs, Paris, which depicts the arrival of Humāy at the court of the Emperor of China, the setting being a flower-garden. This picture, here reproduced as Fig. 191, and dating from about 1430, is a good specimen of the school of Herāt, a charming blend of Ming prettiness and Persian grace both in the drawing of the figures and in the floral decoration. " The figures themselves," writes Monsieur Kühnel, " have become flowers, and bloom naturally in the midst of this splendour of flowers and perfume." It may have been painted by Ghiyāth al-Dīn Khalīl, who went to China three times in the suite of embassies from Transoxiana, and there had opportunities of studying Ming technique (Fig. 192 and 193).

The combination of Chinese subjects and Iranian motives is no less happy, in our opinion, in the illustrations to the famous *Apocalypse of Muḥammad* in the Bibliothèque Nationale (*Supplément turc*, No. 190), written in Jaghatai Turkish in Uighur script and illuminated at Herāt in 1436 for Shāh Rukh; the faces of the angels and of the celestial centauress al-Burāq among the clouds, which are treated in the purely Chinese " chi " style, have the fresh roundness and slanting eyes of the Chinese type; while the Prophet's face and those of his disciples, on the contrary, are of an elongated, delicate type which is essentially Arabo-Persian. The whole composition produces a wonderful impression of fervour and mystic emotion. In such works as these, the Sino-Iranian school of the Timurid age reminds us of the celestial visions of Fra Angelico. In the paradise

FIGURE 245
Buzurgmihr playing at chess.
— *Godard* Shāh-nāma. *Photo, Laniepce*

FIGURE 246

Struggle between Khosrau Parvīz and Bahrām Chūbīn.
— *Godard* Shāh-nāma. *Photo, Laniepce*

of the pure in heart the angels of Herāt have a place beside those of the master of Fiesole (Fig. 194 to 197).

More purely Iranian are the miniatures in a manuscript of Khwājū Kirmānī, executed by Junaid Naqqash al-Sulṭānī at Baghdād about 1396, during the reign of Timur, which are now in the British Museum; in this connexion we may mention various scenes of court life, showing the women's quarters, as gay and animated as an aviary — pages which already foreshadow the similar scenes of the school of Bihzād; there is also a duel scene, delightfully Gothic in feeling, between two horsemen who have dismounted to settle their dispute in a clearing, against a delicate forest background recalling the wooded backgrounds of the French fifteenth-century miniaturists, as well as Benozzo Gozzoli or Fra Angelico. This manuscript also contains several miniatures of " dīwān " scenes by another hand, which bear witness to the elegance and refinements of aristocratic life in Iran under the Timurids; we may mention in particular those delightful scenes of a gallant on horseback beneath his lady's castle, with the lady appearing on a terrace amid a grove of trees surrounded by a flight of birds, in which the lovers frequently represent Bahrām Gūr and his lady-love, or Khosrau and Shīrīn. In these works we already find all the almost excessive delicacy, somewhat unreal charm, and at times rather cold prettiness of the classical Persian miniature. In our opinion, there is more strength and movement in two pages from a Shāhnāma formerly in the Schultz collection, one of which has passed into the possession of Monsieur Martin, the other into that of the Kunstgewerbe Museum in Leipzig, the former representing Rustam asleep in the shade of a magic forest, while his horse, the celebrated Rakhsh, drives off a lion by his unaided efforts, and the latter, one of Rustam's victories.

Let us note in conclusion that, though Persia was dominated in the fifteenth century by the Timurid schools of Herāt and Samarqand, she had none the less not forgotten the very different tradition of the

FIGURE 247
Mystical scene.
— *Godard* Shāh-nāma. *Photo, Laniepce*

'Abbāsid artists of the earlier school of Baghdād. We need no other proof than the page from the Vever collection here reproduced, representing a charming female figure lying beneath a tree in a blooming garden, surrounded by her handmaidens (Fig. 198); both the type and the workmanship have an indefinably Italian suggestion, which reminds one of the "*Pietà*" from the same collection which we mentioned above.

FIGURE 248

Illuminated page from a *Shāh-nāma* in the André Godard collection.
— *Photo, Laniepce*

We have omitted the name of the greatest of the Timurid masters, Bihzād, from this hasty sketch, for the reason that he marks the close of this age and forms a link between the Timurid period and the Ṣafawid period, between the ancient school of Herāt, the art of which he carried to its supreme pitch of excellence, and the future schools of western Persia, all of which were afterwards to claim him as their founder.

Kamāl al-Dīn Bihzād, the greatest of Persian painters, was born at Herāt about 1440 and was the pupil of Pīr Saiyid Aḥmad of Tabrīz. From 1469 to 1506 he lived at Herāt in the service of the last of the Timurids, Husain

FIGURE 249

Transoxianian art, about 1500.

— Sarre collection, Berlin. By kind permission of the owner.
— After Kühnel (trans. Budry): La Miniature en Orient (*Cassirer and Crès*)

FIGURE 250

Young prince. Copy of an original by Sultān
Muḥammad, made by Aghā Rizā, about 1570.
— *Bibliothèque Nationale. Archives photo-
graphiques*

Bāiqarā, whose minister, 'Alī
Shīr Navā'ī, was his patron.
We shall see later how, after
the fall of the Timurids, he
attached himself to the for-
tunes of the new shahs of
Persia of the Ṣafawid dy-
nasty and went to live at their
court at Tabrīz.

From what may be called
Bihzād's "Timurid period"
date his two splendid portraits of Sulṭān Ḥusain Bāiqarā, one of which, in the
F. R. Martin collection, is a
mere unfinished drawing on
a green ground; here, for the
first time in Persian art, we
meet with a real portrait —
a person studied for his own
sake, with his physical characteristics and psychology,
such as the Japanese and the
Chinese alone knew how to
produce in Asia at that time.
The same distance separates
this masterly drawing from
the works which went be-
fore it as separates the illuminations in the mediæval
French Books of Hours from
the portraits of Jean Fouquet, or even François Clouet. From
the same period of Bihzād's life, about 1467, date the illustrations

FIGURE 251

School of Rizā 'Abbāsī (?).

— *Vever collection. Photo, Pivot*

FIGURE 252

Confidences. School of Rizā ʻAbbāsī,
seventeenth century.

— *Bibliothèque Nationale. Photo, Giraudon*

to the *Ẓafar nāma* (Book of Victory), a history of Timur by Sharaf al-Dīn ʻAlī Yazdī, now in the Boston Museum, which represent Timur on his throne, a reception in Timur's palace, an assault on a fortress, a cavalry attack, or the building of a mosque; here we have the whole life of the Transoxianian conqueror, as administrator, as leader in war, and as patron of the arts, passing before our eyes with a realism, a historical exactitude, a sense of movement and of the life of crowds, which are really amazing. The epic feats of the Timurids were then quite recent and must still have haunted men's minds — for Timur died in 1404, whereas the illustrations in the Boston manuscript date from about 1467 — but, above all, they now found no mere illuminators and calligraphers to render them, but an artist of genius, who possessed as marked a personality as our Giotto and was as great an innovator as the latter.

FIGURE 253

The Court of Solomon. Persia, sixteenth century.
— *Vever collection. Photo, Pivot*

FIGURE 254
The Court of Solomon. Persia, sixteenth century.
— *Vever collection. Photo, Laniepce*

FIGURE 255

The Queen of Sheba watching the dancers. Persian, early sixteenth century.

— *Vever collection. Photo, Pivot*

In the same vein, again, are Bihzād's illustrations for a manuscript of Sa'dī's *Bustān* dating from 1487, now in the Royal Library at Cairo. Among other miniatures, this work contains some banqueting-scenes and interiors of mosques, with figures each of which is a little masterpiece of drawing, elegance, and psychology; besides a painting of grazing mares which, with the marvellous cavalry scenes in the Boston Museum manuscript, places Bihzād among the best painters of horses in Mongol times, on the level of such artists as Chow-Mong-Fu. Monsieur Armenak Sakisian also attributes to Bihzād some pages from a manuscript of Niẓāmī's *Khamsa* in the British Museum, dated 1442, among which is a remarkable battle scene of Arabs mounted on camels, worthy of the same painter's representations of cavalry engagements.

Among the works attributed to Bihzād by Monsieur Martin, but some of which Messieurs Migeon and Sakisian prefer to ascribe to one of his contemporaries, Qāsim 'Alī of Herāt, and others perhaps to Aghā Mīrak, are the illustrations in another manuscript of Niẓāmī's *Khamsa*, dated 1434, now in the British Museum, some scenes from which, worthy of Bihzād himself, we may admire in Kühnel's album — Alexander and the Seven Sages of Greece, Sulṭān Ḥusain Bāiqarā in the character of Alexander, etc. The copy of this work dating from the beginning of the sixteenth century which is now in the Library of the Union of Soviet Republics at Leningrad, also contains a few miniatures of the same school, noteworthy among which is one of Majnūn and Lailā among the animals, reproduced by Professor Sarre — a pure, tender scene set in a landscape with all the charm of the legends of St. Francis. Lastly, several critics attribute to Bihzād two great portraits of captive princes, now in the Doucet and Koechlin collections respectively, the latter of which Monsieur Martin inclines to think may be that of the last ruler of the Aq-Qoyunlu, who was put to death by the Ṣafawids in 1502 (Fig. 199 to 202).

FIGURE 256

Solomon and the Queen of Sheba. Transoxianian art, early sixteenth century.
— *Vever collection. Photo, Laniepce*

FIGURE 257
Apocalypse of Muḥammad. Persian,
sixteenth century.
— *Demotte collection. Photo, Laniepce*

In order to complete what has to be said about the regions of eastern Iran, it would be as well to say a few words about the art of the Shaibānids before passing on to the history of Persia under the Ṣafawid dynasty. For the Shaibānid dynasty, which occupied the throne of Transoxiana after the Timurids, from 1500 to 1599, continued, as the latter had done, to patronize the arts to the utmost of their power. The founder of the dynasty, Muḥammad Shaibāni (1500–9), and his successor, Quchqunjī (1510–30), extended their protection to artists and poets. It would be a mistake to believe that under their rule Transoxiana suddenly lost its artistic glory, which passed to Ṣafawid Persia. Moreover, the Shaibānid painting of Transoxiana and the Ṣafawid painting of the early years of the sixteenth century are closely connected with each other. To convince ourselves of this it is sufficient to recall, for instance, the scene of

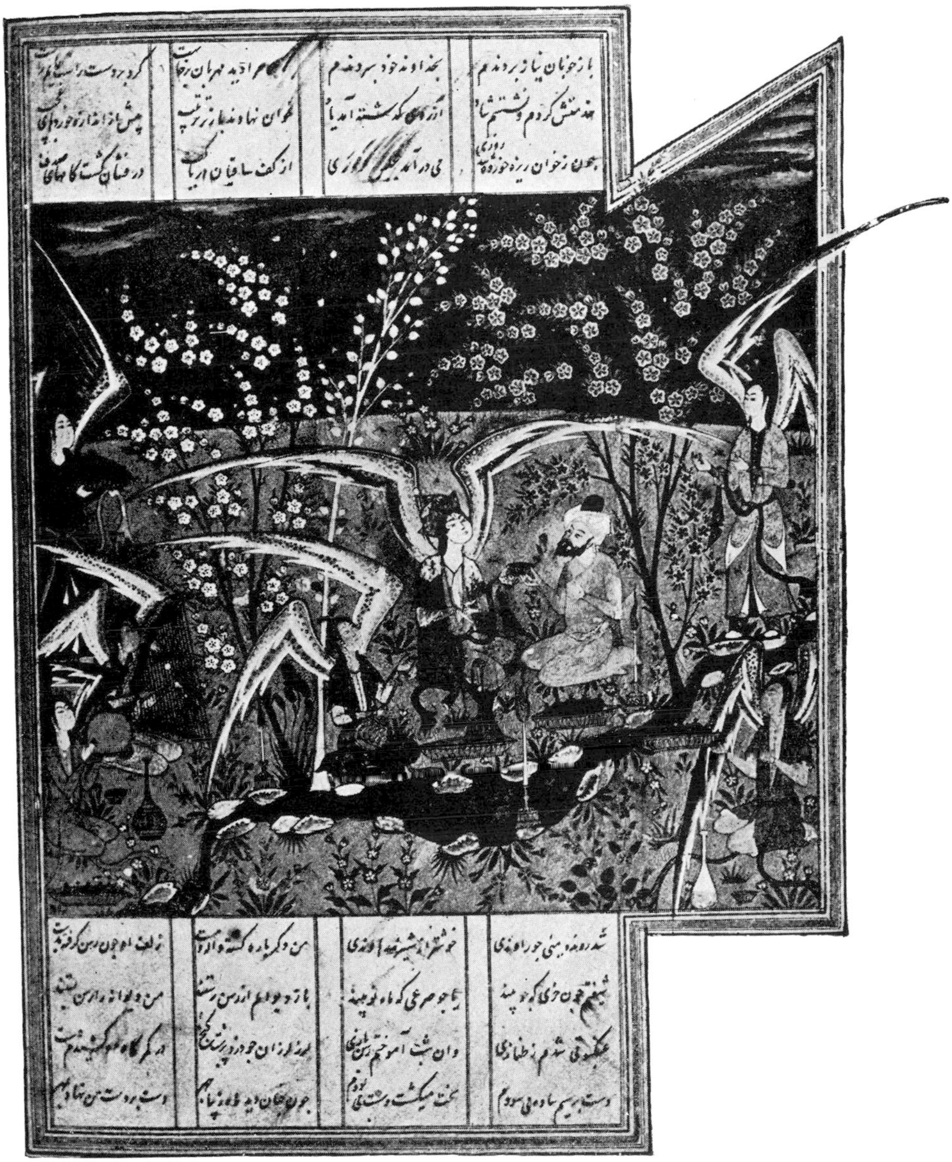

FIGURE 258

Mystical landscape. Persian, early sixteenth century.
— *Vever collection. Photo, Laniepce*

Bahrām Gūr hunting the wild ass, which we reproduce here from a *Dīwān* of Mīr 'Alī Shīr Navā'ī which appeared at Herāt about 1526 or 1527 and is now in the Bibliothèque Nationale; such a work might well be classed either as Shaibānid or as Ṣafawid did we not know that at that date Herāt was a dependency of Persia and not of Transoxiana. On the other hand, there is very little to distinguish from a Ṣafawid Persian painting the picture of the sultan Sanjar reining in his horse in the midst of a landscape of flowering trees to listen to an old woman's petition — painted at Bokhārā for the Shaibānid 'Abd al-'Azīz by "Maḥmud and Muḥammad" in a manuscript of Niẓāmī dated 1545, and now in the Bibliothèque Nationale (Fig. 203). The charm of the floral setting, the grace of the figures and their horses, the delicacy of the features — which positively reminds us of Clouet — and the realism of the portrait of the old woman are in every respect worthy of the finest productions of western Persia.

Nor is the Persian and Turkish poetry of the Timurid period unworthy of the painting of the same age. Two names in particular are worthy of attention, those of the famous Persian poets Ḥāfiẓ and Jāmī.

Ḥāfiẓ was born, no doubt at Shīrāz, about 1320, and spent his life in that city under the rule of the Muẓaffarid princes, several of whom were his patrons. He died at Shīrāz in 1389, after it had recognized the domination of Timur. This poet, the Anacreon of Persia, is justly regarded as one of the greatest Iranian lyric poets.

The themes which inspire him are the eternal themes of Persian classical poetry. He celebrates the beauty of his beloved Shīrāz, the grace of the river of Ruknābād, which waters it, and of the promenade of Muṣallā, which is one of its ornaments. He tells of the sweetness of his garden (see Fig. 204): " The night was about to fade when, drawn by the perfume of the roses, I went down into the garden to seek, like the nightingale, balm for my fever; in the shadow there gleamed a rose, a rose red as a veiled lamp, and I gazed upon its countenance." Above all he sang the beauty of the women and boys of Shīrāz: " The rose is lovely only because the face of my beloved is lovely. . . . What were the grace of the greensward and the breeze that blows in the garden were it not for the cheek of my beloved, which is like a tulip? The honeyed mouth and radiant image of my beloved would be nothing without her kisses and her caresses." Here we no longer find the pessimism of Khaiyām, who calls upon love and wine to drown his tears; nor is it the mystic love of Saʿdī; it is a song of infinite sweetness, telling of human love in a moonlit garden haunted by nightingales and carpeted with jasmine, narcissus, anemones, tulips, and roses, all expressed in a poetry very near to our own: " In the darkness of the night I sought to unloose my heart from the bonds of thy tresses, but I felt the touch of thy cheek and drank of thy lips. I pressed thee to my breast, and thy hair enveloped me like a flame. I pressed my lips to thine and yielded up my soul and my heart to thee as in ransom." And, to sum up: " Pleasure, youth, and song among the roses, such is thy lot, O Ḥāfiẓ. The messenger has no mission save to deliver his message."

The other great poet of the Timurid period, Jāmī, was born near Herāt in 1414 and died in that city in 1492, after enjoying the favour of Ḥusain Bāiqarā. He was the last of the Persian classic poets. He too sang most of the themes treated by the masters of earlier days, such as Yūsuf and Zulaikhā, Lailā and Majnūn, or the adventures of Sikandar — that is, Alexander the Great. Thus at the height of the Timurid domination the soul of Persia remained true to all her great traditions. In spite of their Turkish origin the Timurids were liberal enough to foster this historical continuity, which was to assert itself still more strongly under the genuinely Persian dynasty of the Ṣafawids.

SAFAWID PERSIA

SINCE THE MIDDLE OF THE ELEVENTH CENTURY IRAN, WITH ONLY
a few exceptions, had owed obedience to scarcely any but Turkish or
Mongol dynasties. Yet, as we have seen, Persian civilization was so
full of life that it imposed it-
self upon all its Mongol or
Turkish masters. At the opening of the sixteenth century the
Ṣafawids, a family of purely
Persian race, coming originally from Āzarbaijān, finally
succeeded in overthrowing
foreign domination and restored to ancient Iran the control of her own destinies.

FIGURE 259
Al-Burāq. Persian, sixteenth century.
— *Vever collection. Photo, Pivot*

The Ṣafawids were all the
more suited to stand for an in-
carnation of Persian nationalism because they belonged to
the Shī'ite sect, and Shī'ism
had remained for eight centuries the true religion of the
Persians, their rallying cry
against their Arab or Turkish
masters, all of whom alike had
been Sunnites; in time this re-
ligious distinction had come to correspond with a racial one, so much
so that, by the sixteenth century, Shī'ite had become synonymous with
Persian. Hence, so soon as the Ṣafawids raised the standard of Shī'ism,
their cause was regarded as a national one throughout the whole of

FIGURE 260

Royal audience in a garden. Persian, second half of the sixteenth century.
— *Vever collection. Photo, Giraudon*

FIGURE 261
Royal feast in a garden. Persian, second half of the sixteenth century.
— *Vever collection. Photo, Giraudon*

FIGURE 262

Royal audience. Manuscript illustrated by Farrukh-beg, end of sixteenth century.
— *Vever collection*

Persia. This circumstance explains their rapid success. The first Ṣafawid shah, Ismā'īl I (1502–24) started by wresting Āzarbaijān, 'Irāq-i
'Ajamī, and Fārs from the Turkoman horde of the Aq-Qoyunlu in
1502 and the following years. Eastern Persia (Khorāsān) was, as
we have seen, in the hands of the Shaibānids, who had taken the place

FIGURE 263
Bahrām Gūr hunting. School of Herāt, about 1527.
— *Bibliothèque Nationale. Photo, Giraudon*

of the Timurids. In 1510 Ismā'īl I crushed the Shaibānids at Marv,
threw them back to the northern bank of the Oxus, and annexed
Herāt and Khorāsān, and the whole of Persia was now free. Ismā'īl's
last years were devoted to defending her against the Ottomans who
had invaded her western frontiers.

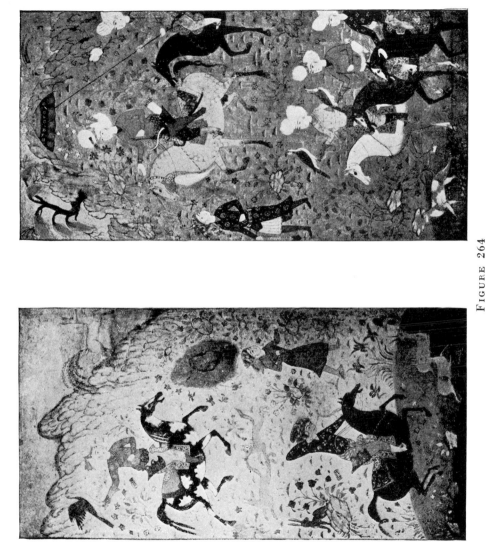

Figure 264

Royal hunting-scene. Persian, sixteenth century.
— *Vever collection. Photo, Laniepce*

From this time onward, up to the end of the dynasty, the struggle
with the Ottomans was carried on in a succession of savage wars
alternating with peaces which brought no more than a truce and had
all the character of a war both racial and religious, a duel between
the Turk and the Iranian, a struggle between Sunnite and Shīʻite.
The danger to the restored Persia was at times all the more grave because, while the Ottoman Turks were assailing her on the west, in
Armenia and on the Tigris, the Üzbeg Turkomans were taking her in
the rear on the east, from the direction of Khorāsān. The life of Tahmāsp I (1524–76), the son and successor of Ismāʻīl, was spent in
withstanding this double peril, though this did not prevent him
from showing himself one of the most enlightened sovereigns of
his day and, in particular, a sumptuous patron of Persian painting. But on the accession of Shāh ʻAbbās I, about 1585, the
double danger from the Ottomans and the Üzbegs had once more
become very grave, the Ottomans having invaded Āzarbaijān; and
the Üzbegs Khorāsān. ʻAbbās I (1587–1629) at once showed himself one of the greatest sovereigns in the history of Iran. Having reorganized the Persian army, he crushed the Üzbegs near Herāt
and drove them out of Khorāsān in 1597; next, in 1603, he in like
manner drove the Ottomans out of Āzarbaijān, and in 1623 even
out of Baghdād. He could then devote himself to the arts of peace.
His foreign policy aimed at encircling the Ottomans by causing
Persia to enter into a concert of the eastern Powers. At home he
set on foot a scheme for the material revival of his kingdom by
borrowing European methods, especially in military matters. Lastly,
as we shall see below, he filled his capital, Isfahān, with splendid
buildings.

In spite of the despotism and debauchery of the successors of
ʻAbbās I — Safī (1629–42), ʻAbbās II (1642–67), and Sulaimān
(1667–94) — they in general followed the same policy. Though they
failed to keep Baghdād, which finally fell into the hands of Turkey,

FIGURE 265
Hunting-scene. Persian, sixteenth century.
— *Vever collection. Photo, Vever*

they maintained their Iranian heritage intact. Beneath their rule Persian civilization continued to shine with a brilliant radiance; their court at Isfahān, as we shall see, continued to be an artistic centre of the highest order, particularly as regards painting. Following the

example of 'Abbās I, they also endeavoured to establish regular intercourse with the western states and gave an excellent reception to European travellers — witness Tavernier and Chardin. But during the reign of Sulṭān Ḥusain (1694–1722), the Afghans, who had hitherto been subject to the Ṣafawids, revolted against them. In 1722 they invaded Persia, seized Isfahān, and deposed the Shah.

This was the end of the dynasty of the Ṣafawids. The Afshār Nādir-shāh, who drove out the Afghans and restored the kingdom of Persia, was

FIGURE 266
Country scene. Persian, sixteenth century.
— *Vever collection. Photo, Vever*

not slow to set aside the Ṣafawid princes and himself assume the crown in 1736. In spite of the vigour of his government and his victories, which carried the fame of Persian arms even as far as India, this adventurer of genius reigned for too short a time to accomplish a lasting work. After his assassination, in 1747, the highest hopes were entertained of the purely Persian dynasty of the Zand, which held western Persia from 1750 to 1794. The Zand prince Karīm-Khān (1750–79) was distinguished for the restorations which he carried out. He adorned Shīrāz, the royal residence, with a number of famous buildings and caused the monuments of the past, such as the mausoleum of Sa'dī and the tomb of the poet Ḥāfiẓ to be piously restored (Fig. 223 to 225). But the Zand reigned for too short a time. They were overthrown by the Turkoman dynasty of the Qājār (1794), who, in spite of their praiseworthy efforts, found it impossible in the changed circumstances to restore to Persia either the political power or the artistic glory of the Ṣafawid period; so that the Ṣafawid period, the great age of Isfahān, remains the golden age of Persian art.

Under the Ṣafawids Persian architecture received a considerable impetus, owing to the activity of 'Abbās I, who caused Isfahān to be rebuilt on a new plan, with a whole series of buildings intended to render his fame eternal; the centre of the city was marked by a great open space, the Maidān-i Shāh, round which stood the "Gate of Many Colours," or Ala Qapy, which opened into the royal palace, the Mosque of the Ṣadr, the clock-house, the royal mosque, or Masjid-i Shāh, and the Qaisāriya, or Imperial Market (Fig. 206 to 210). The royal palace, the eastern end of which opened on to the Maidān (Fig. 212), had running along its southern side gardens and parks about which were scattered pavilions, the most famous of which is that of the Forty Columns, or Chihil-Sutūn, the walls of which are adorned with paintings. In another part of the city 'Abbās I planted an avenue of monumental proportions, the Chār-Bāgh, or " Four Gardens," running from the neighbourhood of the park of the Chihil-Sutūn (Fig. 213 to 215) to the garden of Hazār-jarīb, or " Thousand Acres," which was also lined with palaces, stone water-pools, and playing fountains (Fig. 216).

The Masjid-i Shāh shows the typical plan of the classical Persian

FIGURE 267

Page from a Persian manuscript of the sixteenth century.
— *Vever collection. Photo, Vever*

FIGURE 267b

Page from a Persian manuscript of the sixteenth century.
— *Vever collection. Photo, Vever*

mosque, in which the ancient mosque with four arcades is replaced by an arrangement in which the square central court has four great *eivāns* arranged like the arms of a cross, each one at right angles with the centre of one of the four sides of the court. The *eivān* through which one enters is preceded by a gigantic porch, open across its whole width and to its full height. Moreover, in the Masjid-i Shāh, in addition to the *miḥrāb* in the sanctuary or *eivān* on the far side of the courtyard, there are two halls running along the sides of this sanctuary parallel to each other, each of which has its own *miḥrāb*, as have also the two *eivāns* to the right and left, as well as the two halls connecting the *eivān* through which one enters with these two side ones; and since each of these halls containing a *miḥrāb* is surmounted by a cupola, the royal mosque, as Monsieur Saladin points out, is really formed of a harmonious group of seven distinct mosques. " The whole," he remarks, " is a masterpiece of classical purity and taste." As for the outward adornment of the mosque, the Ṣafawid artists have lavished upon it all the wealth of their enamelled materials: bricks, earthenware mosaics, and tiles (see the concluding section).

The beauty of the Ṣafawid palaces resides not only in the purity of their architecture and the brilliance of their decoration, but also in the charm of their setting. In this respect, again, we do not learn so much from actual photographs of them as they now are — for time has done its work — as from the accounts given by European travellers who felt the full impression of them at the time when they were built. For the Chār-Bāgh we may quote the words of the Frenchman Chardin: " This avenue was planted and embellished with a great number of sumptuous edifices by order of Shāh ʿAbbās and under his immediate supervision. . . . This great avenue, which may be called the public promenade of Ispahān and is the most beautiful that I have ever seen, is watered by a canal which flows down the middle of it. . . . The sides of this charming avenue are formed by beautiful and spacious gardens, each of which has two pavilions. The streets, too, which cut across it in several places, are broad channels of water, planted with a double row of tall plane-trees. . . . The avenue leads up to the king's pleasure-house. . . . When the fountains are playing in this beautiful garden, nothing grander or more beautiful could be seen, especially in the spring, in the season of the earliest flowers, for this garden is full of them, especially along the canal and round the stone basin."

But 'Abbās I was not content with embellishing Isfahān. In 1613 he also built a wonderful palace at Ashraf, in Māzandārān, in the middle of a park which is still known as the Bāgh-i Shāh (the Shah's Garden) — a second Chihil-Sutūn, of which traveller after traveller has described the charm. The proximity of the mountains of Māzandārān has made it possible to surround the kiosks of this royal residence with playing fountains, artificial rivers and lakes. And here again the genius of the architect was enhanced by that Persian taste for gardens which we may remember in Sa'dī and Ḥāfiẓ (Fig. 217).

Under the Ṣafawid age there also flourished a fine school of painting. It should be noted that this school is directly connected with the Timurid school of Herāt. After the fall of the house of Timur, Bihzād, the last and greatest painter of the school of Herāt, who lived from about 1440 to 1524, attached himself to the Ṣafawid shah Ismā'īl I and followed him to Tabrīz, where he ended his life. Here the old Timurid master handed on the heritage of a century of glorious traditions to the artists of the young kingdom, together with all the rich resources of the old miniaturists of Khorāsān and Transoxiana. In fact, a whole galaxy of pupils was formed by his teaching and became in their turn celebrated masters; we may mention among his disciples Shaikh-zāda Khorāsāni, Mīr Muṣavvir of Sulṭānīya, Aghā Mīrak, and Muẓaffar 'Alī, the last of whom was afterwards entrusted with the decoration of the palace of Chihil-Sutūn at Isfahān.

FIGURE 268

Page from a Persian manuscript of the sixteenth century.
— *Vever collection. Photo, Vever*

FIGURE 269

Page from a Persian manuscript of the sixteenth century.
— *Vever collection. Photo, Giraudon*

Like Bihzād, Aghā Mīrak seems to have started his career in Khorāsān — hence his name *al-Khorāsāni* — no doubt just as Bihzād
had done at Herāt. Like him again, he settled at Tabrīz, at the court
of the earlier Ṣafawids. From about 1539 to 1543 he was working
in this city for the Ṣafawid shah Tahmāsp at the illustrations for a
manuscript of Niẓāmī's *Khamsa*. From this manuscript comes the
" Ascension of Muḥammad " now in the British Museum. On this famous page the Prophet, in acordance with the tradition of the school
of Herāt, is enveloped in an immense aureole of gold, which mounts
upwards quivering like a great flame; he is riding on the back of the
virgin al-Burāq, who has the body of a mare, and is galloping upwards into the azure heaven like some antique Pegasus; having
traversed the clouds in this fashion — which in the present picture
are drawn in the Chinese fashion, in the " chi " style — and passed
even beyond the orb of the sun, he is now seen rising into the blue
of the firmament, guided by the archangel Jibrā'īl, while other
angels fly before or behind him carrying presents. Seldom, in our
opinion, has religious art risen to such heights in the creation of
a mystical atmosphere. The imagination is transported by this
new " vision of Ezekiel " far above our planet, beyond the cloud
formations, beyond even the world of the stars, straight into the
heaven of Allah. Just as certain works of Hindu art — for instance,
the Maheśamūrti of Elephanta — seem to us the very incarna-
tion of the pantheist Absolute, so the British Museum " Ascension
of Muḥammad " seems to us the purest embodiment of the
transcendental dream of the monotheistic religions; it is like the
work of a Fra Angelico possessing all the power of Michelangelo
(Fig. 226).

Quite apart from this inspiration of such a special and rather
exceptional nature, Aghā Mīrak and the painters of his school stand
out by reason of their many *dīwān* scenes — that is, scenes of court
life — notable among which are those in a very fine manuscript of

FIGURE 270

Page from a Persian manuscript, middle of the sixteenth century.
— *Jean Sauphar collection. Photo, Librairie de France*

FIGURE 271

Feast in a palace. Persian art, sixteenth century.
— *Demotte collection. Photo, Laniepce*

FIGURE 272

The swing. Persian art, second half of the sixteenth century.
— *Vever collection. Photo, Giraudon*

Niẓāmī, illustrated by Aghā Mīrak himself and dating from about 1524, which is at present in the possession of Monsieur F. R. Martin, the great historian of Persian art (Fig. 227). In the light of these works we can distinguish the new contribution made by Aghā Mīrak to Persian miniature-painting. His figures, as has justly been observed by Professor Kühnel, are already more slender and graceful than those of Bihzād. Under his hands the noblemen, beautiful youths, and lovely ladies assume that elongated and aristocratic elegance which was to continue to be so fashionable in the art of Isfahān (Fig. 228). As a set-off to this, these portraits lose something of the sincerity of Bihzād's figures. They are in obvious danger of lapsing before long into the conventional and the precious. But we must admit that this very preciosity is not without its charm; it is analogous to the age of Botticelli, following upon that of Giotto.

The court of Shāh Tahmāsp, who reigned at Tabrīz from 1524 to 1576, offered a refuge to yet another master, Sulṭān Muḥammad, who also enjoyed the sovereign's favour and was his official adviser in matters concerning painting. Sulṭān Muḥammad was a court painter, in whom the tendency towards elongated aristocratic forms and graceful attitudes of studied unconstraint, which we have already noted in Aghā Mīrak, appear to be still more pronounced. We may obtain some idea of this new style from several portraits, dating from about 1530 to 1540, in the Vever and Koechlin collections, representing beautiful youths reading, sometimes leaning against a flowering tree, sometimes just seated in Eastern fashion, smelling a flower. The Vever collection also contains a splendid portrait, painted by Sulṭān Muḥammad himself, of Shāh Tahmāsp reading (Fig. 229). And it is the aristocratic taste of Sulṭān Muḥammad that also inspired the illustrations to a *Shāh-nāma* of about 1537 in the Edouard de Rothschild collection, especially that of Rustam capturing the

FIGURE 273

Binding of a Persian manuscript, sixteenth century.
— *Vever collection. Photo, Pivot*

FIGURE 274

Miniature from a *Shāh-nāma* of the Shīrāz school. Persia, sixteenth century.
— *Vever collection. Photo, Pivot*

FIGURE 275

Page from a *dīwān* of Ḥāfiẓ. School of Shīrāz, first half of the sixteenth century (?).
— *Veer collection. Photo, Pivot*

horse Rakhsh, besides the series of scenes of Shāh Tahmāsp out hunting reproduced in F. R. Martin's album (Fig. 230).

The triumph of these tendencies is complete in Ustād Muḥammad of Herāt, a pupil of the last-named master. Among the works attributed to him we need only mention the lady picking a lily, in the Sambon collection, and the two lovers in a flowering tree, formerly in the Goloubew collection (Fig. 232), both of which are models of Botticellian refinement. But at the same time Ustād Muḥammad has left some drawings in quite a different style, scenes of country life of a calm and restful simplicity and an absolute purity of line, set in a delicious landscape, which form part of the Marteau bequest to the Louvre; or, again, some humorous sketches worthy of Toba Sojo — for instance, his scenes of strolling players and bears, now in the Library of the Union of Soviet Republics at Leningrad.

We cannot leave the age of Shāh Tahmāsp without mentioning a splendid *Shāh-nāma* of the school of Herāt, dating from the reign of that monarch and presented to Monsieur and Madame André Godard by H.M. the King of Afghanistan. We are indebted to the courtesy of Monsieur and Madame Godard for their kind permission to reproduce fifteen large miniatures from this work. In the first place we have the earliest of the kings, Gayōmarth or Kayumarth, establishing his government among the mountains, a delightful court scene in a flowery glade, among trees and rocks (Fig. 233). Next we have the young Iranian prince Minūchihrī slaying the Turanian leader Tūr, a cavalry combat observed from the life by a contemporary of the Timurid or Ṣafawid wars (Fig. 234). Later on we have the marriage of Zāl, Rustam's father, to the Princess Mihrāb, daughter of the King of Kābul, an epic scene treated in the spirit of a charming social ceremony.

Next in our manuscript come the kings of the Kayānid dynasty, placed on the throne by Rustam; here is Kai Kāwūs attempting, at the instigation of the demons, to conquer heaven in a chariot borne

FIGURE 276

Khosrau and Shīrīn from a manuscript dated 1624.
— *Bibliothèque Nationale. Archives photographiques*

by eagles; this is a wonderful illuminated page, with gold clouds in the " chi " style on an azure background (Fig. 236). Next come the exploits of Isfandiyār, son of Gushtāsp, king of Persia, the page illustrated (Fig. 237) showing the bath of the hero after his victory over the lions; the exploits of the Iranian hero Bījan (Bīzhan), conqueror of the Turkoman chief Nastīhan; Bījan, mounted on horseback, is gazing upon the headless corpse of his enemy; and in this page, under colour of an illustration of the old Iranian epic, we may see a direct reminiscence of a campaign of the Timurid sultans against the Jaghatai tribes, or of the Ṣafawid shahs surrounded by their cavalry squadrons against the Üzbeg invaders (Fig. 238). There is also the episode of Rustam drawing up Bījan out of the pit into which he had been thrown by the Turanians (Fig. 239); the victory of Rustam over the Turanians (Fig. 240); the pathetic scene in which Rustam, after mortally wounding his son Sohrāb, whom he has not recognized, is listening to his last words (Fig. 241); and lastly the death of Rustam, who is falling with his faithful steed, Rakhsh, into the pit full of sharp sword-blades, arranged there by his brother, the traitor Shaghād, with the complicity of the King of Kābul (Fig. 242).

The later miniatures in the Godard manuscript reproduced here are concerned with the legends relating to the dynasties of historical days; that of Shāpūr I taking part in a game of ball in the presence of his father, King Ardashīr, is typical of the scenes representing aristocratic sports, games of ball or polo, which we shall find in such numbers at the courts of the Ṣafawids and the Great Moguls (Fig. 243). We have also Bahrām Gūr winning his way to the throne by slaying the lions which guard it (Fig. 244); the envoy of the Rajah of the Indies playing at chess with Buzurgmihr of Marv, vizier of Khosrau Anūshirvān, a typical *dīwān* scene of the Timurid or Ṣafawid type, which is a marvel of Persian elegance and a regular feast to the eye (Fig. 245); the victory of the Sāsānid Khosrau

FIGURE 277

Khosrau and Shīrīn from a Persian manuscript of the sixteenth century.
— *Bibliothèque Nationale. Archives photographiques*

Parvīz over the usurper Bahrām Chūbīn, typical of those pictures of animated cavalry combats which are the triumph of Timurid painting and early Ṣafawid painting, but which the later Ṣafawid painters were incapable of rendering with equal strength (Fig. 246). In court scenes, indeed, the Ṣafawid painting of the seventeenth century was capable of attaining still greater elegance; its portraits were yet to

FIGURE 278

Persian painting of the second half of the seventeenth century.
— *Musée des Arts Décoratifs, Paris. Photo, Giraudon*

acquire a greater psychological subtlety and a still more perfect grace, but this very refinement was to lead to the representation of the most violent cavalry charges as a sort of sport, hardly to be distinguished from some game of polo, and their art was to lose in vigour what it gained in charm. Finally, in the last miniature reproduced here from the Godard manuscript, we may note the type of the angels and the bold sweep with which they plunge earthward through the air (Fig. 247); on this page the angels themselves appear in rather a different guise from those in the "Apocalypse of Muḥammad" in the Bibliothèque Nationale, approximating rather to a page in the Sarre collection representing a princess waited upon by genii, a Transoxianian painting dating from about 1500, in which Chinese influence and Persian tradition are fused in such a way as to produce a magical and aerial impression, a vision from the dreams of some Ṣūfi poet (Fig. 249).

In general, indeed, the mode of representing flowers and animals in Transoxiana under the Timurids and Ṣafawids bears further witness to this fusion of Chinese and Persian art, combining the expertness of touch of the Ming school with the elegant lightness of Persian drawing. In this connexion we need only mention the

FIGURE 279
The falconer. Persian, sixteenth century.
— *Vever collection. Photo, Pivot*

wonderful painting in the Museum of Fine Arts at Boston of three bears, two on the ground and the other one climbing a tree, which are

FIGURE 280
Persian art, seventeenth century.
— *Vever collection. Photo, Laniepce*

sketched with a virtuosity worthy of the best landscape- and animal-painters of any age.

As we have seen, the apogee of Ṣafawid civilization is to be found in the reign of 'Abbās I (1587–1629). The principal painters of this period seem to have been Aghā Riẓā and Riẓā 'Abbāsī, whom some historians of art consider to have been identical, but whom Professor Kühnel considers to have been really distinct from each other. To Aghā Riẓā, who flourished about 1570, are ascribed some portraits of youthful princes, of a somewhat over-refined delicacy and positively feminine elegance, treated in the manner of Sulṭān Muḥammad's beautiful youths, or perhaps with even more

FIGURE 281
Woman with lilies. First half of the sixteenth century.
— *Léonce Rosenberg collection. From Marteau and Vever, II, 150*

refinement (Fig. 250). To Riẓā 'Abbāsī, who lived about 1630, are likewise attributed some pretty pages and all too beautiful cup-bearers, but also a few works of more direct and popular inspiration, some nude female figures or pairs of lovers locked in each other's

FIGURE 282
Dancing-girl. Persian, about 1600.
*Formerly in the Goloubew collection, now in
the Museum of Fine Arts, Boston.*
— *Photo, Goloubew*

embrace, in the Marquet de Vasselot and Sarre collections (Fig. 251 and 252), and even some *genre* scenes, realistic types, and queer faces of dervishes and goatherds, sketched with all the humour of the Dutch and Flemish schools. For the period of 'Abbās I we may also mention Muḥammad Yūsuf al-Ḥusainī, who flourished about 1580, and Muḥammad Qāsim, who flourished about 1626. For the following period we may mention Mu'īn Muṣavvir, of whose activity we have evidence about 1677–80; and, towards 1700, in the closing days of the dynasty, Muḥammad 'Alī. These latest masters delighted even more than their predecessors in painting figures of an exaggerated elegance, with an almost excessively penetrating glance, invariably beautiful youths, who are treated in a mannered style which reveals the decline of an age; their painting is too intellectual and, for that very reason, rather empty, for its very cleverness has here become no more than the mannerism of a school, exactly as happened towards the end of the Ming period in China.

But it must be recognized that most of the paintings of the Ṣafawid age cannot be assigned to any particular artist or are, at least, of very doubtful attribution. We here reproduce a certain number of these works, most of which we owe to the courtesy of Monsieur Henri Vever. We have grouped them according to some affinity of style or subject. First come the religious scenes: two paintings of the sixteenth century from the Vever collection, representing the court of Solomon, who is surrounded, as is usual in Moslem art, by a group of angels, demons, and animals (these last being particularly picturesque), which his omniscience had made subject to his sway (Fig. 253 and 254). Another painting of the beginning of the sixteenth century in the Vever collection represents the court of the

FIGURE 283
The mirror. Persian, seventeenth century.
— *Demotte collection, Photo, Laniepce*

magician Queen of Sheba, surrounded by angels, among them a wonderful dancing angel, which we may compare with the angels in the Transoxianian miniature from the Sarre collection mentioned above (Fig. 255). There is also a large and very powerful painting in the Vever collection, representing Solomon and the Queen of Sheba seated side by side upon a throne, surrounded by the same assembly of angels,

FIGURE 284

Love scene. Persian, seventeenth century.

— *Vever collection. Photo, Laniepce*

FIGURE 285

Persian art, seventeenth century.

— *Musée des Arts Décoratifs, Paris. Photo, Giraudon*

monsters, and animals (Fig. 256). And lastly, among subjects of a similar nature, we may mention an Apocalypse of Muḥammad of the sixteenth century, in the Demotte collection (Fig. 257); and a prophet waited upon by angels on the banks of a cool stream, also in the Vever collection. And we may note in a class by itself an *al-Burāq* in the Vever collection, represented in the form of a winged centaur- ess, standing erect on her hind feet (the hoofs of a horse) — a charming figure with an atmosphere all its own, in which we can de- tect at once a pagan seductiveness and the mystic emotion of Islam (Fig. 259).

Among the *dīwān* scenes — that is, the pictures of " royal audi- ences " — we are so fortunate as to be allowed to reproduce several paintings from the Vever collection, some of which are still akin to those of the Timurid period in their charming simplicity, though in certain typical details they are already decidedly Ṣafawid; such, in particular, are the details of the costume — for example, the young men have a curl escaping from their head-dress and hanging over the temple; while the turbans become increasingly elaborate, until they reach the extraordinary proportions of those worn by the fashionable young men of the seventeenth century. On the other hand, there are other *dīwān* scenes which, side by side with their Ṣafawid workman- ship, betray an Indo-Mogul influence — for instance, those of Far- rukh-beg, a Persian painter of the end of the sixteenth century, who, as it happens, also worked in India, at the court of the Emperor Akbar (Fig. 260 to 262).

Next come the royal hunting-scenes, a theme which the Ṣafawid school inherited from the Timurid school. The transition stage is pro- vided by the Ṣafawid artists of Herāt in the first half of the sixteenth century, and especially by the scenes of Bahrām Gūr hunting, from the *dīwān* of Mīr 'Alī Shīr Navā'ī, in the Bibliothèque Nationale, the illustrations of which were painted at Herāt about 1527 (Fig. 263).

In paintings of this class we are often struck by the extent to which

FIGURE 286

The lovers. Persia, second half of the sixteenth century.
— *Vever collection. Photo, Laniepce*

the naturalistic tradition of the animal-painters of ancient days still holds its own in these scenes of antelope, gazelles, moufflon, and wild asses grazing or in flight, which are in no wise unworthy of their glorious Assyro-Persian models; or of foxes and hares sketched in attitudes instinct with their native wiliness (Fig. 264 and 265). But we cannot blink the fact that the theme of the chase is treated by the Ṣafawid painters in a spirit of elegance rather than of strength. We

FIGURE 287
The dialogue. Persian art, sixteenth century.
— *Louvre, Marteau bequest. Photo, Pivot*

have only to glance at these agile steeds, which, in spite of their solid proportions, have all the litheness of antelopes and the slender grace of swans; or at these beautiful young huntsmen who ride past in their turbans adorned with aigrettes, with falcons perched on their gauntleted wrists, followed by their high-bred Iranian greyhounds; even in single combat with lions they perform the most improbable feats of huntsmanship before our eyes as though in play. In short, though we once more find in these paintings the great art of representing animal forms which continued from the days of the Sargonids to those of the Ṣafawids to be the Iranian art *par excellence*, the strength and fire of past days have made way for a more and more exclusive pre-occupation with grace and subtlety.

The ancient kings did really indulge in these violent exploits, but it is evident that single combats with wild beasts had now become no more than a sport, an aristo-cratic pastime, a subject adapted for the display of elegant poses and re-finements of cleverness. This ideal triumphs with-out restraint in the rustic scenes, such as those so often represented on the decorative marginal bor-ders in the Vever collec-tion (Fig. 266 to 270). Here young princes, beautiful pages and lovely ladies, smiling cup-bearers, and musi-cians of both sexes in-dulge in collations, sports, and amorous dalliance in meadows carpeted with buttercups, on the bank

FIGURE 288

Carpet of silk velvet. Persian, sixteenth century.
— *Musée des Arts Décoratifs, Paris. Photo, Giraudon*

of some little stream, at the foot of a blossoming tree from which hangs a swing — or, again, as in some Florentine landscape, in the narrow shade of a pointed cypress (Fig. 271 to 272); the antelopes which frolic on the horizon, the foxes slinking behind a rock, are all part of the scene, being creatures as aristocratic as the heroes of these princely idylls themselves (Fig. 273). The Ṣafawid school of Shīrāz introduces a characteristic note of its own into these scenes of garden fêtes, collations, or parties of women, in the shape of touches of a naïveté which, though perhaps studied, is none the less charming (Fig. 274 and 275). At times, too, some epic theme serves as a pretext for a picture full of grace — for

FIGURE 289
Great Mosque, Varāmīn.
— *Photo, Mohsen Moghadam*

instance, King Khosrau Parvīz surprising the lovely Shīrīn as she leaves the bath, a subject which is felicitously treated in a manuscript of Niẓāmī in the Bibliothèque Nationale, dating from 1624 (Fig. 276); or, again, Shīrīn leaning over her balcony to listen to Khosrau, who loiters at her threshold like some simple love-lorn page (Fig. 277). Thus the paintings of these manuscripts in general clothe the festal scenes which took place in the Persian palaces of the sixteenth and seventeenth centuries with an atmosphere of legend that enhances their poetry.

Lastly, the Ṣafawid masters, especially in the seventeenth century, embarked upon large figures treated for their own sake, with no landscape setting, often in the form of simple drawings analogous to those of Clouet. As we have said, there is a whole series of these works which, in accordance with Persian taste, represent handsome young men, pages, falconers, or cup-bearers with plump cheeks and a rather languid grace (Fig. 279 and 280). Sometimes, too, there are lovely ladies with elongated eyes and eyebrows, either alone (Fig. 281 to 283) or listening to the ardent addresses of a lover (Fig. 284 to 286). Sometimes, again, the artist amuses himself by sketching types of old men or scholars with oval faces framed in their beards and wearing a faint, sceptical little smile, full of the poignant wisdom of 'Omar Khaiyām and charmingly reminiscent of Ḥāfiẓ (Fig. 287). And this twofold impression of a sometimes excessive intellectual subtlety and an often exaggeratedly aristocratic grace which we carry away with us as the dominant note of the late Persian miniatures will become even more marked when, in the next volume of this series, we compare Ṣafawid art with the more naturalistic and full-blooded art of Mogul India.

But Persian decorative illumination and painting must be followed out, not only on the pages of manuscripts, but also in the design of carpets; for the greatest miniaturists of the Ṣafawid school were called upon to design cartoons for carpet-weaving. Hence the subjects represented in them are often the same as those of paintings: for instance, the "garden motive" inspired by the tradition of the most ancient Sāsānid "paradises." Above all, we find in them hunting-scenes or combats between animals. "These carpets," writes Monsieur Migeon in his *Manuel d'art musulman*, II, 362, " are sometimes woven of silk, with threads of silver and gold, but most often of very fine and lustrous wool, mixed with silk." Sometimes one of these carpets will recall a well-known picture in its every detail. Thus there is a Persian carpet of the sixteenth century, now in the Friedrichsmuseum

at Berlin, reproduced in Monsieur Migeon's book (II, Fig. 442),
which displays exactly the same elegant conventionalized foliage,
vine-leaves, and animals as those of the frescoes of the Ala Qapy at
Isfahān. The famous carpet with hunting-scenes at Schönbrunn
(Migeon, II, Fig. 443) and the similar one in the Musée des Arts
Décoratifs, Paris (Migeon, II, Fig. 444) are faithful counterparts
of our Fig. 263 to 265. In them we find all the characteristic motives
of Ṣafawid painting: the setting of flowery meads, hunting-scenes
with galloping horsemen pursuing their game, combats of animals,
fleeing beasts, or flights of birds among the high tree-tops, animals
of the deer tribe and horses treated with a slender elegance, or
cypresses with the gracility of a youthful body; we find, too, the same
influence of Chinese decorative art, which is even more persistent
here than in the miniatures: clouds in the " chi " style, dragons with
serpentine convolutions, *fong-huang*, phœnixes and other fabulous
birds borrowed from the China of the Ming period. In addition to
these borrowings from the contemporary art of the Far East, the
textiles with animal subjects take us back to the remotest past of Iran.
We constantly find upon them the motives of heraldic beasts which
first appeared upon the oldest of the Chaldean cylinders, and the
tradition of which was handed on by Sāsānian fabrics.

But the geometrical and floral decoration is peculiarly magnificent. Even if nothing had survived to us of Persian painting, even if
all the carpets with animal motives had disappeared, the great carpets adorned with flowers, or mosque-lamps would alone suffice to
prove that a pure and marvellously tasteful classic style had developed in this country. This decoration is indeed a delight both to the
eye and to the mind. "The types of these highly conventionalized
flowers is borrowed, from the lily or the sunflower [see Fig. 288];
they grow upon long, thin stems, which have at times the rigidity of
ironwork. We have also bouquets of narcissi, tulips in vases, or
mosque-lamps hanging by chains" (Migeon). Besides this stiff floral

FIGURE 290

Fresco from the Chihil-Sutūn, Isfahān.

— *Photo, Sevruguin*

decoration, which seems to have been particularly popular in the region of Qum, we may mention another style, of a more flexible and supple order, which was characteristic of the carpets of Isfahān and of Herāt. " Here," says Monsieur Migeon, " we find freely designed peonies and foliage with fine, flexible stems or ribbons running between them." Such carpets as these enable us to understand better than anything else the famous formula: " The Persians are the poets of flowers." The causes of this preference are deep-lying: the very nature of the country, which is in part desert and waste, has contributed towards making the gardens of Persia so many " paradises," to use the old Greco-Achæmenid term. All those who have travelled across the plateau of Iran will remember how against the background of these mauve-coloured solitudes a single Persian flower, appearing miraculously beside a prattling brook, is an oasis in itself. As Monsieur Demaisons writes, " The Persians draw and arrange flowers with a charming lightness and grace. They paint them in delicate tones that are in subtle harmony with the soft shades of the backgrounds. It must be admitted that Persian fabrics but rarely possess the brilliance of other Oriental stuffs, but they surpass them all in their predilection for delicate tones and subtle harmonies, as well as in the ingenuity and choiceness of invention."

This liberation of floral motives from the bonds of convention seems to be the characteristic contribution of Persia. For, though it clung to conventionality in its representation of human and animal forms, Iran was surprisingly naturalistic in its treatment of flowers. Yet the sources of its inspiration came from very far afield — from the conventionalized forms of Byzantino-Arab art. " When floral designs appeared, they were for long confined within the inflexible geometrical limitations which were the heritage of Byzantium, and thanks to which the motive is conventionalized to an amazing degree and borrowed from a flora utterly unreal. Then, little by little, the whole thing becomes more flexible; the lines lose some of their

FIGURE 291
Old Mosque, Hamadān.
— *Photo, Sevruguin, Teheran*

rigidity, and from the fourteenth century onwards the style of decoration becomes more naturalistic, thanks to a real observation of floral
forms — confined, it is true, to a small number of types: the carnation, the hyacinth, the tulip, the wild rose, and the peach-blossom ”
(Migeon in the review *Les Arts,* No. 16). From this point of view
these carpets may be regarded as no more nor less than the wonderful
sward of some secret garden of Isfahān or Shīrāz, transported with
all its voluptuous delights to the paradise of Allah.

There is a third style of Persian carpet, which has “ a great central
medallion with highly conventionalized and extremely stiff floral
decoration.” This style, we may remark, has close affinities with the
faience casings of the great mosques of Isfahān. In both alike, the
effect is as of an illuminated page enormously magnified (see Fig.
248). The impression produced by these carpets is simply magnificent. “ Nothing could be more remarkable,” writes Monsieur Migeon,
“ than a fine carpet of this school. The composition displays a lavish
imagination which is quite fairy-like. Yet, crowded and intricate
though the motives are, they are none the less subject to rigorously
logical laws of symmetry. No painter’s work could achieve such
supreme harmonies and rare touches of subtlety as that which the
great weavers of Isfahān display in these enchanting works.”

Lastly, as Mr. Pope has demonstrated, the carpets incorrectly
known as “ Polish ” must also be attributed to seventeenth-century
Persia. On account of their richness these carpets, woven in silk on
a background shot with gold and silver, with a pattern of conventionalized foliage and arabesques, were offered as presents to the
courts of Europe by the Ṣafawid ambassadors.

Persian painting is hardly known in Europe except from the miniatures, so people forget that it is also found in the form of fresco. The
frescoes which adorn the whole interior of the Chihil-Sutūn at Isfahān
are among the most remarkable productions of Oriental art.

FIGURE 292
Mausoleum of Bibars (1277), Damascus.
— *Photo, E. de Lorey*

The frescoes of the Chihil-Sutūn are of two kinds. In the principal hall are some very large mural compositions, covering the whole of the upper range of panels, the two chief of which represent the victories of Nādir Shāh over the Afghans and Hindus, while the remaining four, which are also of quite considerable proportions, depict one of Shāh Tahmāsp's battles, the reception of ambassadors from the Great Mogul, and two fêtes at the court of Isfahān, in one of which appears Shāh ʿAbbās (Fig. 290). This last scene is of rare magnificence, owing to the splendour of the tones of gold and the richness of the fabrics. As for the reception of the Indian ambassadors, it is a genuine historical document, the racial characteristics of both Persians and Indians being rendered with scrupulous fidelity; while the portraits of the ambassadors are treated in the very style of the contemporary Indo-Mogul school; one might almost be looking at some miniature of the court of Jahāngīr in the Vever collection, magnified into a life-size painting.

But the smaller pictures at Chihil-Sutūn constitute the most interesting part of the paintings there. These are, as a rule, a little over a yard wide by half a yard high and run along the walls at a height of about two yards from the ground. The subjects are generally of an idyllic character — for instance, some princess of legend, reclining at the foot of a tree in a garden full of bloom, resting her hand on a wine-jar or dreaming of her lover; a little farther on he has joined her and is offering her a goblet; sometimes the two lovers, joined in a fond embrace, invite each other to drink; in one of the pictures the young man is succumbing to the power of wine, while his mistress, still palpitating and with her hair in disarray, regards him with a somewhat ironical glance. Or, amid a rocky landscape adorned with trees, on the deep-green sward lit up by flowers, like that which we see in the pictures of Benozzo Gozzoli or Ghirlandajo, a young woman is stretching her arms luxuriously as she lies in the grass — a fair, voluptuous form, with the long lines of a figure of Botticelli's, wearing a close-fitting robe of a dull red and a golden girdle. The face is instinct with desire, and the whole treatment already suggests that of the Italian masters. Or we find another fair lady, leaning languorously against the branch of a tree in a sinuous pose, while she listens with dreamy eyes to the verses of her lover. Next we come to a gem of the purest water: against a background of rocks, a princess seated under a tree upon red and gold cushions in the deep-green flowery grass, is touching her eyelashes with kohl; her right hand is tracing the delicate line, while the left hand holds the mirror; the face, of a warm pallor with golden tones, set off by a head-dress of tarnished gold, is bending over the mirror; the body, clad in a long robe of creamy yellow and dull gold, of faded hues, is half reclining in a nonchalant pose of infinite grace. This drooping grace, these elongated forms, these long eyes with their black lashes, the softness and magic of these colours faded with age, produce an impression analogous to that of Botticelli's most lovely figures, or even, if we may say so without blasphemy, of the Indian figures of Ajaṇṭā. Another female figure, seated in a similar attitude, is opening a wine-jar; she is dressed in a long robe of old gold with a rosette pattern, and leaning back against cushions of a dark green with a similar pattern or of a dull red. Farther on is a picture which is a triumph of marvellous tones of colour; a lady in a purplish chestnut robe, adorned with a pattern of clouds in the Chinese " chi " style, is offering a goblet to a charming prince clad in a cream-coloured robe with tones of old gold, on which, as on a piece of Damascus ware, are scattered little bouquets of flowers in blue, pink, and green.

One peculiarity of these pictures, which seems at first sight to be a mere convention, is the shape of the bare, jagged, fantastic rocks, which serve as a setting to most of these scenes. But as a matter of fact this is really a sign of close observation. From Qum to Shīrāz, all along the routes across the desert forming the interior of Iran, may be seen these strange apparitions, these chains of ghostly-looking heights, which at times give the landscape the aspect of an extinct planet. What is more, these characteristically Iranian rocks are here treated a little in the Italian style, like those of the Florentine pre-Raphaelites; and the dark-green grass, lit up by the brilliance of the flowers, is, as we have already noted, like that of Fra Angelico's and Benozzo Gozzoli's pictures.

For Italian influence is undeniably evident on all sides. In the outer gallery of the Chihil-Sutūn, on the right-hand side, is a nude woman, seated under a tree, with her feet in a stone pool, with her body bending over the basin of a fountain, in the middle of which stands a bronze satyr, like an unexpected reminiscence of Giorgione's "Concert" or an imitation of it which has strayed to the Forty Columns of Isfahān. Farther on there is a picture of a young mother giving the breast to her *bambino,* which reminds us of some Madonna of the Umbrian school. Farther on again are some hunting-scenes with figures like musketeers escaped from the barriers of the Louvre; and a last surprise awaits us when we come upon great full-length portraits of gentlemen dressed in plumed felt hats, ruffs, laces, orders, and high boots in the Louis XIII style, which might almost bear the signature of some Italian imitator of Van Dyck or Philippe de Champaigne.

Nor is it possible to discuss Safawid art without referring to the decorative mural paintings which cover all the galleries, apartments, corridors, and ceilings of the Ala Qapy at Isfahān. The vine-leaves, conventionalized foliage, chain patterns, arabesques, flowers, rosettes, medallions, and peacocks' tails which are here displayed in a thousand fantastic forms are arranged in designs of unerring taste. The technique of Safawid miniature-painting, as here adapted for the purpose of fresco, rises to the level of high art, and it is curious to see how, by its twofold impression of elegance and grandeur, it ends by giving us a foretaste of a sort of Persian Louis Quinze style.

We may add that in these same mural decorations of the Ala Qapy, among purely floral or geometrical motives, we come upon charming groups of deer, antelope, and gazelles passant, treated with the same realism and elegance as in contemporary miniatures. The same remark applies to the sly foxes sitting upon their hind quarters, or to the birds of every kind — *sīmurgh*, peacocks, doves, nightingales, etc. — which perch in the corners of the ceilings or nest in the convolutions of the vine-leaves. In these, too, we again find the full influence of the traditions of miniature-painting described above.

Lastly, in order to understand the twofold science of Persian colour and ornament, nothing is so profitable as a study of the polychrome mosaics of faience which cover the whole of the Ṣafawid mosques, interior and exterior alike, and especially of the Masjid-i Shāh at Isfahān. The predominating tone of this celebrated building is blue, and the mosque, with its colonnades and its dome, rises heavenward a perfect symphony in blue. But on closer examination how many different colour-notes, how many subordinate symphonies of colour, each complete in itself, go to make up the harmony of the whole!

The deep blue, with sprigs of yellow and green flowers, which forms the general tone of the entrance is quite a different shade from the softer blue which adorns the honeycomb mouldings, and this difference of tone is brought out with supreme art by the pointed arches of green grooving running across the intervening space in a line that seems to thrill with life and vigour; still different is the iridescent blue which adorns the two side panels of the door, with its decorative motive of a peacock's tail set off by a white medallion and four green bobbin-shaped motives; or the greenish blue, sprigged with yellow, of the projecting jambs to the right and left of the door; or, again, the sky-blue which serves as a background to the great inscription in white from the Koran which frames the whole door, a blue which is lent a most striking value by the decided green of the minarets. We may unreservedly admire the perfect harmony with which these varied fancies, all these shades of blue and green, are marshalled and blended with effortless ease in the grandeur of the whole, that celestial symphony of blue rising up to the azure sky.

It must, indeed, be realized that we have here the culminating achievement of ten centuries devoted to the study of æsthetic refinements. In order thoroughly to understand this Ṣafawid classicism of the seventeenth century, it is necessary to go back to the earliest classical age of Persia, the great Seljuk art of the twelfth century, as we still see it in the Mosque of Varāmīn, dating from the early fourteenth century (Fig. 289). And since we have mentioned this venerable edifice, may we express the hope that its noble architecture and the last remains of its marvellous blue faience decoration may be rescued in all haste, before it is too late.

We may also give utterance to another aspiration of a similar kind, in which all travellers will join — to the effect that the great Persian mosques may cease to remain closed to archæologists and artists. While the sanctuaries of Turkey — even the sacred Eyub — of Syria, and of Palestine — even the Mosque of 'Omar — are thrown freely open to travellers, the mosques of Persia remain stubbornly closed, thanks to the fanaticism of a few mullahs. While the Sunnite creed, though more strict in theory, throws open its sanctuaries to our respectful admiration, the Shī'ite Church, which purports to be perfectly liberal, persists in these prohibitions which belong to a past age. May we hope that the enlightened rulers who now preside over the destinies of Persia will put an end to a state of things which cannot but do her harm in the eyes of foreigners.

What is the final impression that we may carry away from this rapid review of Persian art?

Richer schools are to be found in other parts of the territories of Islam. The Ayyūbid school of Damascus gives proof of a more vigorous, virile, and constructive sense of beauty in its strong treatment of fine stone. The Osmanli art of Brusa and of certain mosques of Stambul — the Suleimāniye, or that of Sulṭān Ahmed — has greater power and poetry of inspiration, as well as more substantiality. But Persian art is the privileged possessor of an uninterrupted tradition which we have tried to make clear, linking up the Assyro-Achæmenid period with that of the Ṣafawids. What is more, it grows directly out of its native soil in a way that transcends all human factors. It is inseparable from the very land of Persia, where, against an ever-present background of mauve and golden desert, set in a frame of rosy mountains, a few dead mountains standing out against the horizon like some landscape in the moon, a slender stream of water, a few poplars, and an old crumbling wayside inn suddenly assume a totally unexpected artistic value.

And in addition to this incessant reminder of the desert, there is the light air of the high plateaux with its incomparable purity, which adds an unvarying delicacy to every tone. Against this sky of a tender blue the favourite colours of the Persian architects acquire an extraordinary value — the mellow tone of the brick of the ancient mosques of Hamadān and Varāmīn or the fairy-like blue of the great domes of Isfahān or the gold of the dome of Qum, brooding and solitary in the infinite space of the desert. A profound harmony exists between this country and its art, an intimate relation which transcends human factors and will survive them, for here ruin assumes the aspect of the very soil of the country, while the desert itself possesses the tones and appearance of its ruins.

But the sphere of Iranian culture is not confined to the territory of Iran proper: Persia, Afghanistan, and Transoxiana. It also extends over an immense outlying zone, including Turkey in the west and Moslem India in the east.

As we have already pointed out, the Turkish conquest of Asia Minor in the eleventh century and of Thrace in the fourteenth century in many respects involved the Iranization of these two countries so far as culture was concerned. And especially after the Turks had wrested Bithynia, with Brusa, Nicæa, and Nicomedia, from the Byzantines between 1326 and 1338 — pending the capture of Constantinople in 1453 — they gave free rein to their natural genius. The shores of the Bosporus and the Sea of Marmora, once the haunt of the young gods of Greece, were enriched by the Ottomans with new sources of beauty. "The Greece of sun and landscape" was seen by the Ottoman Turk through the medium of Oriental reverie, and acquired a new melancholy from these conquerors, who bore within them the nostalgia of the gloomy steppe and of boundless horizons. From the palaces of Byzantium they could always hear, beyond the waters of the Bosporus, in the direction of Scutari and verdant Brusa, " the nightingale lamenting on the cypresses of Asia." For during their long sojourn on the borders of Iran the Ottoman Turks, like the Seljuks before them, had been deeply affected by Persian influences. Persian classicism was to them what Hellenism was to our northern races. They peopled the Mediterranean landscape with all the tender and miraculous forms imagined by the Persian poets. For them the verses of Saʿdī and Ḥāfiẓ echoed through the gardens of Brusa and Stambul as through the rose-gardens of Isfahān and Shīrāz. Thus Persian culture, fine, delicate, and rare, became acclimatized on the shores of the Sea of Marmora, with its mosques cased in faience mosaics, its brilliant arabesques, the elegance of its kiosks, and the sweetness of its secret gardens. And perhaps, on the whole, we have reason to bless the vicissitudes of history for the fact that, just as Iran had once been thrown open to Greco-Roman civilization, so ancient Byzantium in turn came to know the culture of Persia, with the result that at the gates of Europe there still remains a corner of the earth which, lulled by the great dream of the East, for long escaped the tumult of our civilization and almost ignored the flight of time.

Let us first call up before us the Elysian vision of Brusa. Verily we have here the paradise of Iranian Islam, which the great sultans whose desire it was to sleep beneath this earth had no need to seek elsewhere. Where, we may ask, is the paradise of Allah, the dream of Saʿdī? It is no more nor less than this light air, this blessed soil,

FIGURE 293
Façade of the Green Mosque, Brusa.
— *From Diehl:* Constantinople (" *Les Villes d'art célèbres* "). *Photo, Sebah*

these peaceful trees, these gleaming brooks, this tender sward, as soft as that of Bihzād or of Fra Angelico. In this setting the Osmanlis sought to effect a fusion between the best Syro-Egyptian traditions and those of Persia. The cruciform plan of the famous Green Mosque, or Yeshil-jamiʿ, at Brusa, built between 1414 and 1424, is directly derived from the Ayyūbid and Mameluke *madrasa*, simplified and, as it were, condensed into a more massive form; but the esplanade planted with trees upon which this building opens tells us that the spirit of the Persian "paradises" reigns in this spot. And so soon as we enter the mosque, the whole of Persia lies before us. The decoration, which consists entirely of faience mosaics, is purely Persian. What a delight to the eye, what an exquisite and exhilarating feast to the spirit, is this symphony of colour, dominated by one uniform tone of vibrant green, harmoniously combined with turquoise-blue: the whole of the lower part of the walls is faced with hexagonal tiles of this soft green, set in blue. Above this, as far as the ceiling, which is also lined with faience, we have the same predominant colours, diversified by the myriad fantasies of medallions and rosette patterns, garlands, conventionalized foliage, and sprays of flowers, in a colour-harmony which is a blend of every shade of green and turquoise-blue, enhanced by yellows, whites, and blacks, as well as a deep red which is the characteristic note of Ottoman ceramics. We find the same "Persian fête" in the Yeshil-türbe, an octagonal monument erected behind the Green Mosque to serve as a mausoleum for Sulṭān Muḥammad I (1421), which was formerly covered both within and without by a similar mosaic of faience in which greens and turquoise-blues predominated.

On crossing over to Europe the Ottomans discovered Byzantine architecture. In their first shock of admiration they adopted and adapted it — and the result was St. Sophia. But suddenly they experienced a revulsion of feeling, and soon there appeared the characteristic type of the Ottoman mosque, on the Byzantine plan, but with Persian decoration. Here again, however, the Turks were not content with a servile copy of Persian or Syro-Egyptian motives. They derived fresh methods from Iranian technique, just as the Moguls did afterwards in India, so that, without going outside the sphere of Persian æsthetic canons, a Turkish art developed, with an originality all its own. Thus, borrowing at once from Persia and from Mameluke Egypt the principle of stalactite decoration, they invented a stalactite of their own, the rectilinear or crystalliform stalactite, which was their own idea. Similarly, the use of faience mosaics, which at Brusa were still a mere copy of Persian work, " assumed quite an original character when it occurred to the Turks to transpose the coloured decorations coming from Persia on to a white background, as fine in tone as porcelain, in such a way that the colours harmonized admirably with the brilliance of the white marble casings."

Thus, thanks to their use of marble and to the general solidity of their materials, as well as to the boldness of their architectural conceptions, the Ottoman mosques have a grand and majestic character attained by no other Moslem school. The Suleimāniye Mosque at Constantinople, due to Suleiman the Magnificent, was built between 1550 and 1566 by the famous Turkish architect Sinān, who was born in 1489 at Kaisariya in Anatolia, of Greek parents, and was architect to sultans Selim I, Seleiman the Magnificent, and Selim II. He died at Constantinople in 1578, but his favourite pupil, Yūsuf, was summoned to India by the emperor Akbar and, as we shall see in Volume II of the present work, had a share in the formation of the Mogul architecture of Delhi and Agra.

This famous mosque looms above the whole history of Islam, both in space and in time. In a few lines full of real poetry Charles Diehl, the great French writer on Byzantine art, has celebrated " its imposing proportions and the harmonious cadence of the lines of its arches and cupolas, the varied hues of its porphyry columns and marble casings, its arcades outlined with black and white voussoirs, the splendid walls of the mihrāb, lined with faience from the ground up to the springing of the vault, and the wonderful coloured windows which light up the far side of the sanctuary." In spite of his deep love of Byzantine art, this famous scholar recognizes the superiority

FIGURE 294

Suleimāniye Mosque, Constantinople. South façade.
— *From Gurlitt:* Die Baukunst Konstantinopels. *Photo, Ernst Wasmuth A.-G., Berlin*

FIGURE 295

Suleimāniye Mosque, Constantinople. Interior, facing north.
— *From Gurlitt:* Die Baukunst Konstantinopels. *Photo, Ernst Wasmuth A.-G., Berlin*

of the Suleimāniye to St. Sophia: " When one finds oneself in the vast nave of the mosque of Suleiman, beneath the lofty dome, before the *miḥrāb* with its stalactites of gold, on which the coloured windows cast the mysterious half-light of a Gothic cathedral, the emotion which one feels is intense and unforgettable." The triumphant mastery with which the architect has succeeded in raising these ordered tiers of cupolas and minarets lends this building a soaring movement which is not to be found to an equal extent in any of the mosques of Syria, Egypt, or Iran. This soaring quality of the Ottoman mosques is perhaps even more striking in that of Sulṭān Ahmed at Constantinople, built in 1610, in which " by the piercing of the lateral façades with openings, the repetition of the semi-domes of the apse and the pronaos, and the superimposing of the pierced cupolas one above the other," the architect has arrived at an impression of extraordinary lightness in the interior. Apropos of the transformation of " Persian faience " into " Ottoman faience," we may draw attention to the polychrome effects of the interior of the Mosque of Ahmed: the faience has a white ground, adorned with flowers, "carnations, hyacinths, and roses of blue and tomato-red, climbing up sprays of green; tulips and carnations drooping from bowls, panels on which grey cypresses are entwined with vine-leaves and bunches of grapes." A comparison of these motives with those of the mosques of Isfahān will show what Ottoman art has added to the old traditional motives of Persia.

Thus the Ottoman mosques succeed in suggesting the same impulse towards the divine as our Gothic architecture, but expressed in terms of Moslem æsthetics and mysticism. Nothing could be more opposed to Gothic art and mediæval theology than the religious and artistic ideal of Islam. Yet in this atmosphere, for all its difference, we are suddenly struck by a sense of equivalence of values and analogous spiritual states. A fine Ottoman mosque, such as those of Soleiman or Ahmed, is a work of such a majestic simplicity — which

FIGURE 296

Mosque of Sultān Ahmed, Constantinople.

— *From Gurlitt:* Die Baukunst Konstantinopels. *Photo, Ernst Wasmuth A.-G., Berlin*

FIGURE 297

Mosque of Sultān Aḥmed, Constantinople. Interior, facing east.
— *From Gurlitt:* Die Baukunst Konstantinopels. *Photo, Ernst Wasmuth A.-G., Berlin*

we may call the simplicity of the absolute — that the mind is inevitably brought face to face with a metaphysical problem, resolving itself in beauty. It is true that we still feel ourselves to be within the general setting of the Persian æsthetic ideal, and the deep charm of our surroundings, all the varied hues of the faience decoration, are an intimation that the mystic sensualism of Iran still forms the accompaniment to our metaphysical reverie. But the dream of the genuinely Persian schools did not go beyond transporting the rose-strewn sward of Iran into the paradise of Allah. Here, on the contrary, the intense harmony of the work, the purity of this Turco-Persian classicism — reaching as it does such a pitch as to be the equivalent of the Greek canon — simply ravishes the soul and throws it into an illimitable ecstasy — an ecstasy devoid of violence or of anguish, an ecstasy which knows nothing of the Christian duel between matter and spirit, or of the bitter inward conflicts of our Gothic; for in the quietist philosophy of Islam, smiling nature and the sweetness of earthly things are but an expression of the goodness of Allah. And so it comes to pass that the sublime theology, the absolute monotheism, of Islam unconsciously joins hands with Greek paganism; and on this ancient Hellenic soil, to which the Ottomans brought the dreams of Persia, they came at last, by the devious ways of Islam, to restore the cult of material beauty. Thus these great mosques of the classic Ottoman period are the expression of all prayer and of all beauty.

Having shown how in the West the æsthetic ideal of Persia became the inspiration of Ottoman art, it remains, in the next volume of this series, to point out how in the East it gave rise in like fashion to Indo-Mogul art. From this twofold comparison it is perhaps already permissible to deduce a conclusion which we may formulate as follows: the Persian æsthetic ideal, which in its own native land remained, for lack of durable materials, to some extent confined to the spiritual realm, required fresh means of expression if it was to find its full realization. The Tāj (see Volume II, Fig. 73 to 246), like the Suleimāniye, is, as it were, the soul of Iran incarnate in the body of India or of Greece.

Isfahān, palace of Hasht Bihisht
October 31, 1928